THE NAKED TRUTH
ABOUT THIS BOOK

"Harvey Mackay is one of the top motivational writers of this era. He has been an inspiration to me, as well as to thousands of others."
—NORMAN VINCENT PEALE

"Harvey Mackay combines the smarts of a self-made man with the rhetoric of a football coach to give us the straight-skinny on how to get a raise or turn a Rolodex into a sales campaign, be a great manager or launch a new business. He is fast, smart, funny—and frighteningly right."
—GLORIA STEINEM

"Breezy counsel from a master salesman . . . From page one to page [384], BEWARE THE NAKED MAN WHO OFFERS YOU HIS SHIRT moves like a car out of control, taking the reader on a wild ride through the subconscious of a supersalesman. . . . Read NAKED MAN for its Norman Vincent Peale–POWER OF POSITIVE THINKING value."
—USA Today

"Harvey Mackay is one of those people who seems to have a good answer for everything."
—St. Louis Post-Dispatch

"I love this book! Mackay strips away the veneer and hits us between the eyes with the naked truth about succeeding in the real world. Impossibly, he delivers more in his second book than in his record-shattering first, which has never been done before."
—KEN BLANCHARD
Author of THE ONE MINUTE MANAGER

I found that the world is our mentor and people like Harvey Mackay keep passing along their message. . . . If only we will listen . . . I did, and am better off for it."
—PAT RILEY
Head Coach
Miami Heat

By Harvey Mackay

Swim with the Sharks Without Being Eaten Alive
Beware the Naked Man Who Offers You His Shirt

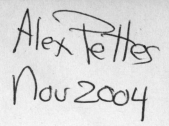

HARVEY MACKAY

BEWARE THE NAKED MAN WHO OFFERS YOU HIS SHIRT

Do What You Love

Love What You Do and

Deliver More Than You Promise

FAWCETT COLUMBINE • NEW YORK

A Fawcett Columbine Book
Published by Ballantine Books

http://www.randomhouse.com

Library of Congress Catalog Card Number: 96-96645

ISBN: 0-449-91184-5

This edition published by arrangement with William Morrow and Company, Inc.

Manufactured in the United States of America

First Ballantine Books Mass Market Edition: February 1991
First Ballantine Books Trade Edition: August 1996

10 9 8 7 6 5

To my wife, Carol Ann, and our
children, David, Mimi, and Jojo,
who unfailingly deliver more than
they promise and who are the very
heart of my life

Acknowledgments

I'd like to thank the following people who have helped in a myriad of ways in the preparation and writing of this book.

First, to my sister, Margie Resnick, who was "on call" throughout the writing process. Her insight made her a never-failing judge, and that judgment proved to be key to the writing process.

Thanks to my friend and agent Jonathon Lazear, who does his best to make the rough edges a little smoother.

My thanks and admiration go to Adrian Zackheim of William Morrow and Leona Nevler of Fawcett/Ivy Books. Their editorial guidance has been invaluable.

To Ron Beyma, whose insight, perceptions, and intuitions are always 100 percent.

To Lynne Lancaster, my "coach," who has a keen eye; I wouldn't want to do without her "chalk talks."

To Vickie Abrahamson and Wes Janz, two super-creative people who helped me immensely with positioning.

A respectful thanks with admiration to writer Maya Angelou, who unknowingly gave me the idea for the title when she spoke on Martin Luther King, Jr.'s birthday in Minneapolis and quoted a wonderful African proverb.

To Nancy Doran-Bren and Linda Ferraro, a special thanks for all the support of every kind shown to me throughout the writing of *Naked Man*.

To Larry Hughes, chairman and CEO of Hearst Trade Books Group, and Al Marchioni, president and CEO of William Morrow, thanks for your continuous votes of confidence.

To Lisa Queen and Will Schwalbe, the two best subsidiary rights brokers I've had the pleasure to work with.

ACKNOWLEDGMENTS

———————————•———————————

My admiration for her patience and creativity to Cheryl Asherman. And likewise to Susan Halligan, whose clever promotional plans are always on the mark.

Thanks go to Diane Ekeblad for her enthusiasm and good work and to Judy Olausen, photographer extraordinaire, who dropped everything for our cover shots.

My thanks to Dave Mona for his sound advice and good humor; David Martin for nearly instantaneous proofreading turnaround; to Ron Simon, Marv Scherzer, and Howard Liszt, whose keen wisdom has been most helpful; and to Loma Cohn for her patience and expertise.

All in all, the best team all around.

—HARVEY B. MACKAY

Contents

1   It's Not Just a Game After All   1
    Lesson 1   Chalk Talk 101   3
    Lesson 2   The Greatest Compliment I Ever Got Was a
                Standing Ovation of Boos   9

HARVEY MACKAY'S SHORT COURSE ON GETTING STARTED   17

2   Sharks, Shark-bait, Shark-proof   19
    Lesson 3   Some New Thoughts About Sharks—You
                Were a Shark Once, Too   21
    Lesson 4   Take This Job and Love It!   24
    Lesson 5   Five Things to Do When You Ask for a Raise   27
    Lesson 6   Five Things to Ask for After They Turn You
                Down for a Raise   31
    Lesson 7   How to Stay Employed   33
    Lesson 8   Deliver More Than You Promise   35
    Lesson 9   There's No Such Thing as Customer Tennis   38
    Lesson 10   The Rule of Ten Thousand   40

3   An Employee's Manual of Self-Defense   43
    Lesson 11   Beware the Office Bully   45
    Lesson 12   Loose Lips Sink Ships   50
    Lesson 13   Don't Hang Your Star on a Superstar   53
    Lesson 14   The Upside of Downsizing   56

HARVEY MACKAY'S SHORT COURSE ON WORKING YOUR
WAY UP   63

4   You're a Lot Better Off Being Scared Than Being Bored   65
    Lesson 15   The Missing Ingredient   67

CONTENTS

Lesson 16   This Isn't the Army: Volunteer   88
Lesson 17   "Garbage Collectors to Receive $30,000 per
             Year"   92
Lesson 18   The Mackay 33™ for Employees   94

5 The One Person Who's Always Happy to Teach You a
   Lesson Is a Tough Competitor   103
Lesson 19   Follow the Fleet   105
Lesson 20   The Most Valuable Tool a Seller Can Have   108
Lesson 21   It's Not What's Up Front, It's *Being* Up Front
             That Counts   111
Lesson 22   Harvey's Odds on Beating Your
             Competition   114

HARVEY MACKAY'S SHORT COURSE ON RUNNING THE
SHOW   117

6 A Manager's Manual of Self-Defense   119
Lesson 23   Seven Clues on How to Roll Up Your
             Sleeves the Right Way   121
Lesson 24   Tell Me the Whole Story   125
Lesson 25   You're Not Managing Change, You're
             Managing Conflict   128
Lesson 26   You're Not Running for Election   131
Lesson 27   Why Nothing Gets Done After You Duck Out
             Early for the Weekend   133
Lesson 28   Your Company Is No Better Than Its
             Reputation in the Community   135
Lesson 29   The Mackay 33™ for Managers   137
Lesson 30   People Don't Care How Much You Know
             About Them Once They Realize How Much
             You Care About Them   147
Lesson 31   Superman Doesn't Live Here Anymore   150
Lesson 32   You Won't Have to Spend a Lifetime with
             Someone Hired by the Hour   154

CONTENTS

7 An Entrepreneur's Manual of Self-Defense 155

Lesson 33 Make Yourself the Happiest Guy in the Place 157

Lesson 34 If It's Your Company, Then It's Your Problem 158

Lesson 35 Don't Confuse Charisma with a Loud Voice 160

Lesson 36 Meet Your New Boss: My Son 162

Lesson 37 The Small Businessperson's Guide to Nichemanship 164

Lesson 38 The Pat on the Back Is Back 167

Lesson 39 When It's Time to Say Good-bye, Make Sure No One Takes Your Company as a Going-Away Present 169

Lesson 40 The Setup 173

Lesson 41 One Thing You *Do* Learn at Harvard Business School 176

HARVEY MACKAY'S SHORT COURSE ON LONG-TERM SALES CAREERS 177

8 The Sale Begins When the Customer Says Yes 179

Lesson 42 Don't Say It If You Don't Mean It 181

Lesson 43 There Is No Such Thing as a Routine Sales Call 186

Lesson 44 It Takes More Than a Shoeshine and a Smile 188

Lesson 45 Why Can't I Get the Account? 193

Lesson 46 Raymond B.'s Guide to Handicapping the Successful Selling Experience 197

Lesson 47 The Old-fashioned Way 201

9 Sold on Selling 203

Lesson 48 The Toughest Sell—Readin', 'Ritin', 'n' 'Rithmetic 205

Lesson 49 The Best Salesman I Ever Met 208

CONTENTS

Lesson 50   Five-Word Job Description of a CEO: Best
             Salesperson in the Place   211

Lesson 51   You'll Never Know Unless You Ask   214

HARVEY MACKAY'S SHORT COURSE ON KEEPING OUT OF
TROUBLE   223

10 Eleven Ways to Avoid Chapter Eleven   225

Lesson 52   You Only Get One Chance to Make a Good
             First Impression, and Yours Is in the Hands
             of Your Receptionist   227

Lesson 53   Don't Let Your Appearance Cause Your
             Disappearance   230

Lesson 54   How to Keep from Being Tuned Out   233

Lesson 55   There's Big Business in Little Things   236

Lesson 56   Why Waste Waste?   238

Lesson 57   It's Not Your Imagination. The Lines *Are*
             Getting Longer   240

Lesson 58   But Will You Love Me in the Morning?   246

Lesson 59   You Can't Get Dealt a Straight Flush Unless
             You're in the Game   249

Lesson 60   If You Can't Say Yes, It's No   254

Lesson 61   Don't Try on the Pants Unless You're Ready
             to Buy the Suit   257

Lesson 62   They Have to Be Doing *Something* Right or
             They Wouldn't Be in Business   261

11 They Still Keep Score in Dollars   263

Lesson 63   The First Hire After You Hire Yourself   265

Lesson 64   Basic Bird-watching . . . or How to Hire
             an Accountant   267

Lesson 65   The Best Way to Buy It Is to Sell It   269

Lesson 66   Borrowing Trouble   271

Lesson 67   Why Your Ads Don't Work   274

Lesson 68   Buy It Before It's for Sale   281

CONTENTS

Lesson 69   Economics Imitates Art   283
Lesson 70   Put Me Down for the Minimum   286

HARVEY MACKAY'S SHORT COURSE ON PEOPLE   287

12 Beware the Naked Man Who Offers You His Shirt   289
Lesson 71   Four of a Kind   291
Lesson 72   Dealer's Choice   295
Lesson 73   And a New Way of Skimming the Pot   299
Lesson 74   What Did You Say Your Title Was?   300
Lesson 75   The Deadbeat   302
Lesson 76   Who Asked Your Opinion?   306

13 Politicians and Lawyers   309
Lesson 77   A Nonpolitician's Guide to Politics   311
Lesson 78   How to Hire a Lawyer, Part I   321
Lesson 79   How to Hire a Lawyer, Part II   326
Lesson 80   How to Hire a Lawyer, Part III   328
Lesson 81   How to Hire a Lawyer, Part IV   330

14 Missing Persons   331
Lesson 82   Two of My Favorite Role Models   333
Lesson 83   Ms. Butterfly   340
Lesson 84   Capitalism Is Efficient. Prejudice Is Not   342
Lesson 85   There Are No Seventy-Year-Old Burnouts   347

15 Quickies   355
Quickie 1   Everyone Wants to Win on Saturday
            Afternoon . . .   357
Quickie 2   Nothing Works All the Time   358
Quickie 3   Don't Take a Backseat to Anyone   359
Quickie 4   The Cookie Factor   360
Quickie 5   Spending Water Like Money   361
Quickie 6   "It's a Great Country, but You Can't Live in
            It for Nothing."—Will Rogers   363

CONTENTS

Quickie 7   You Pays Your Money, You Takes Your
Choice   364

Quickie 8   Tip on Tipping   364

Quickie 9   Anyone Can Win—Once   365

Quickie 10   Pure Doggedness   367

Quickie 11   One More Reason They Call It "The One
That Gets Used"   369

Quickie 12   Why You Can Run a Twenty-six-Mile
Marathon Even If You've Never Run Half
That Far Before in Your Life   370

Quickie 13   The Mexican Rug Dance Can Be a Lot More
Expensive Than the Mexican Hat Dance   371

Quickie 14   One Line They've Never Heard Before   373

Quickie 15   When You Should Overpay   374

Quickie 16   Notes on Notes   375

Quickie 17   Blame Someone Else for the Good News   376

Quickie 18   Only Elvis Doesn't Read What They Say
About Him in the Papers, and That's
Because He's on the Road   377

Quickie 19   Why PR People Could Use Some PR   377

Quickie 20   You Are What You Aren't   378

Quickie 21   We're Number Three . . . We Try Even
Harder   379

Quickie 22   Why Is It That You Can Never Bring an
Expert to New York?   380

Quickie 23   Tell Me a Secret   381

Quickie 24   Why Some People Never Fail   383

Quickie 25   Spend Some Time in the Trenches   383

Quickie 26   Find One Good Idea, and You Can Use It
Forever   384

Quickie 27   It's a Tradition   385

Quickie 28   It Ain't a Classless Society   386

Quickie 29   Table Stakes   387

CONTENTS

Quickie 30   There's No Market for Bad News   388

Quickie 31   How to Keep Your Train of Thought   389

Quickie 32   How to Get a Banker to Smile and Say
             Yes—or Maybe Not Smile and Say Yes   390

Quickie 33   Memories Are Made of This   392

Quickie 34   Why Communism Is in Turmoil   393

Quickie 35   Why Our System Works Better   394

Index   396

CHAPTER 1

IT'S NOT JUST A GAME AFTER ALL

LESSON 1

•

CHALK TALK 101

Could you or I have managed a major-league baseball team to a World Series championship?

The answer is yes.

If we could have demonstrated a sufficient mastery of the mother tongue to have filled out a lineup card with "Ruth—RF and Gehrig—1B" on it, that's about all it would have taken in 1927.

Occasionally, a team comes along that is so dominant that managing it is as idiot-proof as showing up at the ballpark to watch it crush another opponent.

But miracle combinations like these happen along once a generation.

Unless it's a monster squad like the 1927 Yankees, when a team is playing for a championship, winning is more than a question of talent, or mastering the basics. By the time you

•

reach the top level, you've already got what it takes to do whatever humans are capable of physically performing or you wouldn't be there. At that caliber of play, the winning edge does not run inside the chalk lines. That's where leadership matters, particularly when your leader is, for example, Lou Holtz, presently the football coach at Notre Dame.

If you think otherwise, just look at the record. Before Holtz, Minnesota teams were scraping the bottom of the Big Ten. That's when I got to know Holtz, helping lure him to the University of Minnesota from Arkansas. In the two years he stayed there, he took the Minnesota football team to its second Bowl game in two decades. As soon as he left for Notre Dame, the Gophers tanked again. And what did he do at Notre Dame? Took a dispirited, going-nowhere program, turned it completely around and upside down, and restored Notre Dame football to what it was when the Fighting Irish were to college football what the Yankees were to baseball.

One person, one coach, a nearsighted 145-pounder who finished practically at the bottom of both his high school and college graduating classes, has been the difference.

How does Holtz do it?

You won't find the answer in any playbook. It lies in Holtz's ability to motivate people.

In 1988, an undefeated Notre Dame played an undefeated Miami in South Bend in a game that was generally regarded as being between the two best teams in the country and the key to the national championship. I was there as Holtz's guest, making the rounds with him everywhere as he got his team ready for the game. Though Notre Dame was 5–0 going into the game, it was a four-and-a-half-point underdog to the Hurricanes, a rather substantial spread, particularly since it was a road game for Miami.

The night before, Notre Dame held a pep fest on campus. Twenty thousand fans showed up, an astounding number, considering it was about as many as used to show up, pre-

Holtz, to see the Minnesota teams actually play a game. There we were on a chilly night in South Bend, standing around, singing songs, cheering cheers, and gawking at one hundred overmuscled young men gawking back at us. To wind up the rally, Holtz spoke. His message was brief. He finished by saying, "I just want you to do me a very simple favor. You go find Jimmy Johnson [the Miami coach] and tell him we are going to beat the dog out of Miami."

The crowd went berserk. Here it was. The glory days were back. The legends of Rockne and Leahy were being re-created before our eyes. Bedlam.

I got in the car with Holtz as we drove off to the next stop, a chalk talk to the team across campus. I knew him well enough to speak my mind.

"I must have missed something," I said, "or you have lost it completely. That 'beat the dog out of Miami' quote is going to be jumping off the front of every sports page in the country, and for sure, it'll be hanging on the wall of the Miami locker room tomorrow. Do you really think you ought to rile Miami like that?"

Holtz shot me the kind of look an adult gives a child when he's explaining one of the mysteries of life.

"Look, Harvey," he said, "that isn't what really matters this time. You saw the crowd, but did you see the team?" True, within that crowd, there had been an island of surprising calm . . . the team. As Holtz hit his "beat the dog out of them" line, you could sense a sort of collective shifting of feet and a sigh. The players shuffled off to the bus for the chalk talk. They didn't believe him.

Holtz went on. "No, I know what I'm doing. The last four times we played Miami, they beat us a total of 133–20. Well, I wasn't here three of those four times, but still, they don't believe it's going to change. We had a terrible week of practice. I know what they're thinking, and they don't think they can win. They read the papers, too, you know. Well, so do I, and I wanted to show them, in front of mother, God, and country, that I know they can do it, that I believe in them. If I don't, who does?"

We go to the chalk talk. I'm a fly on the wall in the back of the room. Holtz goes up to the blackboard and writes on it:

WE ARE GOING TO BEAT THE DOG OUT OF MIAMI

He turns around to the one hundred members of the Notre Dame football team and says, "Why did I say that?"

No hands go up.

"Why did I say that?"

One hand. Finally.

"Yes?" says Holtz.

"Well, Coach Holtz, I think it's because we've got a better kicking game."

Holtz turns to the blackboard. He writes:

BETTER KICKING GAME

"Is that it?" asks Holtz.

Another hand.

"Our offensive line gets off quicker than theirs," says someone.

Holtz writes:

OFFENSIVE LINE QUICKER

"Anything else?" says Holtz.

"Pass defense. Their receivers can't shake our defenders."

Holtz writes:

PASS DEFENSE

"Okay," says Holtz. "Who's going to get an interception for Notre Dame tomorrow?"

Five hands.

Holtz shakes his head.

"Haven't you guys been reading the papers? Walsh [Miami's quarterback] has played five games without a single interception. Are you serious?"

The five hands stay up.

Holtz calls off the names of each of the five who have their hands up, writes down a huge "5" on the blackboard.

"Who's going to get a sack for Notre Dame tomorrow?" he says.

Four hands go up.

"Wait a minute," says Holtz. "Walsh hasn't been sacked once in five games."

The hands stay up.

Holtz calls out the names and writes a big "4" on the board directly under the "5."

"Now," says Holtz, "who's going to strip the ball and cause a recovered fumble for Notre Dame?"

Five hands go up. Same routine. Another "5," under the "4." Holtz draws a line under the last number, and adds them up.

"That's four sacks and ten turnovers," he says. "*Ten* turnovers. Hey, we don't have to play this game. We've already won it!"

Well, they did have to play it, and they did win it, 31–30. Eventually, they played for the National Championship of college football. A confident Notre Dame team won that one, too, 34–21 over West Virginia.

Holtz had empowered a college team that did not believe in itself, empowered it with the energy of its fans and with his own self-confidence. And that was the difference. The one-point difference that gave Notre Dame its victory. How tiny the margin between winning and losing, but how great a difference one man—one man with the ability to motivate others—can make. He made no promises of great rewards, no threats of punishment. He just brought out the best in others by getting them to believe in what he believed in—themselves.

I know it can happen because I've seen it happen. And what's most important of all is, you can make it happen, not just for others, but for yourself.

LESSON 2

———————————————————•———————————————————

THE GREATEST COMPLIMENT I EVER GOT WAS
A STANDING OVATION OF BOOS

The New York Times and *USA Today* called it ". . . the biggest upset in the 50 year history of the NFL." The Minnesota Vikings, whose unblemished 0–4 record is the worst of any Super Bowl team, finally won the big one.

Not on the field, of course, but where it counts most, in the pocketbook.

In 1992, Minnesota will play host to Super Bowl XXVI. Estimated revenues to a host city run up to $300 million. No event, not a seven-game World Series, not even a national political convention, can match it. When you figure today's cost of $1,350,000 per minute of TV on Super Sunday alone, fourteen days of national buildup, and two and a half years of day-to-day hype, the exposure is beyond comprehension. A community can get that amount of publicity only if its name is Three Mile Island.

———————————————————•———————————————————

That's why the competition to be host city was as bitterly fought among NFL franchises as any game, and for *much* higher stakes.

That's why the moves and countermoves, even though they were played out on the sports pages instead of the business section, were not a whole lot different than the ones on the corporate battlefields.

And that's why, just as when we were fighting to keep the Twins baseball franchise in Minnesota, I wanted to be a player.

Our basic strategy was right out of Frank Leahy's playbook. When Leahy was coaching Notre Dame in the 1940's and 50's, the collegiate season would unofficially start with Leahy's woeful, doleful claim that this year, THIS DREADFUL YEAR, his team wouldn't win a game. This was greeted with a certain amount of skepticism, since Leahy compiled a 107–13 record, went undefeated seven times, and won five national championships.

Nonetheless, Leahy's poor-mouthing served his purposes beautifully. It focused the media attention away from his players and put a bit more pressure on opposing teams. I'm sure that part of the persona of Leahy's reincarnation, Lou Holtz, is calculated to achieve the same result.

With role models like that, how could we lose?

Publicly, our Super Bowl Task Force members let it be known, particularly to representatives from other cities competing for the game, that our own expectations about our chances were small indeed.

In this ancient ruse, we had the unwitting assistance of our local media, who usually suggest there's something vaguely ludicrous about plain-vanilla Minnesota competing for anything as glitzy as a Super Bowl, and we'd all be better off staying home and watching the game beamed on satellite from some exotic place like Miami or New Orleans. A lead article in the Minneapolis *Star Tribune* described our feeble effort, "The Minnesota Super Bowl Task Force has been outspent and outmaneuvered by other cities vying to host the Super Bowl." Another ennobling defeat. Hurray for nice, nice us.

Only this time, our competition wasn't from the Sunbelt. This was the Once-in-a-Decade-Let's-Throw-a-Sop-to-the-Rust-Belt "Northern Tier" Super Bowl. Our competition was Detroit, Indianapolis, and Seattle. Not to be taken lightly, but like the Twin Cities, none of them a day at the beach in the middle of January, either.

You never, never saw anyone let sleeping dogs lie the way we did with these three. From the beginning of the selection process, twelve months prior to the vote, the front-runner position rotated among Detroit, Indianapolis, and Seattle. We were always regarded as an also-ran, and we gladly, eagerly, accepted the public role we'd been assigned. We lay in the weeds, while the competition swung from the trees, crashing into one another.

Who in his right mind would come to Minnesota in the middle of January? How could anyone take these squirrels from Minnesota seriously?

Let it be known that all twenty-eight NFL owners are very much in their right minds, each having acquired and nursed an asset to where it was worth approximately $80 million, and are not about to blow it by making asses out of themselves in the process of staging their premier annual national attraction.

These guys know how to read the weather maps, too. And believe it or not, Minnesota weather horror stories are as greatly exaggerated as the benefits of oat bran. In fact, we have more sunny days in January than most of the rest of the country. I didn't say warmer, I said sunnier.

But let's face it, this contest was not just about sunshine. It was about politics. The FAX was more important than the facts.

There were twenty-eight votes. We needed fifteen to win.

We started to research the twenty-eight owners.

All our efforts boiled down to the ability to network among these people, and that took a prodigious amount of research. Under the remarkable leadership of chairperson Marilyn Carlson Nelson (who for five years knocked herself out leading the Task Force), we made over five hundred phone calls to the library, suppliers, customers, friends, friends of friends, enemies, a good chunk of the *Fortune* 500, and all of the football establishment.

The result was a scientific discovery of cosmic proportions, the most important word in the English language. Ask one thousand people, and you're not likely to get the right answer once.

You won't find it in your dictionary, either.

It's "Rolodex."

Everyone networks, but your Rolodex is the key to being effective at it.

The next time you meet someone you want to keep in touch with, don't just throw that person's business card in a drawer. Put the information on the old Rolo and add a few personal touches: hobbies, background, family names, kids' schools, whatever. Now, when you talk with him or her, you have it all at your fingertips. You may not be able to recall what color tie you're wearing without looking at it, but you'll be hailed for your fabulous memory by anyone you've immortalized in your Rolodex.

I try to keep the birthdays on file, too, but I don't like to ask. It sounds a little too much like a What's-Your-Sign-Mine's-Leo approach at a singles bar. The easiest way, if you aren't dealing with a *Who's Who* entry, is to ask the person's secretary or spouse. Put it on the calendar and call on the birthday. When was the last time anyone besides Mom, your non-same-gender sibling, and your spouse called you on your birthday?

If the house is on fire, forget the china, silver, and wedding album—grab the Rolodex.

Lyndon Johnson was the number-one networker of all time. When he first came to Washington as a congressional aide, Johnson lived in a large rooming house with a horde of other hard-strapped, ambitious young men just starting up the political ladder. As Christopher Matthews tells it in *Hardball,* every morning Johnson would take a half-dozen trips down the hall to the communal bathroom. It wasn't weak kidneys. He figured it was the best place to make new friends. It must have worked, because those contacts were his springboard to election as speaker of the Little Congress, the organization of congressional aides, and the beginning of an extraordinary career in politics.

But you don't have to hang out in the john. People may get the wrong idea. Stick with the Rolodex.

Unleashing the incredible hidden power of our Rolodexes, our Super Bowl Task Force met, combined our information, and dealt the cards. Who got the "quality calls." Who drew a number from the assigned risk pool. How we would approach each owner.

I got Lamar Hunt, a top pick on any draw, and I am not ashamed to flog the "Doing Your Homework" number one more time by telling you about our meeting. Hunt is the Dallas oilman billionaire who owns the Kansas City Chiefs. Our Rolodex reconnaissance told us that he, and not Pete Rozelle, or some PR guy, was the person who actually came up with the name "Super Bowl." He was playing with his son and a toy called a Super Ball. The proverbial light bulb went on over his head. The rest is history.

When I met with Hunt I managed to inject that into the conversation, and he shot out of his chair as if his pants were on fire and sprinted over to his closet, where he dug out a twenty-year-old Super Ball and a fistful of newspaper clips he'd saved from 1966, confirming that, yes, it was Lamar Hunt who named the Super Bowl. It may not rate with a cure for cancer, but who wouldn't want to be re-membered as the man who named an American institution.

Insignificant, perhaps, but it obviously didn't hurt our chances with Lamar Hunt to have come up with that little tidbit.

The hardest job our team had wasn't rounding up votes; it was keeping our own team together. We had more per-sonality conflicts than the New York Yankees locker room.

The old Vikings management had been ousted by the current management in a series of very public, very messy lawsuits. The dispute had that divorce-court quality that in-tensified the bitterness. The parties were not strangers to each other but had been friends and close business associ-ates for years before they had their falling out.

Most NFL owners, of course, are not strangers to the courtroom. These people didn't acquire their sandboxes without stepping on a few playmates along the way, so they were unshockable as far as the business practices being dis-closed were concerned. Still, they did not want the Super Bowl played in an atmosphere crackling with hostility. Bad PR.

The former Vikings management still had many friends among the NFL owners, particularly the Old Guard. Those friendships amounted to an uncashed stack of IOUs that could be translated into votes if the new owners would per-mit the old owners to help round them up.

It's amazing how the tangible benefits of capitalism can overcome conflicts as no other appeal can. Mike Lynn is en-tirely in charge of the Vikings management and is a savvy and tough-minded administrator. He's not loved by every-body, but he is universally regarded as one of the top gen-eral managers in professional sports. Mike's a practical guy, but he still had to be convinced that one of the previous owners of the Vikings, Max Winter, would have to make a key pitch to the league. There's no love lost between Max and Mike, but Mike was finally convinced that Max was needed. No Max, no Super Bowl.

Lynn found out that no one ever choked to death swallowing his pride.

The day of the big vote, I had to leave the NFL meetings in New Orleans to honor a prior commitment to give a speech in Seattle. I received the fabulous news that Minnesota had won the Super Bowl bid shortly before I walked out to address the audience. That's when I got the tribute I'll never forget. The Minneapolis paper, which had not exactly been cheerleaders for us, came around very graciously after we won, and reported what happened when I was introduced to the group that had hired me to speak to them.

"As luck would have it" the paper reported, "Mackay was being introduced by a member of Seattle's Super Bowl task force. The gentleman introduced Mackay and asked the audience to rise. He asked Mackay to sit down. Then he said something like this: 'I'd like all of you to greet our speaker with a loud chorus of boos.'"

They did. Enthusiastically. It was music to my ears.

HARVEY MACKAY'S
SHORT COURSE ON
GETTING STARTED

CHAPTER 2

───────────○───────────

SHARKS, SHARK-BAIT, SHARK-PROOF

LESSON 3

————————————————————•————————————————————

SOME NEW THOUGHTS ABOUT SHARKS—YOU
WERE A SHARK ONCE, TOO

It all started when we were in diapers. Remember how we were treated in those days? When we made our wishes known, the world as we knew it listened. When we wanted to be fed, by God, we were fed. No waiting around for the dinner to get done or the waiter to notice us jumping up and down and waving our arms. When we were feeling a little damp, we just vocalized our concern, and whammo!, all taken care of.

The diapers we wore in those days weren't the garments of helplessness.

They were made for a shark.

They represent the first, and probably the only, time in our lives when we get exactly what we want just by hollering for it. From the time we take them off, and for the rest of

————————————————————•————————————————————

our lives, we have to figure out other ways of getting people to do what we ask of them.

For the first two decades after we get out of diapers, the people who put us in them get even by making us jump through every hoop they can dream up. We aren't sharks then, we're shark-bait.

Not until we grow up and go out on our own do we enter a third phase. Then we become shark-proof. Our former diaperers still talk. We still listen. Sometimes. But we get to decide. The shark/shark-bait relationship weakens, and if we are lucky, we begin to view each other less as rivals for control over our lives and more as loving lifelong friends seeking the same objectives.

The endless cycle of asking and being asked, getting and giving, manipulating and being manipulated is built into every human relationship, even the most innocent and loving.

Whether you're the shark, the victim of the shark, or his equal depends on gaining the same knowledge as the person you're dealing with, and knowing his habits and techniques as well as he knows yours.

Sometimes we have the edge, particularly when we have clearly defined objectives and superior information. The car salesman will always beat the car buyer, because the salesman has that one vital piece of information the buyer never gets. The salesman knows what the car actually costs. By jiggling around the payments, the trade-in, the options, the dealer prep—all those confusing variables—he comes up with a formula that provides him with a comfortable cushion over that cost figure. The moment you have the same information he does, you cease to be shark-bait and become shark-proof.

There are certainly other ways of looking at things. Perhaps you've found that experience is the great teacher that helps you gain knowledge and avoid making the same mistake twice. Not for me, nor for many others. Most of us are such creatures of habit, our mistakes are so ingrained, our character so locked into place, we aren't even smart enough to make *new* mistakes. We keep making the same dumb ones over and over again.

I figure if I only make the same mistake *twice*, I'm ahead of the game. My rule is, never make the same mistake *three* times.

Education can help you avoid the high price you pay for experience. Seminars, tapes, classes, networking are all a lot less painful than learning the hard way.

And I know you can do it.

Not just because you're reading this book.

Because, like everyone else, you were a shark once, too.

LESSON 4

TAKE THIS JOB AND LOVE IT!

After endless years of classes, reports, midterms, finals, it looks as if you're finally ready to learn what it's really like out there in the big, bad world. And for those of you looking again, take heed.

Advice? You'll get plenty of it.

And here's something to remember:

It isn't just dog eat dog out there; it's what Ray Kroc, the founder of McDonald's, called "rat eat rat."

The first thing you'll find is that there are one hundred applicants for the one job *you* want. Worse, you're not graded on a curve here. This is no classroom. Second is last if you don't get the job.

Here's how you can improve the odds in your favor.

Before you set foot in the XYZ Company, you have to do your homework.

Check out XYZ.

If it's a big, publicly held company, it will have an investor relations department. Call and have Investor Relations send you the firm's annual reports and whatever other current releases it has about the company. Most important, ask them to send you copies of the most recent speeches the company's key executives have given or awards or honors they've received.

If the company isn't very big or very visible, you still have plenty of sources you can try. Go to the main branch of your public library. It has a Business Section. Read whatever it has on the company. Many libraries keep clipping files on locally based companies, including the CEO's speeches and awards. Also, check out key names in *Who's Who* or the index to the local paper.

Now, just in case your newspaper doesn't have a published index, go down to the offices of the paper itself, see the librarian there, and ask (or more likely, *beg*, since newspapers tend to be very, very protective of their private files) for permission to look at their clips on XYZ and its executives.

Check your school's alumni office and see who's been placed at XYZ and then call them, meet them, ask them for information.

Ask those up-to-now totally discredited sources of any knowledge—your parents—what they know about XYZ, if they'll network a little on your behalf and find out what they can. In fact, ask your parents or one of their friends to mock-interview you, to find out what your weak spots are so you can work on them. Make sure you have a plan: "Where will this job take me in two years?"

Now you're prepared and armed with the greatest weapon you can have: superior information. You already know more about the company than two thirds of the people you're going to be competing with for that coveted slot.

Next step.

Write a letter asking for an interview. Not to the personnel department, even though your letter will probably end up being sent there. Write to one of the key executives you've been reading about. Tell him or her what you can do for good old XYZ, and don't forget to mention any shared interests you've found in your research.

Many companies hire for style, values, intangibles. It isn't fair; it may not even be intentional. But since you have no track record, what else do they have to go on? So accent the values you have that seem to match the values they have.

Wait a week.

Start calling.

Keep calling until you find someone who will interview you for the position.

You've now flanked about ninety-eight of your hundred competitors, who did nothing more than spotted a want ad in the paper and called the personnel office.

Sure, you may end up in the personnel office, too, but at least it'll be on the basis of a referral by the person to whom you wrote the letter. And the letter itself will precede your arrival, giving the personnel officer something to look at and something for both of you to talk about.

Guarantees? There are none in this life, but there are creative ways to better your chances, and this is one of them.

LESSON 5

●
_____

FIVE THINGS TO DO WHEN YOU ASK FOR A RAISE

Once you've been hired for that position and worked your tail off making sure you're the best darn new hire they ever had, you may decide it's time to ask for a raise. Here are five tips that will give you at least a fighting chance.

1) *Control the agenda.* Almost everyone has an annual salary and/or performance review, but it's amazing how few people are adequately prepared for it. You have to have your act together. You have to find the facts that show you at your best advantage. You have to present them in an intelligent, well-organized manner. And it's going to take some role-playing skills. As a loyal employee, you must go through the boss's checklist first. Don't roll out your heavy artillery during his or her part of the program. If you jump in too fast, you're going to be told, "You're not the only one who's

_____
●

being reviewed, and the company has a set procedure for conducting these meetings."

You'll be shot down before you get started.

Wait. After you've gone through the boss's review agenda, ask to present your own case in your own words.

"I have some additional information that may be useful to you in making your recommendations and decisions concerning my future."

Still the loyal employee, but now the ground is shifting. You're about to put yourself on the opposite side of the table from your employer, but who can refuse "useful information"? It's the Information Age, isn't it?

2) *Keep records.* You must have a well-written, well-documented, names-dates-places record of your major contributions to the company from the date of your last salary review.

Don't try to depend on your memory and then whip something up at the last minute. You'll never get the facts straight.

Do your homework.

Make a daily entry on your desk calendar.

For instance, if you worked overtime two hours to get a special job finished, make a note. Every time, make a note. In a year's time, that is going to be a very impressive and very well-documented number, not just an "I did a lot of overtime" number.

If you performed tasks beyond those in your formal job description, make a note.

If you contributed a new idea, a solution to a problem, a money-saving technique, make a note.

If you received a commendation of some kind, any kind—oral or written—from a supervisor, fellow employee, or customer, make a note.

Put it all together in one big, beautiful package, topped with a summary of the major points, e.g., "a total of 247 uncompensated overtime hours."

It's hard to argue with well-documented facts.

3) *Know the territory.* One of the time-honored defenses against wage demands is, "You certainly deserve it, but we had a lousy year."

Did they?

If it's a publicly held company, get your hands on the annual report. If the company's profits increased, you have a basis for pointing out that it wasn't quite as bad as it may seem. If it's a privately held company that keeps its profitability a closely guarded number, there are still plenty of other comparisons that you can use to make your case. How about the published results of publicly held competitors? "Gee, I'm surprised we did that badly, because the newspaper reported that Mad Dog Envelope Company had record profits."

And there's all that economic stuff that pours out of Washington. The Commerce Department is forever grinding out numbers showing average salary increases in the private sector. It even breaks those numbers down by industry groups. Should you be entitled to less than the average wage increase in your industry? The UAW uses it. The AFL-CIO uses it. You can use it.

4) *Ask for a* specific *number.* This is the hardest one of all, but you have to do it. Most people are very uncomfortable selling themselves like a slab of meat in the marketplace, but if you don't do it, someone is going to do it for you. Or to you. It's not necessarily someone who cares more about you than about saving the company a few bucks.

So put a number on the table. Make it realistic. Have a factual handle. That's what those documented overtime figures or Commerce Department numbers are for.

If you're paid thirty thousand dollars a year and you worked 247 overtime hours in addition to the 2,000 hours you were paid for, then you gave the company a 112.35 percent effort. You gave them 12.35 percent more than they bargained for, and you'd like to think you're worth that much of an increase for the next year, when you'll do the same or better. If you didn't do a nickel's worth of overtime, or anything else, but the government reported that the average annual increase in the manufacturing sector was 5.5 percent and your performance review was satisfactory, well then, you should be entitled to at least the same increase as an average worker.

5) *Don't take "maybe" for an answer.* If you've done your homework, it's not likely you'll get an outright "no." Expect some variation of the familiar tune "I'll Be Seeing You." Or is it the one with the lyric that goes, "But who knows where or when"? Be sure you know where and when.

LESSON 6

FIVE THINGS TO ASK FOR AFTER THEY TURN YOU DOWN FOR A RAISE

Okay, it didn't work.

Now what?

Know that you didn't hurt yourself by asking. Your short-term tactics may have failed, but your long-term strategy is going to work. It's just going to take longer and require more from you than you hoped it would. No matter how cavalier the ultimate no, there are some guilt feelings attached to it.

Like the outfit that put a notice on the bulletin board that read, "Those who are underpaid will be fired last."

You can capitalize on that guilt, helping yourself in other ways and laying the groundwork for a yes in the future.

Here's what you ask for instead of the raise.

1) *Longer hours.* That's right, not shorter hours, longer

---

hours. But you're not looking for a mop job. So far, your overtime hours haven't been worth more to the company. You want your extra hours to be hours that *will* be worth more. Hours in new areas. Hours that give you more responsibility. Greater challenges.

2) *Training.* You want the opportunity to improve your skills and learn new ones. How about the chance to attend a seminar, a convention? How about paying tuition so you can improve your speaking and selling skills? What about computer classes? Will the firm help you learn computer skills and then back them up with the equipment you need on your job?

3) *Hitting the mark.* You want to know what requirements you will have to meet in order to hit your salary goals? Ask. Then ask for another salary review ahead of the normal schedule, "to chart your progress."

4) *Careering.* Are your career goals realistic? Ask. Then ask your boss to set out the firm's ideas for a long-term career path for you at the company and a reasonable timetable for achieving it.

5) *Making the move.* Will management give you strong support in helping place you in another department or another company where your salary requirements and career goals can be met?

The idea here is to get you ahead of the pack, away from the normal processes that the company follows to evaluate salaries. You want to be in the fast-track category. You've designed your own program. You're special.

LESSON 7

•

HOW TO STAY EMPLOYED

Do you feel a slight chill on the back of your neck? Is that the whisper of the ax in the air?

Cutting payrolls has been Corporate America's most meaningful response to foreign competition. With almost thirty-five hundred mergers and acquisitions in 1988 alone, merger activity has been a huge and visible cause of layoffs, but a change in corporate culture is even more of a factor.

The concept of just-in-time delivery has been extended to the work force. The stockpiling of employees, like the stockpiling of parts, is over. Redundant employees are out. The day of the cost analyst has arrived.

The only way to be sure of your survival is to be able to demonstrate that your presence is profitable to the company.

Think of yourself and what you do as a profit center.

•

Whether you're a salesperson, clerk, nurse, computer operator, production assistant, whatever, the essential, inescapable, ultimate question is: Are you bringing in more money than it costs to keep you around?

If you already have to report on this basis, so much the better.

If you don't, you do now.

For some occupations, like commission sales, finding the answer is neat and easy. If you don't perform, you don't get paid. Your value to the company is easy to measure.

But let's make it tough. Let's say you're in a department like personnel that never lays a hand on a penny and doesn't charge back its services to anyone else. Compare your costs with the costs of having the job done by someone or something else.

Your competition may not be another person but another company.

By charging your old outfit hourly rates instead of requiring it to hire a new employee, could another company get the same work done that you do, minus what it costs for your sick leave, vacations, medical benefits, pension?

Ironically, if you are fired in one of these cost-saving moves, don't burn bridges. There's a real possibility you actually may end up doing your old job for your old company—but being employed by a new company at a distinctly lower salary.

Your only protection is your bottom-line dollar value. If you can't honestly justify it, then you'd better start trying by honing your skills, giving yourself an added dimension—like doing the company speaking chores, volunteer work, or training new employees—and/or aggressively moving up the ladder to where you can justify it.

Otherwise, it's just a matter of time.

LESSON 8

———————————•———————————

DELIVER MORE THAN YOU PROMISE

It's the single best way to stay employed.

Smucker's, the jelly and jam maker, has a policy of filling its containers with just a bit more product than the advertised weight. Does anyone weigh them? Probably not. But then, it isn't necessary, because you know it's the company's policy to do more than it has to do. Which may be the reason that I, and a lot of other people, buy Smucker's.

The most successful retailer in the country, Nordstrom—highest margins, best return on equity, all the right numbers—always goes the extra mile for its customers.

Marilyn Savage, a schoolteacher in Oregon, wanted to buy a Nordstrom booklet on how to tie a scarf. Price: $1. Nordstrom was out. Four weeks later, two booklets arrived. No charge. Of course, she now shops at Nordstrom. That wouldn't be so surprising except that she lives in Bend and

———————————•———————————

35

has to drive 160 miles to Portland to get to the store. Do you think Nordstrom got its $2 worth?

Another story from Bend. Same schoolteacher. This time, she totaled her car and barely escaped alive. She wasn't about to buy the same model, so she went to another dealer. He didn't have what she wanted in stock, and he wouldn't order it without her making "a commitment" in advance to buy it. She finally ended up back at the dealer who sold her the car she'd rolled, where her original salesman not only ordered the model she wanted on "spec," but helped her get an additional thousand-dollar settlement from her insurance company on the battered heap.

Where does it say car salesmen are supposed to fill out a prospect's insurance claims? That's a waste of time.

But the fellow who did it happens to be the agency's leading salesman year in and year out. The schoolteacher even baked him a cake when she got her check from the insurance company She bought the car, of course, even though she hadn't made a commitment. Do you think she might have steered a few additional customers his way, too?

Successful people do things others don't like to do.

Lou Holtz has used the same expression every time I've had a conversation with him: "What can I do for you?" It isn't that he always does it, but that he cares enough to want to try. Not many people do. But then, not many people have made it as far as he has.

What kind of attitude do you have toward your job? We all have to do things that we don't particularly enjoy, but we do them to get to do the things we do enjoy. Beverly Sills made her reputation as an international opera singer. As a writer, she had to learn how to handle a new experience, the national book tour. Take it from me, it is not in the same comfort zone as touring with the Metropolitan Opera. It's more like a road trip with the Toledo Mud Hens.

As Sills was winding down a long day of radio talk shows,

newspaper interviews, speeches, bookstore appearances, and autographing, a fan told her how he sympathized with her for "having to go to dozens of cities and meet all these different people." "No," she said, "I don't have to go. I *get* to go. And I don't have to meet them. I *get* to meet them." That's the attitude and personality that made her beloved as a performer and turned her autobiography into a national best seller.

Make them notice you. Don't get the report in on time. Get it in early. It's not that hard, and you have to do it anyway.

Don't try to meet your quotas. Exceed them. Do what it takes to set yourself apart from the pack. Make them need you.

LESSON 9

THERE'S NO SUCH THING AS CUSTOMER TENNIS

"A young man's most profitable investment is to give his best to his employer," said Roger Babson, the New England financier.

Let the boss steal your idea. He'll know where he got it from—and where to go the next time he needs one.

Paul Oreffice, who worked his way up to chairman of the Dow Chemical Company, came to this country as an immigrant after graduating from high school. He had a greater challenge than most people starting up the ladder. He couldn't speak English when he entered Purdue University.

"Go ahead and beat the boss at anything you can," says Oreffice, who is a tennis buddy of mine. "I strongly believe a winner is a winner, and so do most people I know in positions of influence. There is no such thing as playing customer golf or tennis, either with your boss or with a customer."

About two months before the Super Bowl vote, I met Victor Kiam, who owns the New England Patriots. Kiam and I had a tennis match, for no better reason than we're both business authors and tennis nuts. The stakes: a year's supply of envelopes for his executives versus Remington shavers for my employees.

Though I'm not in the same league with him as a business owner (his Remington Shaver Company is more than ten times the size of my company, Mackay Envelope), it didn't take me long to find out we *were* in the same league when it came to tennis. I thought to myself, This guy is going to be voting on our Super Bowl bid; should I dump a few serves into the net just to make him look good?

I didn't do it; I'm a better tennis player than I am an actor. If he sensed I was going into the tank, and he's no dummy, I was sure he'd be a lot more unhappy with me than if he was simply outgunned.

Besides, I'd already given him the perfect alibi.

Just as he was about to make his first serve, I held up my hand to stop him, rushed to the net, jumped over with a copy of his book *Go for It* in hand, and asked him to autograph it.

"Who am I playing here," he asked, "Bobby Riggs?"

No customer tennis that day.

The 350 Remington shavers I won, one for every Mackay Envelope employee, were delivered with a gracious note from Kiam: "Harvey gave me a close shave but not as close as the shave I'm going to give you."

THE RULE OF TEN THOUSAND

When you were a kid, you wouldn't get the pie unless you ate the peas.

As we get older, it gets more sophisticated. They don't threaten to fire you to get a day's work out of you.

But there is a variation of the peas/pie gambit that still gets results. One of the country's most successful college basketball coaches uses the Rule of Ten Thousand. Or rather, ten thousand dollars.

"You miss more free throws than any other starter on this team," he says. "You say you can't make free throws?

"Now, what if I were to pay you ten thousand dollars to shoot above the league average in free throws the rest of the season? Could you hit sixty-five percent?"

"Yeah, I know I can."

"Yeah, I know you can, too. Only there's just one thing.

I'm not going to pay you ten thousand dollars. You are going up to that line, and every time you shoot I want you to think you're shooting for that ten thousand dollars."

A 50 percent free-throw shooter became a 70 percent shooter, for a coach whose teams appeared in the NCAA tournament more often than any other team in his region.

Same problem, different scenario.

"You are late to work more often than any other employee in this section. I've heard all the excuses. They don't cut it. Here's what we'll do. I'm going to bribe you. It's strictly against company rules, but if you are not late to work once, that is, once in the next year, I'm going to see to it that we give you ten thousand dollars. Okay, for an extra ten thousand dollars, can you get an alarm clock that works and remember to set it? Can you get here on time for ten thousand dollars?"

"You bet I can!"

"There's just one thing. You aren't going to be late, but I'm not going to pay you the ten thousand dollars. But I want you to act exactly, exactly, as if you think I'm going to, because now I know you can do it. It's just a question of motivation."

Still the same problem, still another scenario.

This time the setting is your head. The problem, whatever it is, is yours. The boss is on your case. Vague threats. Try the Rule of Ten Thousand on yourself. If you were given an extra ten thousand dollars could you, would you, get your act together?

You can do it after all, can't you?

CHAPTER 3

AN EMPLOYEE'S MANUAL OF SELF-DEFENSE

LESSON 11

—————————•—————————

BEWARE THE OFFICE BULLY

Some people live just to dump on other people.

It's almost a form of rape, a sick way to break through the impersonality of a relationship and violate others.

It can take a variety of forms. Sexual harassment and personally abusive and excessive criticism are common garden varieties often found in the workplace.

Bullies do their thing when it's one-on-one, when they're in a position of advantage or authority, and when they think they've found someone who won't fight back.

You have to neutralize these tactics.

The best way to fight back is to choose your own time and your own battlefield, but not submit to the bully's. A bully can't bully someone who won't let him. *Immediately* break off any contact the moment it starts, turn on your heels, state firmly over your shoulder as you leave, "I'm

—————————•—————————

making a record of this incident." Get as far away from the bully as you can, and as soon as you're able to, head for your desk and write down a thorough, objective record of the entire incident.

Why?

You have now taken control of the situation. You've broken the bully's lance in midthrust. You're gone. When you leave the scene of the crime, the bully doesn't decide what happens next. You do. He is deprived of the pleasure of observing your shock, anger, or submission. He's left unsatisfied, unfulfilled. His attempt to violate you has failed. And he has to sweat out the possibility of your going over his head and raising hell.

With the ball in your court, you now must decide how far to take the matter. It's a safe bet that his supervisor really doesn't want to hear about it; it reflects badly on him as well as on the bully, and you have to be concerned whether it can hurt your own career. No one wants to develop a reputation as a whiner or a squealer.

But, of course, the bully is counting on those considerations to protect him.

So it's not an easy choice, but at least it's your choice, not the bully's. *This time,* you might decide simply to write a memo to the files. In it, you might explain that you didn't pursue matters further because you felt that by breaking off in midair you'd sent the bully a message that would forestall another incident. *But* you're writing this one up just in case there might be a repeat performance.

This time, you might just decide to schedule a meeting with the bully on your turf, time and place of your choosing, tell him about the memo you made and what will happen the next time.

Maybe there won't be a second incident.

If you can, wait until there is one.

But if you have to act, here's how you do it.

Again, and this is critical, make a record.

Then schedule the dreaded meeting with the bully's superior. You have now changed the one-on-one equation and put the bully in the presence of someone who has authority over him. All three of you should be there.

This is extremely heavy-duty action. Take it for granted that your bully's boss does not want to see you and is looking for any excuse to have this matter resolved by the bully and you and in the bully's favor. To act otherwise is to undermine the bully's authority and possibly to get everyone in the soup. Visions of million-dollar lawsuits are flashing through sweaty foreheads.

So if you're going to do it, you'd better do it right.

Read from your notes of the incident/incidents.

If there are two incidents, the notes will prove that you did not go over the bully's head without fair warning and that you held off making a fuss without unilaterally giving the bully a second chance. If there's only one incident, well, so what? It was bad enough that you didn't feel you had to tolerate the risk of this kind of behavior again.

The matter is now squarely in the supervisor's lap. You've probably lost control of how it's going to be handled, but at least you're unlikely to experience another sample of the bully's behavior. If this meeting doesn't put an end to it, probably nothing short of a lawsuit will. You will have to consider the possibility that you may have been wrong or were exaggerating the incident(s).

But if you're still convinced you're right or the behavior continues and you find it intolerable, you've probably reached the point where you should consider seeing your own lawyer.

It could even be a situation in which you're so right, the company thinks it has to prove you're wrong in order to avoid liability.

Here's a big clue: Company lawyers are asking you to

repeat your story to them and asking you to give them signed statements and/or copies of your notes—upon threats of termination if you don't. Smile sweetly and say, "I'll be happy to if *my* lawyer says I should." Don't do it otherwise.

Here's an even bigger clue: You do get fired. (As you will learn, the company regards itself as having defenses, too.) Ask for the reasons in writing. Surprise! It's not for your behavior in connection with this incident, but for an unrelated reason, e.g., "You can't get along with anyone else," or "Your performance is sub-par."

By this time, you have doubtless concluded that 1) you're sorry you brought the whole thing up in the first place and 2) who is Harvey Mackay and how do I strangle him?

Just remember, I'm trying to be straight with you. If the company stonewalls, carrying this matter to its ultimate conclusion is going to require a strong case, good representation, time, money, effort, and guts.

If you have them, you should win. But you might not. As John Kennedy pointed out, life is not always fair.

If you have doubts, you should stop somewhere short of total war.

Of course, the cast of characters may be different. Instead of the Bully, you may have the Snitch, the Slouch, the Slob, the Ungrateful Bastard, the Thief of Baghdad, the Finger-pointer, or one of any number of other less than honorable humanoids to deal with. I never realized the rogues' gallery of workplace losers was so long until Oprah Winfrey invited me to be on her show to talk about office politics. The horror stories I heard from the audience and panel guests told me that office losers are one serious problem. When Oprah drew me out, it was the first time I really saw the bigger picture . . . and how one basic approach handles all sizes and shapes of misfits.

Whatever the type, your technique should be the same: Don't get in one-on-one confrontations, keep records, and hold your fire as long as possible. But when it gets intolerable, go up the ladder and keep hollering until something gets done or until they send *you* a message and you have to decide how hard to push it.

You must remember, too, this approach does not apply to every single personal problem in the world. Life is like the Middle East. Sometimes there is no good solution.

I tend to be aggressive in situations that involve conflict. It has usually, but not always, worked for me. It might work for you.

I guarantee, you will have the opportunity to put it to the test.

You'll find office politics in every office, and I'm including a two-person hot-dog stand in my definition of an office. People are always jockeying for position, and the kinds of people I'm talking about are the only three kinds I'm certain are out there: sharks, shark-bait, and shark-proof. Which one are you?

LESSON 12

LOOSE LIPS SINK SHIPS

This incident involves conflict among employees, but it has a more universal application.

It's a cautionary tale I hope you'll read to your kids, even if you can't persuade them to read the rest of this book.

One of the unhappiest stages on the way to adulthood is losing that baby fat of naïveté that had us believing that everyone on earth except Frank Lorenzo is a wonderful human being who has our best interests at heart.

The daughter of a friend of mine was a recent graduate in graphic arts. She came from a conservative, sheltered Texas family, and she graduated from a conservative, sheltered Texas liberal arts school. She was hired as an intern with a small advertising agency in North Carolina. They told her that if things worked out, if they liked her work after a period of three months or so, they'd offer her a permanent job that would lead to fulfilling her career goal of becoming a full-fledged art director.

This is a fairly common practice in the agency game. Most hires of creative types are made on the basis of their portfolios, and with novices there's no way to tell if the work you're looking at belongs to the kid who's standing in front of your desk or the kid's last instructor. During her trial period, the intern made friends with another woman, an art director who had been there for a couple of years. The art director became something of a mentor to the intern.

"If they offer you a job," said the art director, "you ought to know how much to ask for. You shouldn't take less than $17,500."

"You mean if he offers me less, I shouldn't take it?"

"No way. Ask for $17,500. You're worth that," said the art director.

It turned out the intern was talented and likable. She was offered a job. As soon as she left the boss's office, she rushed over to her newfound friend.

"I'm so excited! He offered me the job, and I took it," she said.

"That's just wonderful. How much?"

"You won't believe it—nineteen thousand five hundred dollars!"

The air froze. The art director believed it all right.

"Nineteen-five? That's almost what I'm getting, and I've been here two years."

The next day the boss called the intern back into the office.

"I'm sorry," he said, "but I can't hire you. I've got a revolt on my hands. We're a small shop, and this is a collaborative business to begin with. You have to be able to get along. Apparently, you went around bragging about the salary we talked about, and now no one wants to work with you. Again, it's too bad, but that's the way it is."

The intern couldn't believe it. Oh sure, she'd known a few like *Dallas*'s Sue Ellen, whose assurance that "you never looked lovelier" was a sure sign you were a fashion flop. But nothing like this art director had ever happened to her before. This was real life. She had been used. She had been had. And she was about to be seriously sidetracked professionally.

So she called her daddy.

And he called the head of agency, explained exactly what happened, and asked him if he wouldn't change his mind and rehire his daughter. The salary wasn't that important.

The answer was still no.

The job was over.

And so we have another sure sign of adulthood. You know you're grown up when you get yourself into a mess that your folks can't straighten out for you.

There are some things that are absolutely no one's business but your own: your salary, your net worth, your medical records, and your sex life.

Don't discuss them with your co-workers.

Discuss them with no one; that is, NO ONE. There is no reason you have to discuss them with anyone. Remember, the definition of a secret is when one person knows . . . . and the walls have ears!

Don't fail to notice that the offices where the deals are made have doors on them. There's a reason.

Don't discuss any business where it can be overheard by others. Almost as many deals have gone down in elevators as elevators have gone down.

The ironclad test of the person you never want to do business with, the total fool or the phony all-hat-and-no-cattle businessman, is hearing him carry on about some big deal where he can be overheard.

Save it.

LESSON 13

———————————————•———————————————

DON'T HANG YOUR STAR ON A SUPERSTAR

A lot of people will disagree with this, because there is no more certain way to gain visibility than to attach yourself to a winner and ride his coattails to fame and glory. The top ranks of the coaching profession are filled with former Lombardi and Woody Hayes and Bear Bryant assistants. I have to admit that being a member of the White House staff carries a certain cachet you won't get from working at Mackay Envelope.

But there are problems.

It's one thing to work for a company run by a top-drawer manager, but it's quite another to serve on the immediate staff of a celebrity type. Stick with the low-wattage personalities.

Charismatic leaders tend to be classic Mr. Outsides. You do the work; they take the bows. For years, yards and yards

———————————————•———————————————

of the Broadway gossip-columnist Walter Winchell's stuff was written by his staff. They may have had the modest thrill of basking in the glow as the great man passed in and out of the office, but neither their salaries nor their subsequent careers reflected their contribution to Winchell's success.

If you do sign on with one of these, know when to jump ship. When you hitch your wagon to someone else, you're stuck with his or her reputation. You lose a portion of your own identity. If your mentor falls, you fall. I'd rather be master of my own fate. I don't think I'd care to be known for the rest of my life as a member of the Nixon staff or the De Lorean team.

An even worse problem isn't when you jump ship. It's when your mentor does.

A friend of mine is a cop. There are more politics in the average police department than you'll ever find across the hall in the mayor's office. Cops are suspicious by nature. It's their calling. They're particularly suspicious of each other. They start forming cliques from the moment they graduate from the police academy. While they're still standing in the reception line, a guy recruiting for the Knights of Columbus makes his way up one end of the line while a guy from the Masons works his way down the other. After dividing by religion, they start subdividing. Plainclothes against uniform. Vice against burglary. Day shift against dogwatch. Everyone not in the front office against the front office. And on it goes.

My friend had a rabbi. Not that he's Jewish, that's just the cops' expression for a mentor. His rabbi was the chief himself. My guy got all the choice assignments. But the minute the chief stopped being the chief, the long knives came out, and not only did my friend's own enemies catch up with him, he inherited the chief's enemies, too. Now, he's off the force. He took a job in another state as chief of a department one tenth the size of the one he dreamed of heading.

The key to this kind of relationship is nimbleness afoot. Think of your place on the superstar's team as a résumé-builder, not as a career, like a law clerk to a judge. They stay a year or two. Then they move on.

The ultimate careerists are the members of the president's cabinet. In the Reagan administration, only one of his cabinet—there were thirteen—served out the full eight years in the same job.

If your own star is going to shine, you can't be standing in someone else's shadow forever. Don't linger. Fly too close to the sun, and you're going to get burned.

LESSON 14

●

THE UPSIDE OF DOWNSIZING

Late 1982 was the beginning of the longest business expansion since the postwar boom of the late 1940's and 50's.

Politicians tend to obscure the reasons, because they focus on the past, pointing with pride or viewing with alarm depending on how they can best dramatize their own roles.

Businesspeople tend to ignore the reasons, because we focus on the future, eyes glued to the horizon, worrying when the next recession will hit. Still, it's important for us to understand the whys. There's a wave out there we can ride, if we know how to climb on.

American-made products have always been vulnerable to foreign competition because of our free-trade policies. We've believed that the free-enterprise system gives us the flexibility to adjust to the challenge of markets open to everyone with anything to sell.

●

That belief was put to the test when the Japanese invaded the marketplace with goods of a quality and price we couldn't match. Like the Japanese themselves after World War II, we had to adjust or die.

We adjusted.

We've all heard about the wonders of Japanese business practices, and heard about them and heard about them. But you don't see many American workers in quality circles, morning calisthenics classes, or singing the company song these days. Even the introduction of new technologies and the rediscovery of product quality, though important, are not where the major changes have been made.

The big adjustment in American business practices has been in the relentless, systematic, ongoing scaling back of the cost of American manufactured goods, principally by holding down the cost of labor. In the past, when labor demanded higher wages, American business, with the automobile industry playing the lead role, put on a little show and then caved in and passed on wage increases to the consumer. And so did everyone else. What was good for General Motors was good for the country. But by 1980, that quaint notion had become untenable; if we were to remain competitive, not only in world markets but in our own house here at home, we had to cut costs.

Labor versus management is where the rubber met the road.

The fork in that road came early in the Reagan administration with the breakup of the Air Traffic Controllers' Union. It was the signal that labor was no longer in the driver's seat; it was the beginning of the end of "the English sickness" in the United States.

That change was reinforced by the recession in 1982. It cooled off inflationary excesses, particularly fat wage settlements.

More recently, the whole structure of American corporate organization has been slowly unraveling. The unbundling of Corporate America is the trend that seems to be creeping up without anyone paying much attention.

More and more businesses are farming out work they used to do in house. The work is being taken over by niche companies specifically organized to do payroll, accounting, pension-fund work, medical records, and the like. It can save both types of companies money. For example, the pension and benefit laws have been structured to force a company to extend benefits down to its clerical employees. It hires a niche company to administer the benefits, eliminating the need for a benefits department within the company. It also provides economy of scale for the niche companies. They don't handle just your accounts; they handle a lot of other people's, too, spreading their personnel and equipment and overhead over a lot more territory.

How are the Japanese going to deal with that? Are they going to ship their Toyotas stuffed with clerks and bookkeepers?

Franchised operations use different techniques to achieve the same low labor costs. Products are prepared on a standardized, assembly-line basis. Minimal skills are required. Turnover is at epidemic levels, which discourages unions. Employees become easily replaceable parts.

It isn't a very pretty picture, but it's the response that got us where we are today, and if you're an employee and expect to compete, you're going to have to find a way to deal with it.

The Bureau of Labor Statistics came out with a study in 1988 that shows that the average college graduating senior will make 10.3 job changes in his or her career. The bureau's also predicting that by 2000, the average graduate will make five *career* changes.

Five years ago, Kimberly joined Hard Edge Software in California's Silicon Valley as a programmer with hot prospects. Hard Edge was a Wall Street darling with wide open spaces and plenty of headroom for a dynamic, intelligent young programmer. There were five separate corporate levels between Kimberly's entry-level position and the top job, director of software development. Kimberly could look forward to a steady climb from programmer to senior programmer, assistant project manager, and deputy software director.

But three years ago, the ground started to shift. Hard Edge did some hard thinking and began to downsize. When Kimberly looked up, she saw her career track being swept away as casually as the wind swept away the tracks of her custom convertible pickup on the back roads of Sonoma.

Today, Kimberly is still a programmer. She works for the software-development manager. (The director's job was axed.) At times, she counts herself lucky to have a job. Other times, she feels trapped. Sound familiar? To a big part of the white-collar work force in America, you bet it does. Overnight, career tracks across America changed lanes—from the express route to the milk run. And that's the way things are going to stay. Computers, competition, unbundling, and mergers are cutting back the number of jobs.

What do you do?

You follow these seven rules.

MACKAY'S SEVEN STEPS TO GETTING OUT OF THE RUT WHEN YOUR CAREER GETS STUCK

1. *Readjust your pace.* If you told a 500-meter sprinter who was 250 meters into the race that he was now going to be running a mile, what's the first thing he'd do? Of course, he would change his tempo, he'd stride differently, pace himself differently. The first thing any sensible employee does in a downsized company is to do the same. Realize the path between promotions may now be longer. The rules

have changed in midrace. Tear your hair and curse the gods if you think it'll help, but the worst thing you can do is make believe it didn't happen.

2. *Analyze your competition.* More than ever, it's important to know who you're up against for those few remaining slots. What are the other people doing? What are they overlooking? Is the next promotion slated to go to somebody outside the company to bring in "fresh blood" and "new perspectives"? Analyze yourself, too. How marketable are you in the outside world? Get to know your value and your options.

3. *Look for sideways growth.* If you can't grow going up, can you build your credentials and experience through lateral moves at the same level so that you can learn new skills? If you're dead-ended in programming, then explore the prospects in marketing. There's never been a company yet that didn't need more sales. Give yourself an alternative route. It's a great way to improve your promotion odds long term.

4. *Study the corporate culture.* Does the company favor a certain way of doing things? Is there a corporate style? At the phone companies, it's called the "Bell-shaped head." When you study the way the winners do it and compare that to the way you do it, you may not like what you see, but you'd better see it.

5. *Take a look at your personal risk factor.* Sure, there are ways to move up faster, but before you leap, look at the risks involved. If your advancement opportunities are fewer, then you may have to find ways to stand out from the rest of the pack, even though you could fall flat on your face trying. Are you willing to propose bold new ideas? Will you take on projects that really stretch your abilities? You can get yourself noticed, and you may get ahead in the process, but your risk of failure increases, too.

I'm for trying. Go the extra mile. It's never crowded.

You'll fail some of the time. If you don't, you're not trying hard enough. If you want to be the leader of the pack, you have to be willing to stick your neck out in front of the others. Sometimes it's risky not to take risks.

6. *Draw up your plan.* Add up all the factors: pace, competition, long-term growth options, risk, and the hard facts about advancement. Then put down your plan, *in writing.*

7. *Measure your results.* If you can, share your plan with your boss, and then measure your own progress on a fixed schedule. If you still don't seem to be going places, it's time to tune up the résumé and look around for a new track to run on.

HARVEY MACKAY'S
SHORT COURSE ON
WORKING YOUR WAY UP

CHAPTER 4

YOU'RE A LOT BETTER OFF BEING SCARED THAN BEING BORED

LESSON 15

●

THE MISSING INGREDIENT

Late last year, I got a letter that pointed out that a formula I wrote—determination + goal setting + concentration = success—was absent an ingredient. The letter was from someone who has pretty good credentials for analyzing formulas. His name is Bob Hahl, and he got his doctorate in chemistry from Harvard last year.

I am writing to mention that a fourth quality which is required for success . . . is courage. That all-important asset, determination, can be undermined by the fear that comes with a new venture. If they haven't anticipated it already, most people meet that fear when they first take on true responsibility. People sometimes then become less ambitious because they feel they don't have the courage. *What people don't know is that courage can be learned.* Aircraft pilots know this to be a fact. The more harrowing rides they take, the less frightened they are on the next one. An acquaintance

●

with fear is an important part of pilot training. Over the years, pilots learn to control their emotions as well as they control the airplane. But it takes effort.

I suspect that many people fail to achieve their goals because they are afraid of the job at hand and don't realize that they can get used to it.

Let me take that one step further. In my opinion, many people fail to achieve their goals not because they are afraid of the job at hand, but because they have grown so familiar in the comfort zone of their job that they are afraid to meet the challenge of a new job.

The greatest acts of courage tend to be committed by entrepreneurs. I have never—I repeat, never—met anyone who left his job, whether fired or voluntarily, who started his own business and regretted it. What these people always regret is not having done it sooner.

That includes people who eventually went bust and had to go back to work for someone else. Last June, *The Wall Street Journal* ran an article about Julian Carnes, who did just that, losing just about everything, including his son's college fund, in a start-up business. He wound up working for wages again—he and his wife now earn ninety thousand dollars—and he says, "I never would have been happy if I hadn't tried it. I'd go back to owning a business in a minute."

Throughout his life, John Huston, the movie director, courted physical danger. He risked his life on the front lines as a foreign correspondent and wartime film director.

Michael Caine, the British actor, once described Huston's success in the movie business in these terms: "John had been through the dam and come out the other side, while most of us feared even getting near the water. Having survived, he never feared anything after that."

In fact, Huston found physical tests of courage exhilarating, and they became the wellspring of his creative impulse, a source of artistic inspiration that never seemed to fail him.

Afraid to try something new? Most of us are. But it's all over so soon that our regrets will invariably be for what we didn't do rather than for what we did. The missing ingredient is courage.

It can change your life. It can change the world. You can do it right here. And now.

TAKE THIS TEST BEFORE YOU TAKE THE PLUNGE

QUESTION 1. DO I NEED A NEW IDEA?

"Yes." Wrong answer.

Not long ago, a young man took me aside and, after extracting a solemn pledge of secrecy, told me he was quitting his job as a stockbroker to start his own business.

"I've got an idea," he said. "I'm going to set up a business selling cut flowers on a long-term contract basis. You see all these advertising agencies and professional offices and executive offices? They have very nicely decorated public areas, and image is important. But what do they have in their reception rooms? Potted plants. Ferns. I can give them fresh-cut flowers for the same amount of money they're spending to rent a moldy old fig tree that somebody comes in and waters once a week."

"Okay," I said. "I guess I understand the concept, but why aren't the established florists in town already doing it? And why would someone buy from you rather than from them?"

"Hey, remember, this is a secret. There's a reason. It's a new idea. That's why nobody's doing it."

"I don't know whether it's a good idea or a bad idea, but the one thing I'm sure of is that it isn't a new idea."

He didn't believe me, of course. Like millions of us consumed with an idea we're trying to bring to life, he thought he had stumbled onto something that had never been tried before.

You don't need a new idea.

"Do the common thing uncommonly well," says Paul Oreffice, chairman of the board of Dow Chemical.

It isn't the quality of the ideas you have that will determine whether you make a success of them, it's the qualities you bring to those ideas. Even people in creative businesses who make a living trying to be fresh and original will frequently find what they think is a breakthrough concept is being done by someone else. That's because so many of us have similar life experiences, plus cultural and educational backgrounds, that we tend to generate similar ideas. A friend told me how he once took a copy of a Leonardo da Vinci painting to a museum and showed it to the curator. The curator took one look at it and told him not only when it was painted, but also the nationality of the copyist—both confirmed when he flipped it over to a signature and date on the back of the canvas.

"How did you do that?" my friend asked, thinking he had run across the world's greatest parlor trick. It turned out to be something more than that. "We're all prisoners of our times," the curator said, "especially a copyist, whose powers of imagination are, by definition, limited. The choice of a subject to copy, the brush strokes, and the emphasis all reflect the tastes and styles in vogue in the time and place he made this copy. The telltale clues track behind him like muddy boots; they shriek from this canvas. How could anyone expect he would be able to escape his own skin?"

The mark of genius, such as Picasso or Beethoven had, is the ability to take an existing form and create something truly original and enduring from it. The mark of talent is the ability to take an existing form and perfect it. Sixty years ago, the best position players in baseball had only four skills: They could run, field, throw, and hit for average. Babe Ruth, the game's one true genius, added an extra dimension: the ability to hit for distance. The game hasn't been the same since.

Warren Buffett, the Omaha investor who turned a borrowed $100,000 in 1956 into over $1.2 billion, has a talent for picking stocks. He didn't do it with new ideas. He put into practice the methodology of Graham and Dodd's *Security Analysis,* a book that's been around for decades. What made Buffett successful was his iron self-discipline and single-mindedness, not unlike Clausewitz's description of military strategy: "Everything in strategy is very simple, but that does not mean everything is very easy."

Buffett illustrates that consuming focus with the story of the poor tailor who scrimped and saved his entire life until he finally had enough money to finance his lifelong dream, a pilgrimage to the Vatican. When he returned, his friends gathered to hear him tell about his trip.

"And did you see the Holy Father?"

"Oh, yes, I certainly did."

"And can you describe him for us?"

"Oh, yes, yes. He was a perfect forty-four regular."

When I finally persuaded my young friend to check out his new idea with the local florists, he found out that it had in fact been tried from time to time, but that they were never able to keep their contracts very long.

"Why not?"

"From what I can figure out, they just didn't want to service them. They can't get much more for cut flowers than for the stuff in pots, and once the fern is there, it's there. You water it maybe every week or so. With the flowers, they don't hold up, and sometimes they even start to wilt in a couple of days. And then, too, the customers start to worry that their own clients and employees will think they're spending too much money on unimportant, frivolous things, so they get nervous and bail out."

"In other words, you think the florists are just too lazy to service them and too weak at selling to reinforce their customers' original decisions."

"Yup."

"Well, I can't see that those are insurmountable problems. You're going to have to care enough to take care of your customers. That's the simplest and the hardest thing anyone in business has to do. There's no mystery to it, but it's hard because you can't slack off. Your product is highly visible. Maybe you can skip a watering on a fern, but with flowers, if you miss your schedule just once or give your customers one inferior delivery, it's going to be noticed, and you're history."

"Yup. And if and when the economy turns down, it may not be so rosy, pardon the pun. Cut flowers aren't exactly sacred cows when expenses are being cut."

"And you're going to have to make sure that if it works, your wholesaler is not going to compete with you. So you might need more than one source of supply."

"Yup."

"But you seem to have done your homework. If you're well capitalized, I can't think of any good reason why you shouldn't make it."

Except that I *could* think of a reason.

It would all depend on him, his single-mindedness, his drive, his determination, his desire to succeed, his concentration, to the exclusion of all the other pleasures and responsibilities he had—and his courage.

If he had those qualities, he had come to the right place. The number of households in the United States with a net worth in excess of $1 million doubled between 1980 and 1987. Proprietors of small businesses made up the largest single category of millionaires.

The best way I know to judge is this: You have to want it more than you want anything else in the world.

And most important, you have to be sure you *never get it*.

The successful people I know always have a carrot in front of them, slightly out of reach, no matter how many carrots they already have. When he was thirty, Lou Holtz wrote down a list of 107 lifetime ambitions on a slip of paper. They ranged from owning a 1949 Chevy to being invited to the White House for dinner. By the time he was fifty-two, he had achieved eighty-six of them. Do you want to bet whether he'll make the other twenty-one? And when he does, if he'll tear up the original list and write down another 107?

Curt Carlson, the ultimate entrepreneur of the Carlson Companies, dreamed of achieving $1 billion in sales. When he did it, he revised his sights to $2 billion. He made that and then his next goal of $4 billion. Now, he's aiming at $9 billion. Somehow I have trouble believing he'll quit when he hits it.

What happened to the budding bud entrepreneur?

The last time I saw him, he was still employed at the same place where I'd met him, the dream of going into business for himself still just that, a dream.

"I just couldn't pull the trigger," he said. "I still think it would work, but you know, I've got a pretty good job, super retirement plan and all that. Maybe I'm better off staying where I am."

Maybe.

But I think I know what was missing.

There is no "off" switch on a tiger.

New ideas. They're wonderful if you can come up with them. But your best chance of success is working the hell out of some old values.

QUESTION 2. WHO ARE MY CUSTOMERS?

"Everyone." Wrong answer.

No one has had "everyone" for a customer since the old *Life* magazine went out of business, which is why it went out of business. If your concept is going to succeed, you have to identify a realistic target audience, big enough to be profitable yet small enough for you to service it thoroughly.

QUESTION 3. WHY SHOULD ANYONE WANT TO BUY MY PRODUCT OR SERVICE?

"Everyone needs it." Wrong answer.

Find an unmet, unanswered need by identifying a market segment that isn't being served or is being served inadequately.

For 125 years, the post office served "everybody"—unprofitably. Federal Express identified a market among business users who needed fast, guaranteed, time-sensitive deliveries, a segment the post office had neglected. Others woke up, including, ironically, the post office itself, and saw that they could further segment the market Federal Express had discovered. The post office sheared off the price-sensitive segment by offering the same service at a lower price. Then came FAX machines, whose manufacturers sliced the pie into even smaller wedges by aiming at the businesses that aren't satisfied with overnight deliveries but want instantaneous deliveries, the super time-sensitive segment of the market.

All of them, except the post office, are profitable. None of them, except the post office, bases its principal business strategy on trying to sell to "everybody."

QUESTION 4. WHO IS MY COMPETITION?

"There isn't any." Wrong answer again.

Yes, there is, or else you're aiming for the quill-pen and buggy-whip crowd or some other obscure market that doesn't exist. If there's a market for your product or service, someone is supplying that market. He may be using another product. Or he may be using a nearly identical product that you can beat on quality, performance, or service. Either way, the existence of competition is a good sign, not a bad one. Nobody ever set a world's record competing against himself. Now, all you have to do is to find a way to do it better.

QUESTION 5. WHAT ADVANTAGES DO I OFFER A CUSTOMER OVER THE COMPETITION?

This one's multiple choice: Product? Quality? Location? Convenience? Service? Price? Selection? Customer satisfaction? Cleanliness? Store design/layout? Reliability? One is not enough. Sometimes, *all* are not enough. See the next question.

QUESTION 6. WHAT ADVANTAGES DOES MY ORGANIZATION HAVE OVER THE COMPETITION?

Management? Product? Service? Financial strength? Reputation? Recognition? Marketing? People?

Let's examine marketing a little more closely.

Take fast-food restaurants. There's a reason McDonald's spends billions on advertising and promotion. It works. It kills competition. If you are aiming for the same market niche as McDonald's, you're automatically on an endangered-species list. You can beat McDonald's on every single comparison I've listed above in question 4, and it still can bury you if you don't have the advertising dollars to pull customers through your doors.

Now, can you beat better-financed competition with superior customer advantages? Yes, but don't try to do it across the street from a competitor with marketing savvy and pockets far deeper than yours.

QUESTION 7. DO I HAVE A BUSINESS PLAN?

They teach courses in B school on this one, but let's simplify matters. Fortunately, all the soft sciences, and entrepreneuring is not exactly nuclear physics, are alike in one respect: The organized thinking on the subject follows pretty much the same outline. You'll find this form used in marketing, business planning, even social work. Call it a plan, prospectus, offering circular, business outline—it doesn't matter much what you call it. We'll use a plan for a new magazine as our hypothetical example. It goes like this:

Situation Analysis

Describe the current state of the industry in which you intend to compete. Start with an overview of the industry generally, its profitability, the status of key competitors, the outlook for the next few years, whatever hard facts you have on the success/failure of recent start-ups. Then you'll narrow your focus and survey the market segment at which you're aiming.

Objectives

Describe what you intend to achieve, e.g., obtain above-industry-average return on invested capital by publishing a magazine and collateral services on career/lifestyle/fashion choices for upscale overweight men and women.

Target Audiences

Describe who you intend to have as your customers. For example, in the magazine business, there are two income streams: people who buy the magazine and people who advertise in it. So your targets may be: Urban adults/25–59; Income/$30,000+; Education/high school+; Overweight. It helps if you can *quantify* your target. How many are there? How many do you expect to reach?

Describe who you want as your advertisers, such as men's and women's specialty sizes and diet products. Describe who you *don't* want, e.g., see-through-lingerie and sexual-aid manufacturers.

Mission Statement

Here's one that you think you can skip, but it's really the core of the whole thing and the one part you'll look at five years later and wish you had followed. For the hypothetical magazine, it might go like this: "To be the recognized national source for providing ongoing communication, advice, reinforcement, products, and services to working men and women concerned about their weight, and to make an above-average return on invested capital for the magazine industry group."

Objective

Now, it's beginning to fall into place a little, isn't it? Obviously, your objective is to publish a magazine and use it as a foundation for related products and services. It isn't to build a network of magazines across the entire universe of magazines, or even across the fashion or career category. If you grow, you want to grow by expanding your penetration in this market segment, which leaves you all sorts of possibilities, like manufacturing products, publishing books, holding seminars, building spas, and so on.

Strategy and Tactics

I always used to get strategies and tactics mixed up. Maybe I still do, but I think if strategy is the "what" you are going to do, then tactics are the "how" you will get your message across. In this case, tactics will involve a number of separate steps. First, you'll conduct market research to determine the size of your targets and their needs. It might help to know whether they actually want a magazine. Here's the time to find out, not after you've blown your life savings.

Maybe you're better off providing some other service. Maybe you'll find people won't buy it on the newsstands because they're embarrassed to ask for it. Maybe potential advertisers prefer general-circulation publications. Here's where you have to tackle the question of how you distinguish yourself from the competition. Weight Watchers is not going to roll over and play dead the day your magazine debuts.

This is also the place to do a little market research on titles, a very, very sensitive and enormously important decision.

When I wrote my first book, my contract with my publisher, William Morrow, read that the title had to be "mutually agreeable." It wasn't. The publisher did not like the title I'd submitted, *How to Swim with the Sharks Without Being Eaten Alive.* One, it was too long. Two, it didn't tell the reader what the book was about. Three, it was confusing. The casual reader would think it was about skin-diving. Four, five, six, seven, eight, nine, and ten. They didn't like it. They didn't like it. They didn't like it. It sounded weird for a business book. Business-book titles should tell you ten ways to do something, like this lesson heading. We held a meeting. We took a vote. The vote was 11−1. Against. I was the holdout. But remember, one was all it took. It had to be *mutually* agreeable.

Being a reasonable sort, I had to accept the remote possibility that eleven professionals who ran one of the most successful publishing houses in America might have a better idea of what would sell books than an unpublished envelope manufacturer.

But I wasn't ready to accept it yet. So I hired the firm of Janz/Abrahamson to conduct market research on the title. They had a dozen creative people read a fifty-page excerpt from the book; then they conducted focus groups. The participants came up with a list of eight hundred additional titles to choose from and were not told which one I had chosen. They picked *How to Swim with the Sharks Without Being Eaten Alive* as their number-one choice.

I went back to Morrow armed with the most powerful weapon you can possess in any negotiation: superior information. And finally reached a "mutual agreement," just as the contract read. I got *Swim with the Sharks Without Being Eaten Alive.* They got to delete *How to.*

Execution

Describe your product in detail. Price/frequency/content/sizes/colors/availability. Everything. Again, back to the magazine, just for an example. In some cases it helps to have a dummy issue—which is what some actually do in the magazine business. Here's also where you describe how long it will take to get up and running as well as contingency plans for what might go wrong (something always does).

Budget

Here we generally enter the realm of fantasy. Whatever you estimate, it will cost twice as much. This should include your sources of capital, your projections on cash flow, income, and expenses in the form of *pro forma* income statements and balance sheets, up to the point of profitability and beyond.

Measurement

These are generally statistical standards. For example, you are aiming at a circulation base of 150,000 by the sixth month of publication; 300,000 by year two, and so on. You can add fanciful standards here as well if they're meaningful to you: e.g., the frequency with which the publication is quoted in other publications, the number and quality of the writers submitting material, and so on.

Summary

It's kind of a salesman's close. It can be very simple: "Because of favorable market conditions—the existence and attractiveness of a market segment that extensive market research indicates is not being served—and our ability to develop a superior, market-tested product line that can be rapidly adjusted to meet demand, it is our intention to . . ."

Can you work your way through that outline? Sure, it's not that tough. It serves several very useful purposes. It forces you to think your way through the start-up process and your long-range goals. It's also a document you'll need if you plan on getting outside financing from anyone except your relatives. If it isn't persuasive and effective to an independent outside businessperson, that might tell you something about your real chances for success. Which takes us to . . .

QUESTION 8. WHAT DOES MY BANKER SAY?

Bankers see and evaluate business plans all day long. That's their business. The older and more experienced they are, the more they've seen. Surprisingly, they have probably seen one similar to yours. Ask your banker to point out the strengths and weaknesses in yours. Then ask the Ultimate Question: Would you lend me money to finance this business? If the answer is no, it's not the end of the world. Find out what they would need to say yes. Then tell them you'll be back.

QUESTION 9. WHAT DOES MY LAWYER SAY?

Do you have a lawyer? A lawyer with extensive business experience, not the one who drew up your will. Take your plan to that lawyer and ask him what legal pitfalls are involved in your venture and what steps you can take *now* to avoid them. But always remember, your lawyer is there to protect you but not to make the business decisions for you.

One large law firm has gotten ahead of the curve and set up a separate department of twenty-five attorneys called "the preventive law group," which includes attorneys who specialize in contracts, product liability, intellectual properties, environmental law, health care, and antitrust law. In my opinion, they should toss in a few tax and estate-planning lawyers, too.

Why spend time and money to try to anticipate a problem you never had?

For the same reason you get a checkup at the doctor's when you're feeling fine.

Take the trip today; it may save your hide tomorrow.

QUESTION 10. WHAT DOES MY MENTOR SAY?

If you have done as I suggested and consulted a banker and a lawyer, you're already ahead of 90 percent of the pack. Here's how to be ahead of 99 percent. Find yourself a tiger, preferably someone who's been around the track. So-called retired people are a marvelous resource for this kind of talent. They have access to people with every imaginable kind of business experience, with the time, patience, skill, wisdom, and understanding to help and, sometimes, just to listen. If you're really smart, you'll check out one of the best kept secrets in America. It's an organization called SCORE, which stands for Service Corps of Retired Executives. SCORE is composed of 12,500 retired and active executives in 736 chapters and offices across America who are available to provide free advice to budding entrepreneurs.

When I got started, I'd use anyone who would listen to me, my banker and my lawyer, both older and experienced heads, and a calming influence, my father. The fellows I played golf with on Wednesday afternoons became my informal board of directors. I was shameless in seeking advice; I still am. How can you get hurt asking for an opinion?

I know how important the entrepreneurial instinct to fly solo is. I also know how dumb it is when you confuse that instinct with cutting yourself off from sources of useful advice because they might tell you something you don't want to hear. That's the one weakness that seems to be an almost universal infection among entrepreneurs, but it's so easy to cure, and the nice thing about the medicine is, you don't have to take it if you don't want to. It's always there when you need it.

QUESTION 11. HAVE I DONE AN HONEST SELF-SURVEY?

Do you really want to do this or are you just trying to escape your own problems? Leaving one business to start another is like remarrying. If you dropped your socks on the floor the first time around, your second spouse is going to chew you out just as much as your first one did. Before you make the switch, make sure the problem is not you. It's not what you eat, it's what's eating you that matters.

Running your own business is no endeavor for anyone who feels anything other than the urge to be the first person in the door in the morning and the one they have to drag out of there at night.

J. Willard Marriott, who founded the Marriott Corporation, worked an eighteen-hour day for years. "No person can get very far in this life on a forty-hour week," he said.

"I made some investments that worked, and some that didn't," Rudolph W. Miller, my father-in-law, observed. "I found out one thing: No matter how hard you work for your money, there's always someone out there willing to work twice as hard to take it away from you."

People who make it big in business don't tend to be very well rounded or even terribly happy. But they do have one quality that's lacking in others: They are single-minded. They are successes because they tune out other needs and other messages. No one said it was pretty, but work works.

Did I hear someone say you don't have to be a work-aholic to be successful? That's right, and workaholism also probably will make you something of a less than wonderful human being. But wonderfulness isn't the question here. It's whether you have what it takes to be an entrepreneur. En-trepreneurs don't become workaholics because they have to. They do it because they want to, because it's more im-portant to them than upgrading their character. They're not in it for what they can get out of it; they're in it for its own sake. They're entrepreneurs because they love being entre-preneurs. As the saying goes, find something you love to do, and you'll never have to work another day in your life.

Novelists are the quintessential entrepreneurs. They're totally on their own; the work product of their little cottage industry is locked inside their skulls. Finally, after months or even years, they assemble their handiwork onto a few dol-lars' worth of photocopying paper and go around trying to persuade someone to risk big bucks printing and marketing it. You should know the odds. There are half a million manu-scripts written each year. Only 10 percent of those, or about fifty thousand, ever get published. And of those, only a hand-ful make the best-seller lists. Those are not odds for the fainthearted.

Remember Wayne Dyer? The story of how he got started is almost as famous as his book *Your Erroneous Zones.* He had trouble finding a publisher, but Dyer's faith and guts wouldn't be denied. Still, sales were going nowhere, so he went on the road to peddle his book. He had a little formula. He'd call ahead to a town and try to arrange an appearance on one or more of the local talk shows. Any town, any show, any time. It didn't matter. Then he'd stuff his car full of books, drive to the town, go to all the bookstores, and tell them he was going to be on such and such a show that day, and would wheedle them into taking some books. He'd do his talk-show number and then try to line up an appearance in the next town.

He did it for two years. That was Wayne Dyer's livelihood. Peddling books out of the trunk of his car. One night he was in San Francisco. It was three o'clock in the morning. Another non—prime-time appearance. He was doing a show for the seventeen people in the world who were listening. And it just so happened that one of those seventeen people was Johnny Carson. And Carson loved it.

The next thing you know, Dyer is on the Carson show, and the book goes through the sound barrier.

A few weeks later, Dyer went to his high school reunion. He probably wouldn't have dared show up if the Carson business hadn't happened. But he went. An old classmate waddled up.

"Hey, Dyer," he said, "did you ever get lucky to get on the Johnny Carson Show!"

Lucky? Wayne Dyer made his own luck. If you're going to be an entrepreneur, you have to believe in yourself more than you believe in anything else in the world.

QUESTION 12. WHAT WILL I DO IF I FAIL?

Pray that you do fail.

Few entrepreneurs make it the first time they try. In fact, if you want to double your success ratio, you have to double your failure rate. The careers of many early titans of American industry, like Andrew Carnegie, are marked by spectacular leaps from poverty, hair-breadth escapes, bankruptcies and near-bankruptcies, failed products and concepts. With each broken dream, they learned what they had to learn, dusted themselves off, and started over.

3M, a $10-billion company that makes over sixty thousand products, was founded on failure. The company planned to make sandpaper, but the mineral it mined for the abrasive was worthless, and it was forced to innovate or go under. After a struggle, the 3M people finally made their first big score, a sandpaper that worked wet or dry, called, appropriately enough, Wetodry. In 1929, 3M came up with Scotch tape, originally intended to seal insulation, now a $750-million product annually. *Business Week* quotes the company's first leader and still its guiding spirit, William McKnight: "If management is intolerant and destructively critical when mistakes are made, it kills initiative."

At 3M, initiative drives the company. Approximately one fourth of the company's sales come from products that weren't invented five years earlier—and five years from now, another 25 percent will come from products that don't exist today.

In fact, the company's commitment to pure research is so fierce that they have a program they call "Genesis grants" for funding projects that have no presently discernable commercial application. If a 3M scientist has a project he wants to do, he applies for one of these. The company is currently supporting about one hundred of them at a total cost that runs into the millions. Pure scientific altruism? Of course not. 3M knows that if even one of these ideas turns into a product, it will profit from its investment.

And if none of them do? What if all these projects fail? 3M will still benefit. By demonstrating its confidence in its employees, it creates an environment in which its key scientific minds thrive.

We've all heard the Horatio Alger stories; they're supposed to inspire us, and they should. The interesting question isn't where our heroes found the guts to try again (what choice did they have?), but where their backers did.

Who is going to lend money to a failure?

Banks actually like to wait until you've made your first major mistake before they lend you any real money. They know how much more careful you're going to be the next time. Their faith is reinforced when you can demonstrate courage, resiliency, determination, and a quick learning curve. They're delighted when you acquire them at someone else's expense.

Few of us lead unblemished personal or professional lives. It's the ability to overcome our faults, rather than never to experience them, that counts. Theologians are fond of saying that no faith is worth having unless it has been tested. There is not a sin in the catalog of sins that has not been committed by a certified saint. Committed, faced, and overcome. That's what makes them saints.

What is the great lesson that failure teaches?

Failure teaches you not to fear failure, because if you can survive it to fight again, you haven't failed. You have only heightened your appreciation of success. Nietzsche said it best: "That which does not kill us makes us stronger."

Linda Gottlieb was senior vice president of Highgate Pictures, a now defunct division of Learning Corporation of America. When the company grew much larger, she said, "the traits my boss once found endearing in me, my outspokenness, my strong opinions, my negotiating toughness, became annoying and unacceptable. Suddenly there were staffs under me and around me, and I was supposed to manage people instead of create film projects, which is what I do best."

Soon Gottlieb was gone. She took an entrepreneurial leap and became a feature-film producer. Her pet project, costing $5 million, very modest by Hollywood standards, couldn't get financed until she talked Vestron Pictures into taking a chance.

The picture: *Dirty Dancing.* Gross: $140 million.

"Failure liberated me," she said. "The termination gave me the armor to pursue my deepest dreams."

Unfortunately, if you haven't learned the lesson of failure, you'll invariably get the wrong message from your success.

You'll think you deserved it.

What we should learn from success is to fear it more than we fear failure.

Time and again, I've seen people who believed that once

they succeeded, the condition had become irreversible, like losing your virginity. If they were right once—particularly if they were right when everyone else thought they were dead wrong—then because they decided to do something, it had to be the brilliant thing to do. Baseball general managers who make the great trade one season seldom do it two times in a row. The next one is invariably a clunker. Don Burr, who built People Express around a new concept in commercial air travel against all the odds, crashed when he expanded too rapidly.

Brett Johnson, who had his picture in *Fortune* at the age of twenty-five, turned the humble painter's cap into a teen-age fashion fad by putting the Copenhagen and Skoal snuff label on it, and was out of business the next year, either as a result of underestimating the fickleness of his market, or overconfidence, or both.

The mandate of heaven is not forever. The concept of infallibility does not apply to you and me.

We would like to believe that we've earned our success through hard work, determination, intelligence, and foresight. Certainly, we couldn't have succeeded without them, but many people have the same qualities and never have success.

The truth is, success often occurs for reasons we don't expect, under circumstances over which we have little control and sometimes unrelated to our own efforts.

There is only one other lesson that success should teach us: Be as amazed by your own success as your friends are. If you truly are, you stand the best chance to repeat it.

LESSON 16

THIS ISN'T THE ARMY: VOLUNTEER

James Michael Curley, the late mayor of Boston and the model for the corrupt but lovable pol of *The Last Hurrah,* was responsible for building the Sumner Tunnel, which connected Boston's airport to the rest of the city. With the decision to build the tunnel, money changed hands, some of it making its way into pockets where it wasn't supposed to go. The law was broken. People went to jail, including Curley.

However.

Had the tunnel been built by the book, had the government process been permitted to take its long, majestic course toward a decision untainted by outside influence, you might still be taking the ferryboat from Logan Airport to downtown Boston. And even if the system had worked its way through years of hearings and meetings and votes, the tunnel probably would have cost the Boston taxpayers ten times as much.

There's a lot to be said for democracy, but two of the things you can't say for it are that it's either cheap or efficient.

Sometimes you get good results from bad motives.

Which brings me to volunteering to get ahead.

Some people obviously get involved in volunteer and charitable work because they feel it will benefit them personally. But in my opinion, being right for the wrong reason is a lot righter than doing nothing for the right reason. A good deal of valuable charitable work wouldn't get done but for the social climbers and business opportunists, and if that's what it takes, the benefits to others justify it.

What's the matter with doing well by doing good?

If the purists want to sniff at you because you weren't suffering enough at the charity ball you paid a fortune to attend, so what? Don't think you have to be Mother Teresa or live up to someone else's definition of what is politically correct behavior in order to become involved or help others.

After I became a volunteer, I discovered that networking and volunteering are almost synonymous. There was a sculpture of Curt Carlson that was commissioned for his company's fiftieth anniversary, and I happened to ask the artist how he got the order. He told me that his wife had volunteered for a United Way committee, where she met Curt's wife, Arleen. One thing led to another, and he finally got to meet Curt. Seven years later, bingo, he got the commission of a lifetime. I think that's terrific. How's a sculptor supposed to drum up business anyway, do ice carvings for wedding receptions?

And yes, the most important reference for joining almost

any charitable board in America is still a credit reference, but that doesn't mean you shouldn't join.

And don't give until it hurts. Give until it feels good. It's just as expensive and leaves you in a lot better frame of mind.

A lot of what I learned about selling, public speaking, raising money, working as part of a team, management, and organization—in other words, a lot of what I learned about everything worth learning in running a business—I learned by being a volunteer worker. When I made mistakes, and I made plenty of them as a volunteer, they were part of a learning process that I could apply to my own business situation. And when I learned a new technique, I applied that, too.

The greatest lesson I learned was a selling lesson.

Every volunteer and charitable group needs money, and the last job anyone wants is raising it. People just hate the sound of the word "no," because they take the rejection personally, and fund-raising is a bottomless pit of rejection.

The usual practice is for the volunteer workers to gather round while the head of the group reads off a wish list, made up of $3'' \times 5''$ cards, each with a name on it. Some cards have the names of people who have contributed in the past and the amount of their contribution. Some have the names of prominent people who haven't contributed, but who someone thinks should. As each name is read off and appropriate amounts suggested for each, volunteers are expected to take their fair share of the stack, and everyone goes off to do his or her duty.

This is when you learn how hard it is to be a salesperson.

People are funny about money; you find that even your best friends will treat you differently, to wit, a lot worse, when you ask them for some.

Soon you find yourself in the grip of "call reluctance," insurance-trade jargon for fear of rejection. It claims the majority of insurance salespeople within two years, just time enough to have sold all their relatives and been slammed to the pavement a couple of hundred times by everyone else. If a life-insurance salesperson can survive that long, he or she usually can make a good living at it.

Volunteers who make it through a campaign or two earn the same battle stripes.

The great selling lesson comes down to this: Never say no for the other guy.

It's like the story about the rookie insurance salesman who claimed he made fifty sales calls every day. That's not so difficult when you start out by saying, "You don't want to buy any insurance, do you?"

As call reluctance builds up, there's a tendency on the part of the salesperson to say to himself or herself, "I know this person. He's going to say no. There's no use calling." And he, or she, doesn't.

No call is just as much a no as an actual call that ends up with a no, but there are two differences: You save that small shred of ego from another rejection. And instead of even a 1 percent chance, there is absolutely no chance of making the sale.

You don't have to close every sale to be a success.

Over 95 percent of Publishers Clearing House mailings get tossed. Yet by closing only one out of every twenty-five prospects, it has set the standard for its industry.

When Lou Holtz was coaching at Minnesota, we had the most successful telephone drive selling season tickets in the school's history. We sold six thousand, and it was a big item in the media. What we didn't tell the world was that we had to make seventy-five thousand phone calls to do it.

Measure success by success, not by the number of failures it takes to achieve it.

LESSON 17

"GARBAGE COLLECTORS TO RECEIVE $30,000 PER YEAR"

The day I saw that headline in the local paper, I knew I was in for trouble.

A key employee, Helen, saw it, too.

"Look at this," she said, tossing the paper on my desk. "The garbage collectors are making more money than I am. Either I get what they're getting or I quit!"

"Helen," I said, "I have only one piece of advice for you. I think you should quit and start collecting garbage tomorrow morning, because that's the best way I know of that you can make your thirty thousand a year."

I tried to explain to her that one reason garbage collectors make so much was supply and demand. Most people don't want to be garbage collectors, undertakers, or bomb defusers in Beirut. Every relatively high-paying occupation carries its own special burden, either in terms of image, risk, or the skills required.

Economic theory was not Helen's strong suit, but she calmed down. For a while. Eventually, she did leave for more money. It worked out just fine for her until her hard-nosed union overplayed its hand. The workers went out on strike, the owners finally found the backbone to say the hell with it and hired replacement workers, and six years is a long time to stand in a picket line. But if she's still waiting for her thirty thou to kick back in, that's where she is now.

By the way, thirty thousand *is* a hell of a lot of money to pay a garbage collector, and I once asked a city council member friend of mine why the garbage collectors got so much.

"Because it's the most dangerous job in the city," he said.

"C'mon. You mean people are taking potshots at their garbage collectors? I don't believe it."

"Nope. They have the highest injury and sickness rate of any group of city employees. Higher than cops. Higher than firemen. Lots of back stuff, and it's legitimate, too. You don't see too many old garbagemen. It's a tough job."

I wish I had known that when I talked to Helen. But I doubt if it would have made a difference.

LESSON 18

●

THE MACKAY 33™ FOR EMPLOYEES

Every human institution has its own value system.

If it's a company, you won't find it published in the employees' handbook. Because of our tradition of egalitarianism, we're embarrassed to discuss it, but some industries are practically colonies of one ethnic group or another: steel, banking, and insurance—WASP; construction—Italian and Irish; movies—Jewish.

Other corporate cultures are the legacy of an iron-willed founder. When Thomas Watson ruled IBM, employees were expected to wear white shirts. One day Watson showed up in a blue shirt.

"Do you think this means we can wear blue shirts now?" whispered one executive to another.

"Wait six weeks," said the other. "It may be a trap."

The ultimate expression of the self-enclosed corporate

●

value system may be the story told about M-G-M when Louis B. Mayer was the head of West Coast operations and Nicolas B. Schenk held the purse strings, reigning over the entire company in isolated splendor from New York. In 1941, in the immediate aftershock of Japan's surprise attack on Pearl Harbor and President Franklin Roosevelt's impassioned "day of infamy" speech that propelled the United States into World War II, Mayer gathered the company's executives together.

He spoke movingly, and at length, of the need for building morale, for strong leadership, and for team spirit to guide them forward to face the great challenge that lay ahead for America. Finally, carried away by his own oratory and blinking back tears, Mayer rose to his feet to propose a toast: "Ladies and Gentlemen, to our president . . . Nicolas B. Schenk."

Wherever you're working, or thinking of working, you will be subject to these strange whims and traditions of half-remembered origin. Here's an exercise to put you in touch with them. And I don't suggest you hand in this questionnaire after you fill it out.

In fact, I'd file my copy under the heading "Draft Report on Discontinued Canadian Operations," or better yet, keep it at home.

CORPORATE CULTURE:
AN EMPLOYEE/CORPORATE SELF-INVENTORY

Company Attitudes Toward Employees

1. How is the company's overall treatment of its employees? (Fair? Unfair? Better in some areas than others? Erratic?)

_____

_____

2. How do the company's salaries and benefits compare with similar companies?

_____

_____

3. Working conditions? (Hours? Expect uncompensated overtime? Stress level? Pleasant, clean, modern offices and surroundings?)

_____

_____

4. How much opportunity is there for advancement? How much encouragement?

_____

_____

5. What is the company's attitude toward education? (Pays tuition? Maintains employee library? Basis for promotion?)

_____

_____

6. What is the company's attitude toward minorities? Toward women? Are they in supervisory positions?

_____

_____

7. What kinds of performance does the company value most highly? (Sales? Cost-cutting? Leadership in community affairs?)

_____

_____

8. What is the company's attitude toward outside activities? (Encouraging? Discouraging? Indifferent? Selective?)

_____

_____

9. What kinds of personal behavior and attitudes does the company value most highly? (Volunteer work? Family? Male bonding? Expensive clothes and cars? Conventional lifestyles? Partisan political activity?)

_____

_____

10. What kinds of personal behavior and attitudes does the company value least highly? (Labor unions? Sexist behavior? Unconventional political/personal values?)

_____

_____

11. What is the company's turnover ratio? (High for the industry? Low? Normal?)

_____

_____

Self-Awareness and Relationships

12. What is the company's reputation in the community?

_____

_____

13. How does the company's self-image match its reputation in the community?

_____

_____

14. What is the company's supervisory style? (Expects you to know what you're doing? Heavy-handed?)

_____

_____

15. What is the company's style when critiquing and reviewing an employee? (Fair? Unfair? Seldom? Frequent? Consistent?)

_____

_____

16. How does the company react to criticism from its employees? (Tolerant? Intolerant? Responsive? Unresponsive?)

_____

_____

17. How does the company react to criticism from others? (Press? Shareholders? Customers? Labor unions?)

_____

_____

18. How does the company regard its competition?

_____

_____

19. How is the company regarded by the competition?

_____

_____

20. How much do "office politics" affect the way decisions are made?

_____

_____

21. How does the company communicate important policies to its employees? (Through supervisors? Group meetings? Written communications from top officers? Grapevine? Read about it in the paper?)

_____

_____

22. Does the company communicate important policies to the public? Is it effective? What techniques are used? (Advertising and PR? Secretive, purposely maintains low visibility? Executives hungry for personal publicity?)

_____

_____

Goals and Aspirations

23. What are the company's long-range goals? (Industry leadership? Merger? Provide a living for members of the owner's family?)

_____

_____

24. What is the company doing to achieve these goals? Is it effective?

_____

_____

25. What is the company doing to communicate these goals? Is it effective? (Employee recognition? Compensation? Displays? Company publications?)

_____

_____

26. What individuals/other companies does the company hold up as role models? Why?

_____

_____

27. What is the most effective means of securing advancement?

(Merit? Other?)

_____

_____

28. What are the company's greatest strengths?

_____

_____

29. What does the company do to capitalize on those strengths?

_____

_____

30. What are the company's greatest weaknesses?

_____

_____

31. What is the company doing to correct those weaknesses?

_____

_____

32. What is the company most proud of? (High profitability? Innovative products? Customer service? Paying big dividends? High salaries? Ego trip for top executives?)

_____

_____

33. Are you proud to be working for the company? Would you
rather be working somewhere else? Why?

_____

_____

You can see why this one has some potential for disaster.
So why bother?

You should bother if you're concerned about the direction your company, and therefore your career, is taking. You should definitely bother if you have responsibility in any of the areas that need improving. Ideally, supervisors should also ask their people to fill these out, on a Don't-Sign-Your-Name basis, of course.

The people who are in an ideal position to use this questionnaire are those who haven't yet gone to work for the company. They can vote with their feet if the answers aren't satisfactory. I don't suggest anyone ask these questions point-blank of whomever is doing the hiring, but before I'd commit my professional life to a company, I'd certainly try to get as many answers as I could indirectly.

What if you're already employed by the company but have very little real authority to change the corporate environment?

You still might want to fill this out. If you're working for a good outfit, this will only confirm it. If not, it might give you the encouragement you need to jump to another lily pad.

The Mackay 33 copyright © 1990, Mackay Envelope Corporation

CHAPTER 5

THE ONE PERSON WHO'S ALWAYS HAPPY
TO TEACH YOU A LESSON IS A TOUGH
COMPETITOR

LESSON 19

●

FOLLOW THE FLEET

My first real job, after I escaped from pushing a broom—
which was the core of the curriculum at the Quality Park
Envelope Company's Learn-the-Business-from-the-Ground
(actually, the Floor)-Up Sales Training Program—was junior
salesman. I was twenty-one. To me, an envelope was something you used when you didn't want your girlfriend's parents to read the letter. Most of my other significant writings
could be handled nicely by a picture postcard.

I studied the phone book for leads for a week. Then my
father suggested that I might try to ingratiate myself with
one of the battle-scarred veterans of the envelope wars on
the sales staff. The next morning, I waited in the company
parking lot, and after the first Cadillac rolled in, I followed
the driver into the bullpen.

He was the least friendly man on the payroll. In the pre-

●

105

ceding week, I had not been able to get so much as a grunt out of him. While I stood at attention at his desk looking at the bottoms of his shoes, he casually finished a cup of coffee and the funny papers. They must have been extremely funny that morning, because he finally granted me the much-coveted grunt.

"I wonder if I might ask you a question?" I began.

"So ask."

"Is there any advice you might give me, to get started, I mean?"

"College boy, aren't you?"

"Well, yes," I said.

"Do you think your customers are? Is that why you wear that fancy little class ring?"

I hadn't really thought about it, but obviously he noticed a lot more than I realized. About me. About our customers. In those days, most buyers didn't have college degrees. I slipped the ring off my finger and into my pocket.

Another grunt, somewhat friendlier.

He got up from his desk and crooked his finger in a "follow me" motion.

"You're not doing anything today," he said.

We went back into the parking lot, got into his car, and to my amazement, drove to our arch-competitor's plant three miles away. Was I so hopeless that he was going to leave me on the doorstep of the Tension Envelope Company with a note pinned to my suit? "Here's Harvey. Try and do something with him. God knows, we can't."

We parked about fifty yards away from Tension's shipping department and waited until its trucks began to exit to make the day's deliveries. The rest of the day, we followed those trucks. What leads we got! They even made a stop at one of my mentor's best customer's. He banged his head on the steering wheel. "When am I ever going to learn? Some buyers are liars. They like to let you think you've got all their business, because they don't want to get locked into one supplier." He could hardly wait to get back to the office to put together a new proposal based on the kind of volume he now realized the customer used.

What would you give to have your biggest competitor's customer list? It's right there, in front of your eyes. All you have to do is learn to work those mean streets.

LESSON 20

●

THE MOST VALUABLE TOOL A SELLER CAN HAVE

More than one buyer.

Twenty years ago, Bob Stein, a University of Minnesota All-American, was drafted in the fifth round by the Kansas City Chiefs football team. Fifth-round draft choices do not command a potful of money. By the time the teams reach down to that level, at least one hundred players have already been chosen. That's one hundred young athletes regarded as more talented, one hundred very hungry young athletes clamoring for a cut of the finite amount of the available bonus money. Because I'd known Bob and his family from about the time he thought a draw play was something you did with a crayon, I was his unpaid adviser.

Everyone on the draft list has a reason why he should be treated as something special and not be signed on the basis

●

of the team's predetermined formula for paying its choices. Luckily for Stein, he had the best reason of all: There was competition for his services. He was a straight "A" student and had been awarded a scholarship to attend Harvard Law School.

I never participated in the actual negotiations. Since what Stein was selling was this strange Jekyll/Hyde combination of Harvard man and mad-dog defensive end, he had to go up against the team's general manager himself. Over and over again, I had him tell the Chiefs that unless they were willing to let go of their fifth-round mentality and step up to the window and pay him like a second-round choice, he'd be tackling Torts next fall instead of tackling blockers. The only mistake I thought he was making during the negotiations, which went on for several months, was heading out the front door every morning at the crack of dawn and taking a ten-mile run to stay in shape.

When I heard about it, I called him down to my office.

"Bob, you don't know how smart these guys are," I said. "If you have to run, go somewhere where they can't see you. Do you think they're going to invest the kind of money you're asking without keeping an eye on you? You're acting like an ordinary jock instead of a guy with a big burning desire to go to Harvard."

"Hey, Harvey. Relax. I want them to see me."

"No, no, you're going to butcher this deal."

"Harvey, wait a minute, will you?"

Stein stripped off his warm-up jacket. Underneath he was proudly sporting a crimson T-shirt with white lettering that read HARVARD LAW SCHOOL.

He got a good contract, the equivalent of a *third*-round draft choice—the guys on the other side of the table were not naïve, either. During Bob's first year with the team, Kansas City won the Super Bowl and he cashed a winner's share check for an additional twenty-five thousand dollars. He's still a winner. Today, he's the president of the Timber-wolves, Minnesota's new entry in the National Basketball Association.

What Bob Stein did was a classic reversal of the normal buyer/seller relationship. He converted himself from being just another low-rent, mean-and-ugly face buried deep on the draft list to being a sought-after prize. Instead of Bob competing for the Chiefs' money with a hundred other guys, the Chiefs competed for his services with another eager buyer.

If you're the buyer, you're always better off if there's more than one seller. If you're the seller, you always want more than one buyer. Whichever you are, make sure there's competition on the other side of the table.

IT'S NOT WHAT'S UP FRONT, IT'S *BEING* UP FRONT THAT COUNTS

If you've ever been curious how lakeless Los Angeles came to have a basketball team named the Lakers, it's a carryover from the days when the franchise was located in Minneapolis. We had been trying to lure the NBA back ever since, and about ten years ago, I was involved in one of those efforts.

It started when my phone rang and the person on the other end began a pitch that went like this:

"Hi, Harvey, my name is John Y. Brown, and I own the Buffalo Braves basketball team in the NBA. I understand you're a person I should be talking to in Minneapolis if I want to move my team there. I'd like to fly to Minneapolis the day after tomorrow to meet with your key civic leaders and government officials so we can look each other over."

I couldn't have been happier if Angie Dickinson had called.

Here was a fellow who had sold Kentucky Fried Chicken to Heublein for $285 million, and who was being talked about as a potential governor of Kentucky. Not too shabby a start for someone still under forty.

I managed to get the Big Cigars together, and with John Y. in tow, we all waltzed over to see our governor. Everyone was duly impressed with one another.

In the next six to eight weeks, many phone calls went back and forth. Brown's message was that we had done a helluva job selling him on the area. Late one Friday afternoon, he called again.

"Harvey, I've decided I'm going to move my Buffalo team to Minneapolis. There's just one possible hitch. I've had a boyhood dream to own the Boston Celtics. This weekend I'm taking my seven lawyers with me and I'm going to Boston, and we're going to try and swap teams. Obviously, if we do it, I won't be moving the Celtics to Minneapolis.

"But believe me, those seven lawyers are going to mess up, so I expect to be in Minneapolis on Monday. But I just wanted to tell you about that in case a miracle happens."

The miracle happened. Over the weekend, Brown swapped the Braves and a lot of the Colonel's non–chicken feed for the Boston Celtics. Was I angry? No. He had told me up front it might happen.

But what if I had read about it in the papers on Monday morning and had not heard about it first from Brown?

I would not have been a happy camper.

If Brown hadn't forewarned us, we would have thought we were being set up all along so he could make a better deal with the Celtics people. We'd been putting our deal together in good faith.

If the Celtics deal really was a long shot, as he had said, he ran a considerable risk telling us anything at all. There are buyers who will walk, instantly, if they find out the goods they're negotiating for are being shopped around and they haven't been told about it.

For all I know, Brown did use our Minneapolis group as a lever with the Celtics owners to persuade them that there were other bidders for the Braves. But by telling me in advance, he gave me the chance to go back to my group immediately, which I did, and retain my credibility with them. The man I'd introduced to them was not dealing behind our backs. In fact, we ended up feeling like insiders. We knew the story, or at least the possibilities, before it broke in the media.

Did we ever put together any kind of deal with Brown? No. I wish I could say we had, but we never did do business with him.

Still, I was reminded of the story when I got a letter from a friend quoting Charles Hendrickson Brower, of the advertising agency BBD&O: "Honesty is not only the best policy; it is rare enough to be pleasantly conspicuous."

I have only one souvenir of the experience: a wedding invitation to the marriage of John Y. Brown to Phyllis George, a former Miss America. Norman Vincent Peale performed the ceremony, and I'll never forget it. The bride was so beautiful I went through the receiving line three times for a kiss. So I guess it wasn't a total loss after all

LESSON 22

•

HARVEY'S ODDS ON BEATING YOUR
COMPETITION

Just show up. . . . You're a winner *80 percent* of the time. Most accounts are won because nobody else is calling on them.

Show up on time. . . . What could be more annoying than a salesperson who can't deliver the first thing he's promised to deliver, his or her own body? Mars, Inc., known around the world for its M & M's, 3 Musketeers, Snickers, and Mars candy bars, is a $6-billion privately held company. This multinational corporation really places a premium on showing up on time. Everyone punches a clock, including the two Mars brothers, and every employee who punches in before 8:30 A.M. receives 10 percent added compensation called "The Punctuality Bonus." Talk about positive reinforcement— that's certainly nothing to "Snicker" at! Do it when you say you'll do it, and you're a winner *85 percent* of the time.

•

Show up on time with a plan. . . . Okay, you're here. So what? You have to know your prospect's strengths and weaknesses and be able to anticipate his or her concerns. Give your prospect a clear understanding of what the product benefits are and the specifics of price/delivery/service. Don't expect to get by with vague, offhand answers to any objections to your proposition. If there are going to be any problems you know about, don't try to lie your way around them; let your prospect know up front. By being truthful and accurate in your answers, you'll get orders that others, who may actually meet the customer's needs better than you, won't get, because they haven't been clear-cut in their responses. Do it right, and you're a winner *90 percent* of the time.

Show up on time with a plan and a commitment to carry it out. . . . If you don't believe in what you're selling, how can you expect anyone else to? Lack of commitment shows through like rust on a used car, and will kill a deal even faster. You have to look, act, and feel like you mean it. That's why motivation is the single common denominator you'll find in all topflight salespeople and the hardest attitude to maintain. If you have it, you'll win *95 percent* of the time.

Show up on time with a plan, a commitment to carry it out, and then execute it. Nothing is more deadly to a sales relationship, or any relationship, than a broken promise. Whatever you say you're going to do, you'd better do it, and if you find you can't do it, then the price/service/delivery concessions better be so generous that the buyer is glad you didn't. Once you've put the other elements together, if you perform, or better yet, if you deliver more than what you promised, you'll beat the competition *100 percent* of the time.

(Odds compiled and guaranteed accurate by Harvey the non-Greek.)

HARVEY MACKAY'S
SHORT COURSE ON RUNNING
THE SHOW

CHAPTER 6

---○---

A MANAGER'S MANUAL OF SELF-DEFENSE

LESSON 23

———————————•———————————

SEVEN CLUES ON HOW TO ROLL UP YOUR SLEEVES THE RIGHT WAY

The era of the clean-desk executive who "sets policy," delegates everything, and then sits back and waves his hand while it all happens is over.

Takeovers, cost-containment, downsizing, foreign competition are the buzzwords of this economic period.

We've re-entered the era of hands-on management.

Here's how today's managers are jumping into the trenches

1. IT DOESN'T TAKE AS LONG AS THEY WANT YOU TO BELIEVE IT DOES.

Challenge the amount of time your people tell you they need to develop a new product or implement a new policy.

———————————•———————————

Honeywell originally thought it took four years to design a new thermostat. When a big customer threatened to walk because the time frame was too long, Honeywell unleashed a "Tiger Team" and had the new thermostat ready in twelve months.

If these new structures work for special projects, they should work for your "normal" organization, too. When a 3M employee comes up with a new idea, he or she recruits an action team to see it through, with salaries and promotions tied to the team's progress.

2. TIGERS HAVE BIG APPETITES.

Put a bounty on innovation. S. C. Johnson set up an internal seed-money fund of $250,000 to help its inside innovators get ideas rolling. 3M awards up to 90 Genesis grants of fifty thousand dollars each year to staffers to work on pet projects and gives them up to 15 percent of their work hours to prove it's practical. Rubbermaid, Hewlett-Packard, Merck, and a number of other companies with a record of leadership in new-product introduction all have similar programs.

3. GET IT RIGHT THE FIRST TIME.

Nothing is more destructive to your bottom line and your relations with your customers than defective products. Test throughout the manufacturing process, and then test again just before shipping. Then test the testers to make sure they know what they're doing.

4. GET IT THERE BEFORE YOU SAID YOU WOULD.

Two kinds of deliveries your customers never forget: late deliveries and early—but not too early—deliveries. Guess which one destroys your credibility and which one pays off forever.

5. MAKE YOUR GOLFING BUDDIES "CONSULTANTS" FOR YOUR BUSINESS.

More and more companies are networking with each other to solve operating problems. Why pay big outside consulting fees or fly by the seat of your pants when you have a ready-made unofficial board of directors (and one that is not worried about personal-liability lawsuits) waiting at the next tee?

6. YOU CAN'T MAKE IT A CADILLAC BY PUTTING THE NAME ON A CHEVROLET.

Not every product is sold on the basis of quality, but if yours is and your quality starts to slip, you're dead. You've got about as much chance of restoring your reputation as Zsa Zsa Gabor has of restoring her virginity. Cadillac is trying to do it by restoring its old land-cruiser image with bigger cars and fins, of all things, but I don't think it will ever regain the market share it lost when it downsized and started building its cars on the same frames GM used for its less prestigious vehicles.

Schlitz may have thought the public couldn't tell one beer from another, but it ran out of gusto and never regained the market share it lost after it changed its brewing process. Howard Johnson has not regained the market share it lost after it failed to upgrade and modernize. Burt Reynolds went from being the nation's number-one box-office attraction to box-office poison by coasting through a string of poorly scripted star vehicles.

Burt Reynolds came back, though. But if you can't cut it anymore, it's time to unload the business while it still has some value, instead of running it into the ground.

Esquire magazine was repositioned and turned around by two hot young publishers from Tennessee when the old management failed to expand its readership or appeal to male advertisers.

Of course, if you're really shrewd, you can mismanage it so badly that the corporate raiders will take it off your hands for you at a big premium.

7. "SUCCESS COVERS A MULTITUDE OF BLUNDERS"— GEORGE BERNARD SHAW.

Tolerate failure. It's the price of success. Philip Morris, generally regarded as one of the best-run companies in the country, has experienced a long string of dubious management moves. *The New York Times* reports that a few years ago, just as the Philip Morris Miller beer division was closing in on Budweiser, the Miller people got overconfident. Anheuser-Busch outworked and outmarketed it and Philip Morris missed a golden opportunity to seize the number-one spot. Philip Morris also overestimated the marketing abilities of its General Foods' acquisition, using dated pitches for its cereal and Jell-O products. Now, with the Kraft merger, Philip Morris will try again. What makes Philip Morris keep doing it? Why is the company still a Wall Street darling? Because though it has stumbled, it has never neglected or mismanaged its principal business, tobacco, and its principal brand, Marlboro, which remains a cash cow for everything else.

LESSON 24

●

TELL ME THE WHOLE STORY

"Okay, Lefty, let's hear it again from the beginning."

"But I already told youse guys what happened a hunnerd times."

"So make it a hundred and one. And don't leave nothing out this time."

Sound familiar? It's the dialogue from 100 cop shows, so make it 101. And it's a technique we can use in real life.

People generally have enough sense not to lie outright. But the truth can be embarrassing. So they compromise. They tell half the truth. They "forget" the rest. Or they "didn't think it was important." One of the better divorce lawyers I know, a fellow who has to deal with the most sensitive kinds of personal problems, has a line he lays on new clients.

"If I were your doctor and if you came to me and you

●

had chest pains and headaches, but you only told me about the headaches, there's a strong chance that whatever I did for you would do you more harm than good. If you want sound advice, you're going to have to tell me the whole story, no matter how embarrassing you think it may sound. That's the only way I can help you."

That's a good way to get someone to level with you if your job is to help him.

But what if he thinks your job is to hurt him?

And you still have the problem of getting at the truth.

Something goes wrong at the office. Some equipment is missing or destroyed.

Here's the part where you better forget the cop shows and the courtroom melodrama.

Because if you push too hard, you'll end up on the wrong end of a million-dollar lawsuit instead of just losing a few old typewriters out of the storeroom.

First, get the written reports from everyone who handled the ball or could have.

You're not looking for suspects, just information.

Then, you interview them individually and have each tell his or her story, again and again, until you're sure you have all the facts.

Before any session gets under way, ask if the participant minds if you have an observer present taking notes, or if you can run a tape recorder, or both. State at the outset that your purpose is merely to find out what happened. Be sure you just ask questions. Be very, very sure you do not conduct yourself in an intimidating or threatening manner, that you do not humiliate or accuse. If you doubt an answer, say, "I'm confused about . . . Do you mind going over it again?" At the end of the session, thank the participant for his or her cooperation.

Will the culprit confess? Will the truth come out just the way it does on TV?

No.

Are you Perry Mason?

No.

And it's not necessary to get back to anyone, either. In fact, you shouldn't do much of anything unless you're sure you have an ironclad, lawsuit-proof solution. And even then, you'd better think twice about taking any action.

But chances are that unless you've got a skilled professional running loose, it won't happen again.

Your objective isn't to find out whodunnit.

It's damage control.

Leave the detective work to the guys on TV.

LESSON 25

●

YOU'RE NOT MANAGING CHANGE, YOU'RE MANAGING CONFLICT

I used to think it was because I'm in a classic low-tech industry, but I spend a lot more time sorting out internal problems than I do coming up with ways to incorporate the latest wrinkle in envelope folding. Even IBM, the model for success in a high-tech, fast-paced, rapidly changing industry, has often let someone else do the pioneering before it entered a market.

Most managers do not manage change. Change takes them by surprise. What we're actually managing is the conflict wrought by change.

When we hold budget meetings at our company, every department has the same request: We can bury those hotshots across town if you just give us more resources.

Production wants more machinery, sales wants a better

commission schedule, delivery wants more trucks, accounting wants more computers, and administration wants to open a branch in Sri Lanka.

There's a built-in conflict of interest between each of the departments and the company as a whole. Each wants to make its goals easier to reach, and there's no question that if it gets what it wants, they will be easier to attain. However, someone else's will be harder, and noses will be out of joint. Instead of teamwork, it's tug and pull, back and forth, day in and day out. But believe me, teamwork really works. The Boston Celtics won sixteen NBA world championships and never once had the individual league-leading scorer on its team.

If you're not careful, running a company can be a lot like running a failed political campaign. In politics, you spend a year and a half running against the people in your own party for the nomination or endorsement or primary, and only three months running against the people in the other party. If you're not careful, you can build up so many internal resentments within your own party among the people you need to support you in the general election, you've lost before the real election is even under way. That's how the Republican party tore itself apart in 1964 when Goldwater was nominated and the party liberals never came home for the general election. The same thing happened four years later to the Democrats, when members of that party's left wing sat on their hands after Humphrey got the nomination.

Before you can beat the guys on the other team, you need to have your own people on board.

Good managers have to sort out these conflicts. You can't just allocate resources and set policy by the numbers. Otherwise, you wouldn't need a manager— an accountant could run the company. Every one of the people running a department is a sincere, hardworking manager in his or her own right. When these managers toot their own horns fighting for as much capital and responsibility as they can lay their hands on, they're really not being selfish. They're doing what they've been trained to do—be competitive. It's hard to curb that aggression, even when they're dealing with members of their own team.

My good friend Ichak Adizes, adjunct professor at the UCLA School of Business, describes the ideal manager's role: "Good management equals united differences based on respect."

But good managers are hard to find. Almost any other talent can be bought by the yard.

LESSON 26

●

YOU'RE NOT RUNNING FOR ELECTION

Every time we get a new president, commentators like to tell us it signals a new trend in personal style. When we had Carter, technocrats were the rage. With Reagan, we had charisma. Now, Bush's kinder, gentler approach is in, charisma is supposedly dead, and the corporate autocrat is a dinosaur. Well, forget it. Everyone has his or her own style, and what works in one institutional culture or one situation may not work in another.

It would be a better world if we could always lead by recognizing and praising the contributions of others. Until we earn our eternal reward, however, we're not likely to reach that better world. This one is still full of goof-offs and assorted bozos. Part of leadership means acting like the head coach when you have to, not just the head cheerleader.

One of Lou Holtz's finest moments came late in the 1988

season, with the national championship on the line. Just hours before the USC game, he suspended two of his stars for coming late two days in a row. They were on the plane back to South Bend while Notre Dame was upsetting the Trojans without them. Autocratic? You bet. But so were Holtz's predecessors, Leahy and Rockne, and it didn't hurt their teams, either. Be as nice as you can be, and as un-nice as you have to be.

LESSON 27

•

WHY NOTHING GETS DONE AFTER YOU DUCK OUT EARLY FOR THE WEEKEND

Did I say a moment ago, "You aren't running for election"? Well, let's amend that a bit. "You're not running for election on the basis of personal popularity." How does your dog miraculously know that you are about to take him for a cherished walk when on other occasions your faint stirrings on the couch merely signal a change of channels? The answer is: While you are watching Old Poon only 1 percent of the time, he watches you 99 percent of the time, That's how he makes his living. Your dog is sensitive to your body language. Don't you think you can expect your people to be at least as influenced by your behavior as your dog?

If you curse and shout, your managers will curse and shout. If you wear gold chains and a pinkie ring, your sales managers will wear gold chains and a pinkie ring (alas, they might wear them anyway). If you overpromise, they'll overpromise. If you're paternalistic and tolerant of feather-bedding, so the people under you will be, too. Your subordinates will copy and perpetuate your style. Your behavior will fix it in place long after you're gone. The corporate culture is you.

LESSON 28

●

YOUR COMPANY IS NO BETTER THAN ITS REPUTATION IN THE COMMUNITY

Not only you but your company as well should set an example. It should be an active, visible supporter of community and civic programs. This isn't feel-good advice. This is practical stuff.

In 1987, corporate raiders tried to take over the Dayton Hudson Corporation, our area's major retailing giant and the parent company of Target stores. Its counterattack depended on securing changes in the state's corporate-securities laws, not a very easy assignment under the best of circumstances. Consider trying to get it done within a thirty-day deadline or having your company vanish into the gaping maw of a corporate shark.

Within a week, the governor had called a special session of the legislature, and the laws were passed 131–5. The raid failed utterly, and for once, the raiders lost their shirts.

●

The company succeeded because it had established a statewide constituency. Every major civic, editorial, political, and governmental voice, right and left, supported its continued independence. Dayton Hudson cashed in chips earned by decades of participating in and contributing to fund drives, volunteer committees, nonprofit boards, citizens' groups, and do-gooder activities throughout the state.

Its reputation for helping others gave it the clout to get help when it needed it.

Major crises such as the one this corporation experienced are rare. More important is how your reputation affects you on a day in, day out basis. Dayton Hudson's stature as a progressive company has spilled over to other areas. It's the most profitable retailer in the area, and one of the most profitable in the country. Customers trust the company. Even though its wage structure isn't outstanding, people want to work there. It has more quality applicants for every slot than any other employer in town. And it hasn't had a major labor dispute as long as it's been in business.

Corporate nice guys finish first.

LESSON 29

●

THE MACKAY 33™ FOR MANAGERS

It should not come as an awesome surprise that the same twisted mind that devised the Mackay 66™ for Customers, the 12 P's Competitor Profile, and the Mackay 33™ for Employees would want to have an equally firm grip on the attitudes and concerns of its employees.

Same approach. Different objective. Here it's to get our managers in touch with the people they manage.

The questionnaire examines three distinct roles: the employee individually; the employee in relation to the people around him or her; the employee in relation to his or her goals.

Once we get the information and analyze it, we have a pretty good handle on how we can motivate our people. Good managers tend to be good teachers. That doesn't mean they have to be Harvard B School profs. As Kahlil Gibran writes in *The Prophet*, good teachers reveal "that which al-

●

half asleep in the dawning of your knowledge," so
ou are led to the threshold of your own mind."
ese reports are absolutely confidential and are kept
ked up. Personnel data is very touchy stuff. We make
are our people use the information carefully. The files
should be kept current and updated every year. Like any
other reports, they're only as good as the people who use
them, so we evaluate the evaluations in conjunction with
our annual management-appraisal process.

Personal Profile

1. What is this person most proud of? (What trophies,
photographs, certificates, etc., can be found at the person's
desk, in the office, around his/her locker or work area?)

_____

_____

2. a. What is the employee's attitude toward education?

_____

_____

b. Is he/she attending classes? Pursuing a degree?

_____

_____

c. How does he/she keep skills current?

_____

_____

3. Is this person a leader? How have leadership skills or deficiencies been demonstrated?

_____

_____

4. What motivates this person? How can we satisfy this motivation?

_____

_____

5. Has this person been briefed on handling confidential information? Describe.

_____

_____

6. How does this person's outside activities, interests, and concerns reflect upon Mackay Envelope? (Memberships, associations, awards, demanding home situation?)

_____

_____

7. How does this person accept criticism? How often do you have to correct the same mistake?

_____

_____

8. This person is most successful at doing his/her job because of (technical skills, perseverance, experience, etc.).

_____

_____

9. This person is least successful at doing his/her job because of (poor attitude, lack of experience, limited problem-solving skills, etc.).

_____

_____

10. The greatest single strength this person has is _____ . Are we utilizing or underutilizing it?

_____

_____

11. How would we feel if this person were working for the competition?

_____

_____

Self-awareness and Relationships

12. How aware is this person of his/her strengths and how to make use of them?

_____

_____

13. How aware is this person of his/her weaknesses and how to deal with them?

_____

_____

14. Is this person regarded as an "office politician" by his/her peers?

_____

_____

15. Who is this person's mentor or role model in the company?

_____

_____

16. Are there people better suited to be a role model? Why? If so, how do we encourage the change?

_____

_____

17. Is this person a team player? In which ways is this person effective on the team? Ineffective?

_____

_____

18. Is this person a natural teacher? If yes, how can we utilize these natural teaching skills?

_____

_____

19. Should this person be a role model for someone in the company? If yes, who? How can this be done most effectively?

_____

_____

20. Is this person an effective spokesperson for Mackay Envelope? Would he/she be comfortable in speaking for the company? If yes, how can we effectively use this talent?

_____

_____

21. What do co-workers say about this person's job performance? In his/her own department? In other departments?

_____

_____

22. How would co-workers react if this person was given a higher level of responsibility?

_____

_____

Goals and Aspirations

23. What does this person want to be doing in five years? In ten years?

_____

_____

24. Given this person's strengths and weaknesses, how realistic
    are his/her goals?

    _____

    _____

25. What have we done to help this person meet these goals?

    _____

    _____

26. Is there any challenge within the company that this person
    can take on to help him/her achieve these goals?

    _____

    _____

27. What training programs outside the company does this
    person need to be prepared for his/her next job?

    _____

    _____

28. What on-the-job training opportunities exist to prepare this
    person for advancement, and how do we specifically plan to
    use them?

    _____

    _____

29. Does this person believe anything or anyone is blocking his/her future with our company? (A person, a past problem, lack of education, etc.?) Is this concern realistic?

_____

_____

30. What has been this person's level of achievement against past goals?

_____

_____

31. Do you feel this person will do better or worse in the next-highest level of authority than in his/her present job?

_____

_____

32. Has there been clear and open communication of our goals? Describe what was said and when.

_____

_____

33. How do you feel the goals of this person match up with the goals of Mackay Envelope?

_____

_____

You'll note there's nothing very fancy here, no trick questions or attempts at deep Freudian analysis. We even make the space for the answers fairly skimpy, so the writing—and reading—required isn't too demanding.

Still, we do have a hidden agenda.

Managers learn something filling out these reports beyond how to evaluate their people. The questions are a means for communicating our standards for job performance, to teach managers that they have to focus on people in an objective, fair, reasonable way. They're designed to help managers avoid sexist, racist, ageist judgments like, "You're too old to get ahead"; or "She'd be perfect for the job, but I hear rumors that she may want to have a baby"; or "When I heard he signed that union card, I knew he'd never want a job in management."

All it takes is one knucklehead spouting stuff like that, and you're dealing with shattered morale, ruined careers, and the possibility of years of painful and costly litigation.

Don't just ask a manager to fill out this report on others. The first person he should fill it out on is himself. If his perception of himself is a hoot, how much can you rely on his perceptions of others?

Read through enough of these reports, and you'll often find out more about the people who wrote them than the people they're writing about.

If all of the people John describes in his reports seem "insecure and concerned about their future," it may suggest that John's management style makes them feel that way.

Do you have interdepartmental friction? Here's a way to find out the cause. Have the managers fill out questionnaires on someone else's people. For instance, if the managers of production and accounting seem to regard everyone in marketing as "arrogant and abusive," that may give you a clue as to how the manager of the marketing department is training his people to deal with other employees.

No one's immune. Is there a fuzzy understanding of the company's goals? Then it's a pretty good indication the CEO has done a lousy job of communicating them.

When these reports are properly prepared and used, they can generate some real breakthroughs.

Here are a few war stories.

A loading dock isn't usually where you find people sticking around for the gold watch, but ours would have made a fast-food mop job look like a lifetime appointment to the federal bench. The reports told us why. According to the foreman's answers, he didn't think there was a single employee on the loading dock, not a single one, whose strengths outweighed his weaknesses, or who could be expected to perform well at a higher level. He thought they were all stiffs. And that's how he treated them, too. Once he left, performance improved dramatically and turnover returned to normal.

At some other companies, these reports provided answers they didn't expect. The picture of a child on a desk explained why a recently divorced young attorney refused an important promotion. It involved too much travel, taking away time she wanted to spend at home.

A simple question about two rocks used as bookends, and an EDP programmer revealed he was an amateur geologist, looking for a transfer to the Southwest.

A junior PR staffer who had always seemed under-employed yearned to become more visible. A hundred-dollar-a-month expense account put him on the luncheon circuit in touch with community leaders and on several major nonprofit boards. His company may lose him to politics before long, but what the hell—it helps sometimes to have a friend in city hall.

This works. It tells you things you need to know and can't learn any other way.

Don't limit the use to negative intelligence. We try to find a way to recognize as many employees as possible and give them special status, like writing them up in an article in the house organ or signing them up as the company representative at a seminar. These reports are a gold mine for that sort of information. Employees should know they're used for that purpose.

LESSON 30

PEOPLE DON'T CARE HOW MUCH YOU KNOW ABOUT THEM ONCE THEY REALIZE HOW MUCH YOU CARE ABOUT THEM

By now, some of you reading this book probably are saying to yourselves that gathering information about employees and prospects just isn't your style. It's prying and snooping into the affairs of others in personal areas that are simply nobody else's damn business.

Well, I disagree.

I'm not interested in keeping the spirit of J. Edgar Hoover alive at Mackay Envelope. We have a different purpose in mind.

These information tools really have only one function: to act as a memory tickler for managers and salespeople to aid them in their relations with their employees and prospects. Behind each fact in each form there should be a live, caring

---

human being who wants to know about people so he can *motivate* them, not *manipulate* them.

I concede that getting information is a lot easier than handling it correctly. I've stuffed this book with reams of forms, but I can't emphasize enough how useless, even dangerous, they are in the wrong hands. Keep them away from the junior detectives, the curious, the meddlers, the busybodies, and anyone else without a need to know. Better yet, don't hire that kind of manager or salesperson in the first place.

But how incredibly effective they can be when they're used properly.

Let me give you an example.

When our factory manager roams the plant and approaches our machine operator, Mary, and asks her about the high proportion of rejects she's running, I want him to be able to say in the next breath, "Mary, congratulations on your daughter Joanie's high school graduation last week. Does she have plans to go to college?"

Suddenly, the fact that Mary's operator number showed up in a batch of duds is not the same as a spaceship malfunctioning on the launch pad. We're making envelopes here. Not launching satellites. Whatever happens, happens. It won't be the end of the world. And handing Mary her head won't get them made any better or any faster. Giving her some reassurance, along with whatever corrective action is needed, is the best guarantee she'll get back on track.

Corporations spend zillions on management training, schools, conferences, seminars, workshops—and books like these—but the one skill that can't be emphasized and taught enough is human relations. It is the bedrock element of the work product of every business. Mess it up, and I don't care how good your strategic plan is, how superior your product line, or what your balance sheet looks like, you're heading down.

The bad news is, I can't begin to tell you all the war stories about how a misstep in this area simply ruined a good employee's performance permanently. Jack Shewmaker, former president of Wal-Mart, tells about the manager who turned down an employee's request to take a few hours off for a family event. The company got all the time it had paid for, but it lost it back a hundredfold in ill will and lack of future productivity that the manager's callousness generated.

The good news is, human-relations skills can be learned. I don't mean sending your managers to some seminar where they come back pumped up for a day or two and then it's business as usual. I mean *every day* and *every contact* has to be made with human-relations considerations uppermost among your managers' and salespeople's minds. There isn't a manager from the top on down who couldn't improve in this area. Caring is contagious. Help spread it around.

LESSON 31

———————————————●———————————————

SUPERMAN DOESN'T LIVE HERE ANYMORE

There may be no such word as "can't" in your vocabulary, but there ought to be a "shouldn't." It applies to situations where you can get someone to do the job better than you can.

A plumber in our neighborhood runs an ad in the local paper that reads, "We fix leaks, stoppages, and your husband's repairs."

I'm guilty. I have to bite my tongue every time I bring my car in for work to stop myself from telling the mechanic exactly what's wrong. If I don't, I get charged twice, once for what I tell him is wrong, and then again for what he has to do when he fixes what's really wrong.

But that's just the little, personal stuff. Where it gets serious is when you play Superman or Superwoman down at the office.

———————————————●———————————————

Sure, you can probably do your subordinate's job—if you have to. But isn't that why you hired the person? Let your subordinate do it. If you know how, explain how. Even demonstrate how. But don't do it yourself.

Even the best managers and motivators can become impatient and grab the reins if they see an assignment being botched. Coach Lou Holtz wanted to teach his punt-return man how to handle a kick. Lou demonstrated. I'm sure the kid learned a good lesson when Holtz broke a finger in eight places. So can you.

If you don't know how, find someone who does.

It is not an admission of personal inadequacy to get advice when tough business decisions have to be made, such as site selection, financing, reorganization, acquisition, or a key hiring.

I am as skeptical as the next person of the quality of a lot of professional advice that is sold in this country. Many who call themselves experts aren't. Many who *are* experts aren't consulted at all.

Dr. Thomas Self is a gastroenterologist who teaches at the University of California at San Diego. According to *Pediatric News,* he surveyed one hundred pediatricians and family doctors who said they regularly prescribed the "BRAT" diet (bananas, rice, applesauce, and toast) and asked them, face-to-face, so they couldn't look it up, what BRAT stood for. "A very high percentage really didn't know . . . , with answers ranging from B stands for bratwurst to T stands for tea."

Unfortunately, many of those who pass as experts are used as false fronts so frequently that the credibility of the breed has become widely suspect. The expert is hired to suggest potential locations for the new corporate headquarters—giving the CEO the necessary cover to pick the one closest to his home.

Before you hire outside help, do what the outside people

will do as soon as you hire them. Ask the people who know you best. Your own people. Make it standard operating procedure for your sales staff to tell you when a product has had it or what features your customers are looking for in a new line. Recognize them and reward them when they do it.

Ask your customers. Customer focus groups are stunningly effective in uncovering customer concerns on a wide range of issues and great PR to boot. You cared enough to ask.

Ask your peers. Most small and medium-sized companies have similar problems. They're organizing "thought swap shops" and cross-pollinating with other firms in their communities to come up with new ideas.

You are surrounded by experts, people who use your products in ways you weren't aware of, people who make their living from them. They all have opinions. They may not be big-picture people; the opinions might be limited to some small area of expertise. But they may raise issues you never thought existed. The guy who pushes the broom may notice the escalation in wastage from a new design long before the cost accountant does.

And it doesn't cost a nickel to ask.

You may not like what you get, but you will never offend anyone by asking for an opinion, and you will never come away knowing less than you did before you asked.

As a novice writer, I knew I needed advice. My adviser suggested that he could arrange for the attendees at the Stanford Publishing Course to criticize my manuscript as part of their classwork. There were eighty-one of them, experienced editors and publishers spending part of a summer at Stanford polishing their skills. They literally shredded my book, but I doubt if it ever would have been published if I hadn't used their criticism to rework the material.

The higher up you are on the ladder, the more likely it is that you're hired for your judgment and your ability to inspire others, not your technical skills. Bass are where you find them. So is information. Don't try to do it all yourself. Don't cut yourself off from any potential source.

The more experts, the more varied the points of view, the more complete the picture you'll have, and of course, the more contradictory their advice will be. You can handle it if you break down their work product into its three parts: new information, analysis, and conclusions. First, throw away the last page, the one with the conclusions on it. Think of experts as the six blind men describing the elephant in the old grade-school classic, or as opposing lawyers in the courtroom. Each is forced to deal with the same set of facts, but they emphasize them and analyze them differently to reach different conclusions.

You have to serve as the jury. Use experts expertly. Pick up on their information and analysis. Reach your own conclusions. That's your job. Just enlarge your definition: An expert is someone who knows something you don't.

YOU WON'T HAVE TO SPEND A LIFETIME WITH SOMEONE HIRED BY THE HOUR

Nothing is more aggravating than going into a negotiation and finding that your support team, your lawyers and accountants, aren't as strong as their opposite numbers on the other side of the table. You can change them, of course, and I have, even knowing it's a sure sign of weakness.

Just remember, as bad as it is at the time, there's going to be a next time, and now you know whom to hire. During a two-and-a-half-year negotiation, I went through two sets of lawyers before the deal was concluded, and I was eventually able to hire the lawyer on the other side.

It was worth the wait.

Upgrading is not limited to cars and houses.

CHAPTER 7

———————————○———————————

AN ENTREPRENEUR'S MANUAL OF
SELF-DEFENSE

●

MAKE YOURSELF THE HAPPIEST GUY IN THE PLACE

Obviously, if you're not, you shouldn't be running it. But no one is able to be up every minute of every day.

How do you overcome the inevitable drag on your spirits of doing tasks you hate but that have to be done?

I do it by playing a trick on myself. It's the old peas/pie routine again. If I have to do something I don't like, I make it a point to be especially nice to myself later by doing something I really do like. The same day. What will it be, Harvey? I think about the possibilities all the time I'm plowing through the monthly reports on loading-dock shrinkage and ninety-day-plus receivables of more than five thousand dollars from accounts outside the metro area. Then, four hours and six aspirins later, I'm ready to give myself a new tennis racquet, dinner out, or whatever mad and capricious delight strikes my fancy at the moment.

You're a helluva guy. Reward yourself. No one else is going to do it.

●

•

IF IT'S YOUR COMPANY, THEN IT'S YOUR PROBLEM

Some people who go into business for themselves fantasize that they've finally made good their escape from the drudgery of whatever they've been doing. Don't kid yourself. It's going to get worse before it gets better. Save the money you were going to spend on the upscale office furniture and the brass plate that reads PRESIDENT. You won't be needing them for a long time. I can guarantee you'll be doing more dog work your first few years of running your new business than you ever did in a lifetime of fitting into some corporate slot where modern broom-handling techniques, mop methodology, wastebasket and filing systems, and sundry other skills you took for granted were being taken care of on your behalf.

There is nothing that you should be unwilling or unable

to lay hands on if you have to. Phillip Pillsbury, of the Pillsbury Pillsburys, wouldn't have needed to work a day in his life, but he was active, vigorous, and served as president of the company that bore his name. He accomplished a good deal in his eighty-one years; he'd even been a guard on an undefeated Yale football team. Yet one of his proudest accomplishments was losing the tips of three of his fingers. That marked him as a journeyman grain miller. His hands carried the unmistakable brand of a man who had been employed grinding flour, and whose fingers had been caught— more than once—in the giant rollers. Phillip Pillsbury knew what it was like to do a tough, hard, dangerous job. More important, everyone at Pillsbury knew that he knew it.

Until you get up and running, you'll do everything. You'll learn every job you have to hire for and trace every dollar that goes out. You'd better be the best-informed, best-qualified person in the place. Otherwise, you should be working for the one who is.

DON'T CONFUSE CHARISMA WITH A LOUD VOICE

Some very effective corporate leaders are corporate mumblers.

They're barely audible. People have to *strain* to hear them. That's the idea.

S. I. Newhouse, the media magnate, claimed to have given only three public speeches in thirty-five years. And like many major media owners, he declined to submit to the essential transaction of his publishing empire; he wouldn't be interviewed.

In the days before we had major-league sports franchises in Minnesota, Cedric Adams was as close as we came to having a national celebrity. He was our best-known newscaster and columnist. His son, Steve, owns Adams Communications, and it wouldn't surprise me if someday he makes the *Forbes* 400. He doesn't give interviews, either.

We used to have a police chief around here who hardly uttered a sentence without making some wisecrack about his alleged poverty of intellect. It drove his enemies nuts and helped make him one of the most popular men in town. He was also one of the smartest and most vain, but he managed to keep it beautifully hidden under his self-effacing speaking style.

Irwin Weinberg has been a leading stamp dealer for over forty years, helping to build some of the greatest collections ever assembled for his clients. At one time, he owned the world's most valuable stamp, the one-cent British Guiana, a tiny square of clipped and soiled paper that he sold for nearly $1 million. In a recent newsletter, he wrote:

In the early 1970s, through philately, I was honored with the friendship of Stephen D. Bechtel. He passed away recently at almost 90 years of age. His biography as one of the world's greatest builders (he founded Bechtel, Inc.) has been extensively reported elsewhere as has been his first name relationship with kings and presidents. He often said his proudest accomplishment was the building of the Hoover Dam. I remember so clearly our first private luncheon with him some years ago when in answer to my wife's question, "What kind of work are you in, Mr. Bechtel?" he replied, "Jeannie, you might say that I have been a ditch digger all my life." He then ordered his car to stop at a florist where he bought her a lovely corsage. So like the man—self-effacing and generous as are most truly great men. And that's how I shall remember my good fortune in having as a friend one of the world's heroic figures.

The bigger they are, the less they have to do to prove it.

MEET YOUR NEW BOSS: MY SON

A couple of years ago, the accounting firm of Laventhol & Horvath studied entrepreneurial families and came up with this result:

A full 61 percent said that relatives of theirs were active in the business, and half of them thought they wanted their children to join them in the business.

But forget about marrying the boss's son or daughter as the way into the family business. Of the family entrepreneurial businesses surveyed, 31 percent had a father working with a son, whereas only 7 percent had a son-in-law in the business, 11 percent had a daughter, and only 3 percent had a daughter-in-law in the business.

One of the nice things about the increasingly intense level of competition in business these days is that it leaves less room for deadwood, including that taking the form of chips off the old block.

"There is something that is much more scarce, something finer by far, something rarer than ability. It is the ability to recognize ability," said a man named Elbert Hubbard.

Rare indeed. He must have met some of the people who tried to pass their businesses on to their children. Your success is enough of a burden for your children. Expecting them to follow in your footsteps just adds to the load.

It can be risky to pass it on when you pass on.

LESSON 37

●

THE SMALL BUSINESSPERSON'S GUIDE TO NICHEMANSHIP

As soon as a business buzzword becomes credible, so do the myths about it.

We've been through "intrapreneurship," "networking," Japanese anything and everything, and "nichemanship" is no exception.

Myth one: "A niche has to be chic." Turtle Wax has held a dependable—and sizable—share of the car-wax market for years—a market that is synonymous with something people hate to do. They did it with a product that has a reputation for being more difficult than others to apply, by exploiting a niche out there of people who literally "love" their cars. What better way to show love than by sacrifice, by lavishing care and devotion on the object of one's affections? Working hard to get a shine that shines through. Romantic stuff, huh?

●

Domino's doesn't belong on the Appian Way, but it did figure out how to successfully and predictably deliver hot
pizzas to people before they had a chance to sober up and
go out to get a fancier one. Waste Management made it by
doing something IBM and General Motors do not care to
do—pick up other people's garbage. Niches and glitter have
nothing to do with each other.

Myth two: "A niche has to be new." Fifty-seven percent
of the couples in America have abandoned the traditional
family structure in which the husband is the only breadwinner. Everybody is chasing the working mother and the
two-family income these days. But what about the 13 million women in the traditional homemaker role? Only a fool
would neglect the power of that still-immense market segment.

Myth three: "A niche shouldn't be too narrow." Recently, lawyers and doctors have started to market their
services. Trained as professionals to be aloof from the
hue and cry of the marketplace, they've been less than
eager to embrace such a program. And being cautious and
conservative by nature, they've tended to do it by the
numbers.

In our area, all the hospitals broke from the starting gate
and launched their advertising at about the same time. Each
had done a focus-group-market-survey-patient-profile-ques-
tionnaire number in great depth, and each, separately, found
that the consumer of medical services viewed "compas-
sion/concern about them as an individual" as the single
most important characteristic of medical care.

The "compassion/concern" niche was identified as most
important by 44 percent. Next came another traditional
value, "quality of treatment," identified by 28 percent.

When they launched their advertising, it all tended to
look alike, full of gentle humor and the images of warm,
smiling, happy patients interacting with warm, smiling,

happy doctors and nurses. Everyone was concerned and compassionate.

With a half-dozen or so advertisers all trying to deliver a similar message, none with a product benefit more specific than compassion or concern, consumers couldn't tell one from another.

The research was accurate, but the strategy wasn't.

The campaigns had blurred into one another.

Only two hospitals concentrated on the smaller "quality of care" segment. They were able to increase their market share significantly, even though they were aiming at a much smaller target.

Don't assume that because your niche is larger, it's better.

Wouldn't you rather be fighting for half of a 28 percent segment than one seventh of a 44 percent one?

Myth four: "A niche has to be neat." Not every niche is defined with the sharpness of a surgeon's scalpel. There are liquor stores in the toniest sections of Manhattan, Chicago's Gold Coast, and Beverly Hills that do as much volume in Château Ripple, vintage Wednesday, as Château Lafite-Rothschild, vintage 1895. No one, no matter how wealthy, eats caviar and drinks champagne every day. It isn't that the rich can't afford it; it's that it gets as boring as anything else if it becomes routine. There are a lot more rich folks with palates like Elvis than Epicurus. The trick is not to fill up a niche; it's to fill up a customer.

LESSON 38

•

THE PAT ON THE BACK IS BACK

Your employees shared your dream; give them their share of the rewards. Give them an incentive to perform with profit-sharing and stock-ownership programs. Hutchens Over the Road Suspension Systems doubled its profitability with only a 10 percent increase in sales when management gave employees a stake in the company. Rubbermaid hasn't had a down quarter in eight years. Earnings are expanding at a steady 18 to 20 percent clip, and the company earns better than a 21 percent return on equity. Quality is what distinguishes Rubbermaid's line of household products from its competitors'. Line employees are the key to maintaining that quality. They're constantly on the lookout for defects. Rubbermaid's profit-sharing plan has been in place since 1944.

Both these companies have a win/win approach to labor relations. The employees benefit; the owners benefit.

•

When you have a problem, ask your employees for the solution. "Time after time," says Jack Shewmaker, former president of Wal-Mart, in *Nation's Business,* "I have seen struggling businesses where the solutions to problems were known by employees." And they weren't asked for the answers.

When your employees have a problem, or a family crisis, make it a point to demonstrate your concern, personally.

Be sparing of building structural walls between management and labor. It isn't necessary to make class distinctions such as fancy offices or dining areas based on the corporate hierarchy. Perks should be awarded for performance achievements at all levels, not just management. Sure, there will be times when you need your own separate facilities, but as a general rule, you don't. And the more means you have for staying in contact with your people, the more quickly you'll be on top of their concerns and your problems.

LESSON 39

WHEN IT'S TIME TO SAY GOOD-BYE, MAKE SURE NO ONE TAKES YOUR COMPANY AS A GOING-AWAY PRESENT

Think of the worst hosing you ever gave someone else.

Now, think of what you can do to stop the same thing from ever happening to you.

When I walked out the door of Quality Park Envelope at the age of twenty-six, I took three hundred accounts with me. I could have done Quality Park less damage if I'd backed a truck up to its loading dock and rolled out with the company safe. I walked out the door with its future.

It was fair. It was legal. Yes, it was even ethical. We still have a free-enterprise system in this country. Just because you become an employee doesn't mean you have permanently abandoned any notions of participating in it.

I had no contract with Quality Park. My accounts were

mine. When I started selling, the company didn't hand me any house accounts, it handed me a phone book. My customers' loyalties ran to me, not QP or its products. I could just as well have been selling Kewpie dolls as QP envelopes.

Does that sound a little strident and defensive? Of course it does.

There's an argument for the other side, too. After all, QP did give me a job and a product to sell. And since my intention on leaving was to be on the other side of the table for the rest of my life, I wanted to be sure that, as an employer, I could protect myself from what I had just done as an employee.

I found a lawyer who drew up a fair, simple, and enforceable noncompete agreement. We've been using it almost unchanged for thirty years, which is more than I can say for any other piece of equipment around our place. Some very sophisticated people will tell you that all these contracts are invalid. It's not true. I have the lawyers' bills to prove it, and more important, so have the people who have challenged it unsuccessfully in court.

Each of those points I mentioned—ethical, simple, and enforceable—is vital if the contract is going to stand up. Let me explain why.

First, most noncompete agreements try to prevent the employee from working for *any* competitor *anywhere,* at *anytime.* Well, that just isn't fair. If you're in envelope sales, you should have the right to make a living selling envelopes.

The second problem is that these agreements also often contain cleverly designed restrictive clauses that are really total bans against competing at all. Of course, you can forbid an employee from taking any proprietary property, whether it's an idea, or a plan, or a document. They're the property of the company.

But don't press your luck. Even when contracts allow the ex-employee to go to work for a competitor, if they still forbid doing things like taking the previous employer's strategic plan "into consideration" in his or her new job, they are likely to be overturned. How do you tell if a former employee was thinking about his previous employer's strategic plan? That's like telling someone not to think of the word "hippopotamus" for the next five minutes. The courts won't enforce shams cooked up to keep people from working in the same trade. Out goes the contract.

Resist the temptation to make the restrictions too broad. Your former employees will sneer at them. They won't be enforceable anyway. And with just one bad clause, you could poison the whole contract.

My approach is very different and is based on this premise: Every salesperson at Mackay Envelope is given a territory, an orchard to cultivate. When they come to work for us, there are already trees in that orchard. We planted them. We made them grow. While employees work for us, they can share in the harvest, but when they leave, they can't dig up those trees and take them with them.

So the employment agreement (there isn't room for it here, but I'd be glad to send you a copy) contains the list of the accounts that we're giving them when they come on board. When they leave, they agree they can't take these accounts with them. Because that provision has to be balanced against the salesperson's right to make a living, that limitation applies for one year. I figure that if I can't defend my orchard for any longer than that, the salesperson was right to resign—I'm not worth working for. On the other hand, I know that if I can hang on to the customer for that long a time, even after losing a top hand, I'm likely to keep that customer for a long time to come.

What about the accounts the salespeople developed themselves? The way we deal with that is to limit the territory in which they can compete with us if they leave. For legal purposes, the smaller the better. When we analyzed our market, we found that 80 percent of our accounts fell within the county in which we're headquartered. That became our noncompete territory. It covers a lot of trees they may have planted on their own.

Again, the period is limited to one year.

Oh, by the way, I'm not the first person in the world ever to have dealt with this, so you'd better find out what kind of noncompete agreement binds that superstar you've been trying to lure away from your biggest competitor. You know the one I mean . . . the one who's going to bring all the new business your way.

LESSON 40

———————————•———————————

THE SETUP

Scenario A: A big company you've never been able to crack contacts you unexpectedly and asks you to prepare a proposal for a project that could make your year. It indicates that price is paramount, and there are currently no other bidders for the job. You are drooling to get the company's business. You make it a No-Way-Can-It-Refuse offer. While executives don't quibble over price or ask for any significant revisions, they become quite vague about when they intend to place the order.

Scenario B: A top executive with a much larger and more prestigious firm calls you with the surprising news that he's admired you from afar and he'd like to go to work for you. You enter into negotiations. He asks for an employment contract and you give it to him, but you never seem to be able to sign him up.

———————————•———————————

173

Scenario C: A company you are interested in acquiring dithers endlessly over your excellent offer without suggesting any specific changes. Though the company continues to encourage your interest informally, it's nearly impossible to schedule negotiations.

We're not talking here about a situation in which you knowingly do a mountain of spec work in hopes of converting it into real business, or one in which you're one of a number of known bidders.

This is about long delays and strung-out, halfhearted *second-round* negotiations that often signal you are not a serious contender but are being used to jack up someone else's bid.

Each of these little delaying tactics could be nothing more than a legitimate negotiating ploy. You may still be the one and only. But if you suspect you're being used, you probably are.

The telltale clues of the classic setup are: when the initial contact comes from out of the blue; when it involves someone you've never done business with before, usually a big, fancy someone; when it represents a potentially enormous transaction or a major personnel coup; and when it requires you to submit very specific terms and pricing.

A big, big chunk of new business? No one gives you all his or her business at once. Customers want to see how well you perform before they make a major commitment.

Mr. Wonderful? Superstars do not present themselves on strange doorsteps. You have to dig them out. They do not tend to advertise their availability; they are expert networkers. Looking for a new job? Top hands know that's a lousy time to make new friends. That's why they have the old ones.

I've had my chain pulled twice. Once, by an executive at a New York Stock Exchange–listed retailing firm with sales thirty times bigger than mine. This guy loved the piece of paper I gave him with all the big numbers next to his name, but he stopped returning my calls the second the news of my offer fell into the hands of his real target. I wonder how that happened?

My second charmer was a football coach whose public posture was that I was trying to drag him away from his happy home in the Southland and who privately encouraged me to do just that. Naturally, in his version, I was cast as the potential body-snatcher. I think he owes me an agent's commission for the five-year contract extension I got him.

The deal of the century? Attractive acquisition prospects can be raided by outsiders, but rarely are they shopped around publicly; they tend to get shopworn in a hurry.

In other words, if you are wondering to yourself, Why should I be so lucky?, you aren't. Be honest. Ask yourself, "Even though I may seem valuable to a third party, am I important enough to cause trouble if I get dumped on?" If the answer is no, then you may simply be providing someone else with a free pricing tool.

●

ONE THING YOU *DO* LEARN AT HARVARD BUSINESS SCHOOL

I attended a seminar on entrepreneurship taught by a Harvard Business School professor who told us the ten things he tries to teach students who want to be entrepreneurs.

First thing on the list was "Don't run out of cash." The last thing on the list was "Don't run out of cash." And I'd have to say whatever the eight were in between, you really only have to remember the first one and the last one.

●

HARVEY MACKAY'S
SHORT COURSE ON
LONG-TERM SALES CAREERS

CHAPTER 8

THE SALE BEGINS WHEN
THE CUSTOMER SAYS YES

DON'T SAY IT IF YOU DON'T MEAN IT

The buyer walks into the new-car showroom, and he's just as eager to buy the car as the dealer is to sell it. Then the salesman finds out that the car that's being offered in trade is worth less than the amount of money that's owed on it. Car salespeople call these people "upside down." They're also a nightmare for insurance companies, since these cars have a way of being stolen or smashed up in disproportionate numbers.

Salespeople who overpromise are classic "upside downers." They'll say anything to close a sale, but there's nothing behind their promises. It's a lazy, greedy, dishonest way of doing business. And a totally unnecessary one.

Several years ago, dazzled by the sizzle, in this case, technology, I acquired something without truly understanding what it was or the conditions under which I was acquiring it. My new, non-AT&T telephone system worked beautifully on a stand-alone basis. We could make interoffice phone calls all day long with no problem. But our exotic flower began to wilt when we had to communicate with the outside world. You could call outside, but only when weather conditions and astrological signs were in the proper configuration. It may have been right for someone who only wanted to receive calls, not make them, like a bookie parlor, but in my business we frequently feel the need to reach out and touch someone.

How can you avoid the same mistake?

Too low a price and an unfamiliar brand name are the obvious tip-offs, particularly when they involve new products.

But you already know that.

The more subtle clues are the long-term lease and the promises of technological wonderment that are beyond the layperson's ability to understand.

Had I bought the system, I could have sued for breach of warranty of fitness to perform. Unfortunately, with the lease arrangement, I waived that right. My contract provided for a huge penalty for bailing out for any reason.

Avoid long-term leases with penalty clauses.

Hire a lawyer before you sign a contract. Remember, he's there to protect you.

Hire an independent consultant before you buy any expensive high-tech equipment.

Be wary of any salesperson of a high-tech product who promises he can deliver you more performance at a lower price than major companies with a proven track record. It may work in a test, it may work for a while, but it's questionable if it'll be around long enough to meet your long-term needs.

Take IBM, for example.

The corporate world is littered with the bones of companies that have gone up against IBM and made huge earnings and sales spikes. Their success lasts for a couple of years before they crash.

People wonder why. "Why" is because IBM's corporate strategy is not to attempt to repel all invaders at the moment of attack. The IBM people may do it eventually, but they don't do it instantly. They wait to see what happens. IBM is too big to try to ram every destroyer that crosses its wake. It lets others go through the exertion and expense of finding out if there's a market out there big enough to justify an IBM cranking up a competitive product. If the market isn't big enough, IBM stays out. It doesn't try to compete with everyone. You can't kiss all the girls. But if it is big enough to justify IBM's presence, IBM steps in and, in time, shoves everyone else aside. Napoleon's advice applies to IBM competitors: "Let China sleep, for when she wakes the world will tremble." That's basically why every twenty years or so, the government launches an antitrust suit against the IBMs and AT&Ts. Their very size tends to mash the competition.

Well, I'm a little guy, too, and I think I understand what it is to hear the giant's footsteps behind me, but in my phone-equipment episode, I think the bigger mistake was made not by me, but by the people who sold it to me. I messed up buying my phone system. They messed up their business.

They wound up doing themselves a double disservice. Forget that it was the wrong equipment. By selling us stuff we couldn't use, they missed the opportunity to sell it to someone who could use it. If they'd sold it for what it was, highly sensitive equipment of great technological sophistication, they might have found the right customer for it. By overpromising, by not caring enough to identify the right target, they helped to permanently negate any success their company or their salespeople might have had with us—and ultimately with people who might become valuable customers and who could lead them to more customers.

What did I do? I yanked out the equipment they'd installed in my own office and went back to my old setup. As for the rest of the company, the new system is still in place, temporarily, until I can decide on a supplier. Leading candidate? The biggest phone company in the United States. Once you've been hurt, there's always a tendency to go back home to Ma.

In the movie business, the professionals know that all any amount of hype can do is get enough people into the seats the first week or two to give the picture a chance. From then on, whether or not the movie has legs depends entirely on word of mouth.

Let me give you another example.

Renault and Toyota entered the American market at about the same time, the late 1960's, both of them with inferior cars—the Renault Dauphine and the Toyota Corona.

No one remembers the Toyota Corona. There was very little hype. Promotion and advertising were modest. The car was reasonably priced but not competitive with the popular compact of the time, the VW Beetle. The most memorable feature of these early Japanese cars, and I'm not sure if Toyota was one, were the fuchsia and chartreuse paint jobs, the Japanese idea of what would appeal to gaudy American tastes. When Toyota sensed it couldn't penetrate the market with what it had at the time, it got out and didn't come back until it was able to put together a superior model, both in price and quality. It messed up with its original model. But it didn't mess up its market. It didn't overpromise.

Renault made the same mistake three times. First it tried with the Dauphine, a mechanically inferior model. Then, it tried aggressively to position the Le Car model to rival the formerly popular Beetle. In a frenzy of cuteness and overreaching, it even painted "Le Car" on the side of its cars in

letters about the same size and as tastefully executed as a
"Domino's Pizza" logo on a delivery wagon. Unlike the Japanese, Renault didn't just make an aesthetic misjudgment. It
seemed to be saying that it had THE car, and Americans had
better learn how to pronounce it in French.

Le Car was no Beetle, and le flop was very visible.

When Renault returned again, it was in partnership with
our weakest car manufacturer, actually an assembler by that
time, American Motors. Though the new model, the Renault
Alliance, wasn't a bad car and was priced competitively, it
wasn't good enough to erase the memories of the Dauphine
and Le Car or suspicions that here was another AMC dud.
Renault failed a third time. My guess is that it won't try
again.

The sale really begins when the customer says yes. That's
when he starts to find out what's really under the hood. If
you've delivered what you've promised, you have someone
you can go back to time and again. He's the foundation of
your business, someone who's on the books and doesn't
have to be resold, who knows he can trust doing business
with you. And who wants to.

Good products, bad products. Businesses survive with
both.

But there's one thing no business has enough of: customers.

If you want to have them, what you do *after* the sale
matters more than what you do to get it.

THERE IS NO SUCH THING AS A ROUTINE SALES CALL

Is a sales call from you a classic definition of boredom? Do their eyes glaze over when you show up?

Memorizing the party jokes in *Playboy* won't help. Instead, you might take the professional approach. Before you make that sales call, think of something new to bring to the table. A new proposal, a new product, a new application for an existing product, a new place to go for lunch, a new book. You have to concentrate on escaping the deadliest trap of them all: predictability, the mark of an order-taker. Sooner or later, the order-taker always loses out to the true salesman. That means you have to reinvent yourself in some way each time you show up.

Don Bosold, who reps for suppliers to the mining industry, prepares a card outlining his calls for the week. Bosold has a way of reminding himself of the need to be fresh: At the bottom of each week's card, he writes a single word in large capital letters: ASTONISH.

Bosold also makes notes for his closes. "It has to be natural. It has to be comfortable. It has to sound like you've never said it before. That doesn't happen by accident. You have to literally say the words to yourself until you've got it right. And one other thing, I never, never use the same close twice."

Why?

"For the same reason a coach doesn't announce his plays in advance, because the other team has a much easier time of defending when they know what's coming."

I know what Bosold means about practicing. I once had to ask for money from Curt Carlson, a business genius and the richest man in my state, but not always a little ray of sunshine. My job was to ask for a large donation for the University of Minnesota.

"How much are you asking for, Harvey?"

"Twenty-five million dollars, Curt!" Try rolling that number around on your tongue and see if it doesn't stick to the roof of your mouth like a peanut-butter sandwich the first few times.

IT TAKES MORE THAN A SHOESHINE AND A SMILE

I once wrote ". . . if selling were just a matter of the low bid meeting specs, the world wouldn't need salespeople."

How true.

Even when it supposedly *is* just a matter of the low bid meeting specs, you'd better have more going for you than nice schematics and a firm handshake if you expect to get the order.

A friend of mine makes a comfortable six-figure living selling telephone systems to local units of government, like school boards and county offices.

Now if there's anything that *sounds* totally cut-and-dried, it has to be selling something like a telephone to a county purchasing agent. Sure, it's become a bit more sophisticated and competitive since the AT&T breakup, but a phone system for a county clerk's office is pretty standard stuff, isn't it? And dealing with a civil servant from a sand-and-scrub-pine county that's been on federal emergency assistance for the past fifteen years isn't like working with a tough Chicago building inspector, is it? I mean, these are God-fearing country people, just looking for the right combination of extension lines and hold buttons before they place their orders, aren't they?

Not hardly.

In fact, the farther away you get from so-called big-city corruption, the less likely you are to have any independent observers with adequate resources, like big-city newspapers or two strongly competitive political parties, to keep an eye on the local pols.

And the poorer and more remote the area, the more it tends to be dependent on government as a source of income. That means that orders for government work take on an inordinate importance in terms of the local economy. Where money's involved, no matter how benign the situation appears from the outside, lots of funny things can happen.

Let me tell you how it really works.

My friend, let's call him Mike Sanderson, had been at the game long enough to know that when you submit a bid, you appear in person, as close to the deadline as you can cut it, as a means of preventing anyone from "accidentally" opening your envelope before the close of bidding and passing on the information to a favored competitor. In fact, Sanderson's firm even fields two separate teams, just in case one gets sidetracked on the way to the purchasing agent's office and misses the deadline.

Does that seem a bit overcautious? Not when salespeople have been known to be unable to start their cars or have been arrested—and detained—for "speeding" on their way to critical bid openings. Even taking the normal precautions wasn't enough in one case.

"We had left the city early in the morning to get to this little town in the northwest corner of the state for a 2:00 bid opening," Sanderson said. "We don't like to stay overnight, because then everyone in town knows who you are and the owner of the motel is always the second cousin once-removed of the county agent.

"This time, the county had a new wrinkle. They'd hired a 'consultant' back in the city who was supposed to advise them on the big, complex technical issues. The consultant had already made a pass at us for a little incentive if we wanted to be selected, and when we turned him down, we knew this one would be a dilly.

"The bidding instructions provided the same deadline for submitting to both the consultant and the county, that is, before 2:00 P.M. on the same day. With the consultant and the county two hundred fifty miles apart, obviously their idea was that one of our two envelopes would have to arrive in sufficient time before the deadline so they'd have a chance to open one and relay the information to their preferred bidder.

"Well, of course, we had a guy down in the city whom we instructed to leave off a copy of the bid with the consultant no earlier and no later than 1:59 P.M. We'd be at the county offices then and do the same, and there just wouldn't be time enough to rig the bids.

"Our city guy scopes out the consultant's office at 1:45, and it's locked. He bangs on the door. No answer. He calls him—he was carrying a phone, of course—it's nice to work for a phone company in this kind of situation—and there still was no answer. He couldn't exactly hear heavy breathing behind the door, but he was certain the consultant was in there. Still, no panic. He does exactly what he's been told, he waits. Then, at 1:59, he slips the envelope under the consultant's door.

"We're at the purchasing agent's desk half a state away,

and at 1:59, we hand him our envelope. There's no one else around, but that doesn't mean there aren't any other bidders. At 2:00, I ask him to open the envelopes. He starts stalling. 'Hey, the specs say 2:00 P.M., and it's 2:00 P.M.,' I said. 'If you call your consultant, he'll tell you we got our bid in on time there, too, and it says right here that now is the hour. You have to open all the bids publicly. We're the public. Like now, please.'

"More stalling. It's 2:02. I said, 'If you don't open those bids like immediately, I'm telling you that the world's biggest, baddest phone company is going to start a lawsuit for fraud against your little county that'll end up making headline news in every paper in this country. Time's up.'

"It's 2:03, there's no one else around, the phone hasn't rung, and the purchasing agent finally reaches into the drawer, pulls out two other envelopes, and opens them along with ours. One is blank on the line where the costs were to be submitted. The other is high. We're low. At 2:05, the phone rings. It's the consultant. I couldn't get much of the conversation, but it didn't matter. It was clear the call had come too late to do their buddy any good."

A lot of people, even some salespeople, have the notion that selling is just sweet-talking the prospect into submission. Find the prospect's hot button, say the magic words, smile the magic smile, and the order is yours.

It doesn't work that way.

Selling is not like operating a punch press, where you stand at your machine eight hours a day and turn out a thousand parts. Admittedly, in selling, there is a lot of routine work and one salesperson is pretty much like another when it comes to the daily grind, riding around from here to there, setting up appointments, doing the smile number.

But unlike the punch-press operator, a salesperson may have only five minutes a week that really count.

It's those five minutes a week that separate the good ones from the also-rans.

The real pros are not professional glad-handers. They may have pleasing personalities, but they know that isn't enough. They understand their products and the environment in which those products are sold. Like Sanderson, they've done their homework. And they can be as tough as they have to be, if they know that's what it takes to close a deal.

Charm is not a substitute for knowledge and guts, it is merely a supplement.

WHY CAN'T I GET THE ACCOUNT?

Lyle Cazel has been a manufacturer's rep for the last eighteen years and in advertising, marketing, and merchandising for forty-five years, including tours of duty with two companies that make brand-name products. Now sixty-five, he says he has discovered the secret of youth: a thirteen-year-old daughter.

There are four types of hard-core, hard-case buyers, Lyle says.

1) *The "Political" buyer.* This one wants to take care of his buddies, the people who take care of him with golf trips and other goodies. You can't win with price, quality, or service, because this guy is tuned in to another station. How do you get your share?

2) *The "Send Me the Literature" buyer.* Probably the commonest dodge of them all. Either the guy can't read or

the stuff goes immediately into the round file, but no amount of marketing kits or slick brochures ever generates a return phone call.

3) *The "Circle the Wagons" buyer.* He doesn't want to hear about it. New items? Lower prices? Better service? Forget it. He's sticking with carbon paper for copies, fingers and toes for counting, and carrier pigeons for passing the word.

4) *The "Turtle in the Shell" buyer.* He's afraid to see a salesperson at all. Thinks they're all plaid-suit, two-tone-shoe, high-pressure types.

All these buyers have two things in common:

They're buying from somebody, and when they give you the bad news, the given reason is seldom the real reason. Pick up the paper any day of the week and it's filled with "resignations to pursue personal goals" and "corporate restructurings" and "changes in company policy" and 1,001 other disguises for the truth. The buyer who tells you to "send the literature" isn't starved for reading material; he's brushing you off.

Your objective is to find out why and do something about it.

Publishers' Clearing House, the direct-mail marketer of magazine subscriptions, never stops market-testing. The "grand prize" always includes the option of cash or a house, which, by the way, no one in the history of the contest has ever chosen in lieu of the cash award. Then why offer it? Because market-testing has proven that including the option of a house pulls more responses than a cash award alone, and some houses generate more mailbacks than others. The next time you open your envelope, look and see if your house prize option is the Tudor, the ranch style, or the Colonial. The Colonial is the perennial leader, but PCH is still testing, testing, testing.

Never stop tinkering with your technique. Change salespeople. Send your Turtle the most nonthreatening person you can find. Give the prospect an introductory "special." Offer to do a research project, to evaluate Turtle's advertising, to do a market study, to put on a focus group for Turtle's product—anything to be of service. Create a role for yourself as an ancillary employee.

Your Circle the Wagons prospect isn't immune to change, just afraid of it. Provide a money-back guarantee. Free training. Send samples. Arrange a demonstration. Find out what Circle needs, and then make yourself needed.

Study the competition. What is it that they're doing that you aren't? Permit me to suggest that you read the chapter titled "Know Thine Enemy" in *Swim with the Sharks Without Being Eaten Alive* by (I blush) Harvey Mackay.

We once had a Turtle who wouldn't stick his head out of his shell, and I couldn't figure out why. We had been through our 66 Question Customer Profile (it's in the *Sharks* book) a half-dozen times, and there wasn't a clue. At a focus group to study "meeting buyers' service requirements," our target let it be known that the one thing that annoyed him was a salesman who always cracked dirty jokes. Dirty jokes? I thought that gambit had gone out with joy buzzers, but when I confronted my salesman, he blushed furiously and looked very uncomfortable.

Switching salespeople didn't help this time. We could never erase a bad first impression.

Be a differentiator. If the competition is giving away cases of liquor to get the business, do the opposite. Don't give away anything. You may not get the same accounts that your competition is getting, but there are buyers out there who don't want whiskey or anything else and resent the implication that they do. The competition zigs, you zag. They sell price, you sell quality. Don't play the other guy's game.

Of course, you can always get lucky. There's another kind of buyer we haven't mentioned, the one every salesperson dreams about. Car salespeople call them "flops." They're the guys who walk into the showroom, ask how much the car costs, and without a word of argument, flop open their checkbooks and write out a check for the full amount.

Like Lyle, I've always wondered why there is only one Flop for every hundred Turtles.

LESSON 46

RAYMOND B.'S GUIDE TO HANDICAPPING THE SUCCESSFUL SELLING EXPERIENCE

We used to have a salesman at Mackay named Raymond ("Don't call me 'Ray'"). Not our best, not our worst. He was a real, honest-to-goodness three-piece-suit, Volvo station-wagon kind of guy, unusual in a business where plaids and Cadillacs are standard issue. Raymond had one other distinctive trait: He liked to play the horses.

"Raymond, are you any good at that—handicapping, I mean?" Raymond had been studying the racing form in his office. (I was *not* hovering. We're not running a vacation Bible school here. I was simply curious.)

"Actually, yes. Much better than most. It's really quite scientific, you know."

"Like how?"

"Well, there are factors here, factors that you can isolate

197

for each horse. Certain horses do better on certain kinds of tracks. Certain ones do better at one distance than another. It's a challenge, but I find it fascinating. I've made quite a study of it."

It did sound interesting, if slightly unbelievable, and I wanted to ask him more, but afraid of revealing my total ignorance, I left him to do his calculations. But I didn't stop thinking about what he'd said. If he could do it for horses, why not for people?

There are a lot of different ways to look at how you succeed. Are you more successful at a particular time of day? With a particular kind of person? Selling a product but not a service? More likely to produce with a particular kind of manager? Good on the golf course, but not in the conference room?

Naturally, I put Raymond on the case. I asked him to devise a questionnaire that would permit our salespeople to collect information about their selling experiences.

Here are the results.

Raymond B.'s Guide to Handicapping the Successful Selling Experience

1. The sale versus expectations:
   Was it harder or easier than I expected?
   Was it as successful as I wanted it to be?
   Were the customer's objections the ones I had prepared for?
   (Unsuccessful sellers will prepare time and again for the wrong questions.)
   Was I able to enlarge the scope of the sale?

2. The conditions of the sale:
   How did I get this lead?
   What time of day was it? What day of the week?
   Was it in a business or social setting?
   How long did the meeting take?
   What competition was I up against?

3. The sale as an event:
   How did I limber up, train, practice?
   Did I rehearse my comments?
   Did I work from notes?
   Did I use brochures or handouts?
   As I came to the finish line, how did I go for the close?

4. The sale as an interpersonal skill:
   Did the mood or atmosphere of the sales call change after I did
      or said anything in particular?
   What kind of small talk took place during the call?
   Did the customer seem particularly interested in it?
   Was the customer pleased/not pleased to discuss business?
   How much did the customer talk?
   How much did I talk?
   Was the customer's behavior today different from in the past?
   Did I do anything differently?

5. The customer as an objective:
   What level of responsibility does this person have?
   Do I regard this person as knowledgeable about the products
      we're offering his company?
   What made it easy for me to succeed with this customer?
   What made it tough?
   What should I do differently the next time I call on this customer?

Okay, so it may not be as scientifically drawn up as the past-performance charts in Raymond's racing form, but I guarantee that if you pay attention to the details that this survey asks for, you will start to see some patterns.

You can use those patterns to make important progress toward improving your sales ability.

The trick is getting to know what you're good at and why. Once you have that information, you can either try to find those situations that ideally match your skills and temperament ("Horses for courses," as Raymond would say) or you can expand your skills in areas of weakness—just as the person who counts calories has a better chance of reducing than someone who guesses.

The payoff is this: You've got a big bet riding on you. If you're going to collect on that bet, you have to study yourself as hard as you study your customers.

THE OLD-FASHIONED WAY

In 1843, a journalist from continental Europe visited the famous auction houses of London, including Sotheby's. At that time, the trendy items were rare books. The journalist observed the techniques of the auctioneers, shrewdly manipulating their wealthy clients into a buying frenzy. He filed this dispatch:

> The duties of a London book auctioneer demand various talents not given to all, . . . He must. . . , by tireless effort, have acquired a wide circle of acquaintances He must be able to recognise, at a glance, the enthusiast on whom the words "tall copy" will have an electrifying effect, the one who cannot resist an "uncut copy," the one whose imagination will be fired by the words "first edition," or who will respond to the announcement "bound by Lewis." Everyone who sells books constantly has on his lips the words . . . "a sweetly bound

volume" (or) "a glorious blackletter" ... [but] the art of using them at exactly the right moment and fixing one's gaze on the appropriate listener ... demands tact and a profound knowledge of one's fellow man. ... A smile from the auctioneer will encourage one man, a frown will urge on another, while a shrug will embolden a third. The auctioneer must be able to judge which method has the greatest effect on each potential buyer. He must be able to read the minds of those present and help them translate their thoughts into action.

The amazing thing about that passage is how little has changed in the 147 years since it was written. If anything, most salespeople are much less expert at their craft than the auctioneer, relying more and more on mechanical promotions like brochures and advertising to do the actual selling.

They may help, some.

But when you get right down to it, the salesperson who hits the top of the charts is the one who understands human nature the best.

CHAPTER 9

SOLD ON SELLING

LESSON 48

———————————•———————————

THE TOUGHEST SELL—READIN', 'RITIN', 'N' 'RITHMETIC

I always thought the toughest sell was life insurance, because it's the only product the company would rather you didn't sell to someone who needs it.

Then I got this piece in the mail, and I realized there was one type of selling that was even more of a challenge.

Knowledge.

Here's "A Principal's Advice to a New Teacher," by Robert A. Grager.

To a New Teacher:

A class knows you from what they see in you, hear from you and gather from your attitudes and mannerisms.

Talk clearly. Use the device of repeating if you think there is a need. And PAUSE frequently, allow your students time to

———————————•———————————

collect into a sequence, into some sort of order their impressions of what you have said. Nothing interferes with good instruction so much as confusion, both from without and from within.

Do not expect immediate grasping of your point, illustration, or reference. After all, the material of the morning should be *old stuff to you, but new to your class.* Did you grasp what your lesson contains the first time you met its content?

Hold the attention of everyone. When attentiveness wanders, so does thought and, like a swarm of bees, *one wanderer can lead the hive* into the woods. Be prepared for that! Have something new and arresting up your sleeve—a question, or tell a story, or drop a book, or just stand there in silence if you feel capable of carrying that little trick off, then begin over again.

But don't complain, ever, about *lack of attention.* The fault is yours! You are supposed to be the interesting one. See that you earn the distinction as a teacher. Better to go far afield and retain the respect of the class than to belabor a point on them without interest; for example, if it's the weekend of the big game, the big dance, a student uprising, don't fight it. Surprise them with a choice bit of timely wisdom, give them a five-minute exercise and then let your hair down and talk about what interests them. A good teacher expects a certain amount of such interrupting to his schedule and so plans it, like holidays in industry.

Be *eager,* especially *about your subject,* and being eager, be aware that others may have to learn to share your eagerness. You may have to entice them into a readiness for this eagerness concept, so many of the young being prone to put on the armor plate of sophisticated indifference, but, by and large, the young like to laugh. Laughter can be the salt of learning. Note that I said, "can be," for it takes taste and judgment to know when to laugh, when to frown, when to encourage and when to discourage. That is teaching. Would you have it otherwise? But how monotonous all one tone would be, gay and frivolous or acid sour or learnedly dull—heaven forbid! To be dull is the cardinal sin—like being dead. For living and growing is learning and you are one of the landmarks along the road of learning.

Expect no more than is reasonable. After all, you are not responsible for anything but what you contribute to each member of your classes. However, see that you contribute and do not fall into that common apology for inadequacy by blaming a pupil as "hopelessly dumb, stupid, uncooperative, lacking in foundation, below standard, etc."

You are in charge of your class and its instruction because it is up to you to produce commendable results. There is no need for any accusations, nor for loudness. Do not resort to argument. No two classes are identical, so be aware constantly of any special needs or ways that will help you and yours—and do not hesitate to repair any ill-advised venture. These are young minds you are dealing with and your contact with them is precious, not for an instant to be carelessly treated. Never, never, never go to class unprepared. That is like a carpenter showing up for work without his tools. If you have to face the dilemma of "what shall I do with them third period this morning?" (as you undoubtedly will), be honest. Your lack is understandable and no explanation is necessary. Turn the class over for discussion, for repair of recent weaknesses, or for one of those "games" you should have up your sleeve. But don't try to bluff your way through. It will take months to erase the stain of that shame and some of the blemish you never will remove because it is where you can't get at it.

Okay, class, here's what we do next. Go back through the letter and substitute the word "salesperson" for the word "teacher." Here are your midterm and final exams all rolled into one: Isn't that darn good advice?

LESSON 49

THE BEST SALESMAN I EVER MET

I don't know if Billy Graham ever played baseball, but he has some of the same qualities Eddie Stanky did. Leo Durocher used to describe his second baseman this way, "He can't run, can't hit, can't field, can't throw. All he can do is beat you."

Other ministers tell funnier jokes than Billy Graham, do a better job of illustrating Bible passages and organizing their sermons, but no one is more effective than Billy Graham in making an altar call, getting people to step forward in front of the congregation and make a commitment. Translated from evangelism, that is what is called closing the sale.

Billy Graham started his career as a Fuller Brush salesman.

"It's no accident that Billy Graham came out of the recent scandals unscathed," says Martin Bailey of the National Council of Churches. "Even with his high visibility, he's a man of integrity who is concerned with people."

Graham's personal qualities set him far apart from other evangelists. But Graham is quick to point out that he's just one member of a team, and that team does not merely talk about a high moral ground, they operate from one.

Unlike the other top ten evangelical money-makers, BGEA belongs to the Evangelical Council for Financial Accountability and publishes a financial statement every year. Every penny is accounted for. Graham's personal finances are fully disclosed. His salary is set by an independent board. He gets $59,100 a year and a housing allowance of $19,700, not exactly lavish for the head of an organization that grossed $81 million last year. And he accepts no fees for speaking. His book royalties go into a charitable trust.

Most TV evangelists are not well regarded by other ministers, who see them as predators, siphoning off support for local churches into their own pockets.

Graham does it differently. Graham has taken potential rivals and made allies out of them by unselfishly catering to their needs.

He helps strengthen local congregations, not weaken them. In effect, he says, "My congregation is your congregation."

His crusades are planned with and built around the local ministry. The name of every new convert who steps forward during a crusade is turned over to one of the participating local churches.

Graham also ministers to ministers. He has a program that runs during the first week of each crusade called the "School of Evangelism." Every pastor within two hundred miles of the crusade city is invited to attend a weeklong series of seminars. They feature the best speakers and most successful ministries in the country discussing the personal and professional issues of the ministry. The Graham organization furnishes attendees with free rooms at a good hotel for themselves and their spouses for the entire week and a mileage allowance to and from the city where the crusade is held. For some ministers, it's the only chance they get to recharge their batteries, with one of the best "rechargers" around.

BGEA's headquarters is as nondescript as other evangelists' are grand. It's a collection of aging, purely functional office and warehouse buildings on the edge of downtown Minneapolis. The only signage on the complex is tiny lettering on the front door you wouldn't be able to read from more than three feet away. BGEA's local profile is so low, most people in our area don't even know it's around, although one out of every ten pieces of mail that originates here comes from Graham's headquarters.

What can we learn from Graham?

Selling success is not a function of grandiose personalities and paraphernalia. For decades, Billy Graham has been on the list of the ten most respected Americans. He's maintained his status and high visibility by sticking to the qualities that got him there: sincerity and moral integrity. While others in his "industry" have succumbed to the "holy wars," Graham keeps getting stronger because he's the class act.

Your reputation is your greatest asset. Not product, not price, not service. Everything flows from it: closes, customer loyalty, referrals.

You can earn it only by earning it. Once you do, don't ever let it slip away.

Grant Tinker, who was instrumental in pulling NBC from last to first among networks, had the right idea. "First we will be best," he said. "Then we will be first."

LESSON 50

●

FIVE-WORD JOB DESCRIPTION OF A CEO: BEST SALESPERSON IN THE PLACE

Harry Truman, who was succeeded in the presidency by former general Dwight Eisenhower, predicted that Ike would find the job a little different than he imagined it to be. "It isn't like the Army. He thinks all he'll have to do is say 'do this,' and 'do that.' He'll say it and nothing will happen."

And if it won't happen for the president, and it doesn't, it isn't going to happen for the rest of us, either.

For those of you who believe salesmanship is dead, try to perform the real duties of a CEO without it. Here they are.

1. SELLING THE FIRM AS AN INSTITUTION

The CEO sells the firm to the investment community and the financial press to enhance the value to shareholders and minimize borrowing costs.

●

The CEO sells the firm to the local community and special-interest groups in order to increase business, attract and retain the highest quality work force, develop a support network, and create positive social good.

The CEO sells the firm to the public to establish goodwill among its many constituencies.

2. SELLING THE FIRM'S PRODUCTS AND SERVICES

The CEO sells the company's products and services, believes in them, understands them, uses them, is enthusiastic about them, and is involved in their planning and creation.

The CEO sells the company's products and services as the best choice for its customers and prospects.

3. SELLING AN ORGANIZATIONAL ATTITUDE

The CEO sells the company's goals to its employees and communicates an enthusiastic, winning attitude about the company, its products, and its reputation.

The CEO sells the company's well-being as the best way to secure the employee's well-being.

4. SELLING AND SALES-FORCE MANAGEMENT

The CEO is the sales tone-setter for the organization. He's responsible for developing the sales techniques that will be most effective and innovative and for seeing to it that the style of sales communication matches the high standards of the firm.

5. SELLING THE BUSINESS MARKETING PLAN

The CEO sells change, to meet the changing needs of the customers and the unchanging challenge of the competition. He has to know when to push, when to pull, and how to alter course in a way that everyone on board can understand and support. He has to *be* flexible and he has to *sell* flexibility.

The CEO has to sell the future.

6. SELLING IT ALL

Harry Truman was wrong; Ike did understand that selling policy is just as important as setting policy.

Ike recognized that leading a free people in peacetime was very different from issuing orders to an army in wartime.

Ike was able to sell his program as president because he understood how to use his personal strengths: likability, personal warmth, low-key leadership, and his very non-threatening, gradual approach to change. Historians have criticized him for having moved too slowly, but it was a style that matched the times and was good for a nation still recovering from a long war. What his critics usually fail to mention is that in different times, in a different role, as the leader of the Allied Expeditionary Force in the Normandy Invasion of World War II, he took bold action, successfully, against the advice of many who would have had him hold back. As head of a conglomerate army of competing, overinflated egos from the high commands of England and France, as well as the United States, he had to sell that plan, too. Ike knew how to match his technique to the conditions he was working in. He knew how to sell.

Andrew Carnegie put selling in its proper perspective: "Take my factories and my money, but leave me my salesmen and I'll be back where I am today in two years."

What every CEO has to realize is that "saying it" ain't going to make it so. No matter what authority you think you have, you've got to be able to *sell* it.

LESSON 51

—————————————————•—————————————————

YOU'LL NEVER KNOW UNLESS YOU ASK

Do we ask our customers to tell us how we're doing, or do we just make it up as we go along? We ask. Our customer survey is our most valuable planning and marketing tool.

Here's the complete package:

A Measure of Customer Satisfaction
Mackay Envelope Corporation

Prepared by Keller, Rosen and Associates

DIRECTIONS: After each question, please write the number corresponding to the answer that best reflects your opinion. If a question does not apply to your area of responsibility, write the Not Applicable (N/A) response.

—————————————————•—————————————————

Very Dissatisfied				Very Satisfied	Not Applicable
1	2	3	4	5	N/A

1. How satisfied are you with the following aspects of
ENVELOPES you purchase from Mackay Envelope?

   a. Sufficient styles and types to meet your envelope
needs _____

   b. Promptness in preparing quotations _____

   c. Responsiveness in attending to your special
requests _____

   d. Competitive pricing _____

   e. Artwork preparation _____

   f. Quality of envelope construction _____

   g. Envelope performance on your inserting
equipment _____

   h. Quality of printing _____

   i. Overall quality of products _____

2. How satisfied are you with the following INTERPERSONAL
FACTORS related to Mackay Envelope SALES
REPRESENTATIVES?

   a. Making effective use of the time spent with you _____

   b. Calling on your account often enough   _____

   c. Promptness in returning phone calls   _____

   d. Friendliness and courtesy   _____

   e. Reliability   _____

   f. Developing a long-term relationship with you   _____

   g. Overall performance   _____

3. How satisfied are you with the following TECHNICAL FACTORS related to Mackay Envelope SALES REPRESENTATIVES?

   a. Understanding your business and envelope needs _____

   b. Knowledge of Mackay Envelope products and services   _____

   c. Knowledge of current postal requirements   _____

   d. Making cost-effective recommendations   _____

   e. Overall technical competence   _____

4. How satisfied are you with Mackay Envelope's BUSINESS POLICIES AND PROCEDURES?

   a. Availability of credit   _____

   b. Accuracy of invoices   _____

   c. Timeliness of invoices   _____

   d. Responsiveness to billing inquiries   _____

5. How satisfied are you with DELIVERY of the envelopes you purchase from Mackay Envelope?

a. Availability of standard envelopes/in-stock _____

b. Length of time between placing an order and
   delivery _____

c. Meeting agreed-upon delivery schedules _____

d. Emergency service/filling rush orders _____

e. Notification of shipping delay, if necessary _____

f. Clarity of container labeling _____

g. Physical condition of the shipment on arrival _____

h. Correctness of order as delivered _____

i. Overall delivery performance _____

6. How satisfied are you with performance when you call Mackay
   Envelope to PLACE AN ORDER or for CUSTOMER SERVICE?

a. Speed of phone being answered at Mackay
   Envelope _____

b. Ease of reaching the appropriate person by phone _____

c. Efficiency of Mackay Envelope telephone system _____

d. Promptness in returning phone calls _____

e. Promptness in responding to your requests _____

f. Courtesy and friendliness _____

g. Accuracy of orders _____

h. Overall ease of placing an order _____

i. Availability of order status information _____

j. Availability of delivery date information _____

k. Understanding the nature of the problem to be
solved _____

l. Overall technical competence _____

m. Overall performance _____

7. Please indicate your OVERALL PERCEPTIONS of Mackay
Envelope.

a. Mackay is innovative in the envelopes it designs
to meet customer requirements _____

b. Mackay is meeting our needs for customer-
designed envelopes _____

c. Mackay printing quality is high _____

d. Mackay has an excellent reputation for providing
high quality products and services _____

e. Mackay consistently achieves a high level of
customer satisfaction _____

f. Mackay pricing is competitive _____

g. Mackay business practices make it easy for me to
be a customer _____

h. Mackay keeps the promises it makes to customers _____

    i. I would recommend Mackay as a supplier to
others with envelope needs similar to mine   _____

8a. If you have had experience with other envelope
manufacturers, please rate Mackay Envelope compared to
them.

  a. Envelope quality   _____

  b. Printing quality   _____

  c. Pricing   _____

  d. Delivery performance   _____

  e. Responsiveness to requests for quotes   _____

  f. Availability of order status information   _____

  g. Range of envelopes available   _____

  h. Innovation and creativity   _____

  i. Sales rep effectiveness   _____

  j. Customer Service/ordering by phone   _____

  k. Overall reputation   _____

8b. Please write the name of the envelope supplier who, in your
opinion, offers the best overall performance in terms of
product, service, price, and business support programs.

_____

9. Which three of the following are the MOST IMPORTANT
FACTORS when you select an envelope manufacturer? (Even if
other factors are also important, please mark only the *most
important three.*)

a. Envelope quality   _____

b. Printing quality   _____

c. Pricing   _____

d. Delivery performance   _____

e. Responsiveness to requests for quotes   _____

f. Availability of order status information   _____

g. Range of envelopes available   _____

h. Innovation and creativity   _____

i. Sales rep effectiveness   _____

j. Customer Service/ordering by phone   _____

k. Overall reputation   _____

l. Other _____   _____

10. Please use the space below to provide comments or suggestions about how Mackay Envelope could increase your satisfaction with its products and services.

11. Overall, are you more or less likely to do business with Mackay Envelope today than you were in the past?

    1. Less likely   _____

    2. More likely   _____

    3. Anticipate no change   _____

4. Unsure   _____

Mackay Envelope management will read all customer comments. If you would like your comments identified, please sign below. Without your signed permission, your comments will be used anonymously.

_____

(Signature)

Thank you for taking the time to help us serve you better.

Copyright © 1990, Mackay Envelope Corporation

Does everyone answer? Of course not. We get about a 44 percent response rate. Two weeks after the first mailing, we follow up with a second request to those who didn't reply to the first, and enclose another copy of the questionnaire. That draws another 15 percent, so our total sample is more than half our customers. If the responses are signed, we send an appreciative acknowledgment letter.

Note that we try to touch all the bases here. How we answer the phone is as important to our business's health and well-being as the quality of our product. I've always believed in and practiced the following: "Give me the receptionist, the secretaries, and the security guard, and I've got the power to destroy the competition."

Obviously, there's a lot of envelope stuff here that won't relate to your business, but most of it will. Use it. People who take the trouble to answer these surveys have something they want you to know about how you do business.

Our program is primitive compared to what companies like U S West Communications have done. It's established an ongoing consumer panel called "Direct Dialogue," with a staff headed by Nita Satterlee, a former utilities commissioner with a strong consumer background. Each state has its own "Direct Dialogue" board made up of people who are representative of U S West's customers and who tend to be vocal and even critical of phone-company policies. They're totally independent of the company's control. They meet monthly, set their own agenda, issue their own reports, and have even lobbied state legislatures on behalf of their concerns, sometimes biting the hand that feeds them.

U S West pays them a per diem, funds their research, and listens to what they have to say. "Direct Dialogue" has not only helped U S West stay in touch with its constituency, it's given the company lead time to respond to issues like "frequency of use" fees on local calls and the quality of rural phone service. Had the company simply waited until consumer concerns boiled to the surface, U S West would have wound up confronting angry, fist-shaking phone users at every public hearing. "Direct Dialogue" keeps U S West ahead of the curve. Paying attention to your customers will pay big results.

HARVEY MACKAY'S
SHORT COURSE ON
KEEPING OUT OF TROUBLE

CHAPTER 10

---○---

ELEVEN WAYS TO AVOID CHAPTER ELEVEN

YOU ONLY GET ONE CHANCE TO MAKE A GOOD FIRST IMPRESSION, AND YOURS IS IN THE HANDS OF YOUR RECEPTIONIST

Which is why I periodically have someone call my company so that person can tell me how the call was handled. A recent article in *The Wall Street Journal* told of one receptionist who was reported to have told a caller that "Joe can't talk to you now. He just went down the hall to the men's room with a newspaper." An "A" for accuracy, anyway, but not exactly the best response in that situation.

Dead-end jobs are the toughest jobs in the world. The second-toughest job is trying to figure out ways to motivate the people who have the dead-end jobs. I have a friend who runs a large European hotel chain. He once said to me, "How do you motivate a doorman or a waitress who's been around forty years? You can't. No way." He hires young, fresh, inexperienced types for those positions. What they lack in finesse, they make up in hustle. Except for a handful of elegant topflight restaurants, where the rewards are sufficient to coax faint traces of enthusiasm, you rarely see older waiters and waitresses anymore. The job is just too tough, repetitive, and unrewarding.

I don't think it's as hopeless as he paints it.

Ray Berry, the New England Patriots' head coach, took Polaroids of all the ball boys. Then he had them sign their names on the snapshots. At a team meeting, he passed out the photos and told his players to learn the names that went with the faces.

"The boys know who you are," said Berry. "I want you to know *them*. Everybody's important."

Holtz had a way of getting the same thought across. At the first team meeting he held when he came to Minnesota, he distributed T-shirts with the word TEAM printed on them in big block letters. Underneath, in tiny print, was the word "me."

Senator Bill Bradley of New Jersey tells this story about himself. He's in a restaurant and the waiter brings over the rolls, but no butter.

"May I have some butter, please?"

The waiter gives a slight nod and wanders off.

Ten minutes later, still no butter. Bradley catches his eye.

"May I have some butter, please?"

Still the vaguest of responses, and after ten more minutes, still no butter.

"Maybe you don't know who I am," says Bradley. "I'm a Princeton graduate, a Rhodes scholar, an All-American basketball player who played with the New York Knicks in the pros, and I'm currently a United States senator from New Jersey, chairman of the International Debt Subcommittee of the Senate Finance Committee, chairman of the Water and

Power Subcommittee of the Senate Energy and Natural Resources Committee, and a member of the Senate Select Intelligence Committee."

"Maybe you don't know who I am," said the waiter. "I'm the guy who's in charge of the butter."

However it's done, whether by getting together every morning the way they do in Japan to sing the company song, or the way Berry and Holtz do it, the words have to be drilled into every employee's head: You Are Important No Matter What You Do; Therefore, What You Do Has to Be Done Well.

That's the gospel. Make sure you dispense the rewards of heaven to everyone who gets it, and the punishments of hell to those who don't.

When it's called for, pour on the praise. Praise from the boss may be the strongest motivating force in the civilized world. A congratulatory note or call will take thirty seconds of your time. The employee who receives it will never forget it.

"If each of us were to confess his most secret desire, the one that inspires all his plans, all his actions, he would say, 'I want to be praised,'" said E. M. Cioran, a Romanian-born philosopher.

It's not the only way, but it's still the best way.

DON'T LET YOUR APPEARANCE CAUSE YOUR DISAPPEARANCE

Next to quality, appearance is the single most important factor in selling products. Sometimes it's even more important.

Syndicated columnist Robert Metz says that when the city inspectors come, restaurateur Nick Ottomanelli tells them, "I want a thorough inspection. The other day I offered an inspector a flashlight to inspect the corners. He said that it was the first time in all his years he was ever offered one.

"Quality is no big secret. Anyone can do it," says Ottomanelli, a second-generation butcher turned restaurateur who operates ten food establishments in the New York City area. His secret is he concentrates just as hard on how it *looks* as how it *tastes.*

One of the principal reasons McDonald's has consistently buried the other burger chains is the company's insistence on maintaining the highest standards of cleanliness at every store in the system. Other chains seem to have looser criteria or less control over their franchisees, and their results reflect it. Americans will tolerate almost any indecency under the name of food, but run out of toilet paper or have dirty garbage cans visible, and you're history.

Marv Wolfenson and Harvey Ratner, who paid $32.5 million cash for the Minnesota Timberwolves NBA franchise, built their business on cleanliness, and now own a chain of twelve tennis clubs with 150 tennis courts. You could eat off the floor of any one of them. Even the locker rooms.

By simply putting their people in uniforms and operating clean, cheerful, well-lighted establishments, some businesses, particularly consumer businesses, even get by with marginal products and a less than satisfactory level of qualified, trained help. No one hires people who wear raggedy, stained, down-at-the-heels clothes. Who would want to do business with them?

Fortunately, the ancient wisdom is true: "Seven tenths of good looks is due to dress and three tenths due to nature." You can always look like a winner if you want to, and so can everyone on your staff.

There's a book called *High Visibility*, by Irving Rein, Philip Kotler, and Martin Stoller, and in the chapter titled "What Does an Image Consist Of?" they list

Your appearance
Your name
Your voice
Your body language
Your behavior, and finally,
The content of what you have to say.

If you're selling by phone, you can subtract "Your body language," and if you're doing it by letter, you can also subtract "Your voice" and "Your behavior." But appearance, whether it comes through your advertising, your letterhead, or your clothes, is always what sets you apart from the flock.

Life is not a midterm exam. Before you get to the guts of your message, unless you have the other five areas under control, you aren't going to pass the course.

No one is going to want to do business with you.

Come to think of it, how do we pick our spouses? When was the last time your mate told you he or she married you for your mind?

———————————————•———————————————

HOW TO KEEP FROM BEING TUNED OUT

There are two kinds of people who can't seem to give you their undivided attention: workaholics and "interruptaholics," described by Michael Schrage in *The Wall Street Journal* as people who constantly flit from task to task, never spending more than a few minutes at a time on a single project. They solve problems in fits and starts, rotating like the beam in a lighthouse. It sounds like a dreadfully advanced case of the short attention span, but sometimes it's just entrepreneurial itch asserting itself when the subject is boring or the rest of the team is dragging behind.

Few traits turn others off like the trait of being a bad listener. And few traits attract others like the ability to listen. After Laurence Olivier's death, Anthony Hopkins wrote a moving tribute to his friend for *The New York Times*. In it, he described his first meeting with his idol: "He came forward to shake my hand and I gave him my name. He gave me his full attention. That was another ability of his, to give his full, undivided attention to the moment, as if there were no past or future.

". . . He loved gardening and tree-growing and being with his family. But even in his 'ordinariness' there was that one peculiar quality of concentration. This is what set him apart as an extraordinary human being: He never dismissed anything; he never disregarded anything. Everything held his interest."

Most of us mere mortals would give our right arm for that kind of concentration. Usually, however, we just don't have it.

I'm not suggesting a cure, but if you do have interruptaholic tendencies, recognize that it is not an endearing habit. People enjoy being cut off in midair time and time again about as much as they care to see you take out your teeth. The least you can do is forewarn them. "If I get a call, I'm going to have to take it." "I can give you only five minutes before my next appointment." Whatever. Just don't let someone believe you're going to give him or her a full hearing and then cut it short. That goes beyond rudeness to dishonesty, and eventually it'll cost you.

Curt Carlson fits into the workaholic category, but there's no reason my strategy with Curt can't apply to interruptaholics, too. I finally figured out how to get Curt's attention for thirty uninterrupted minutes. The key, of course, is to get him out of the office and away from the phone.

Here's a variation on the business lunch, the power breakfast, the cocktail party, the golf course, the company boat, and the company box at the ball game. Carlson is constantly on the move, so when I need a big slice of his time, I'll ask his secretary to scan his schedule for a meeting that will take a half hour to reach, and I will drive him to it. Once I get him in the car, he's all mine. (And as an added precaution, I always make sure it's a car *without* a cellular phone.)

Senator Richard Russell was another classic workaholic. The book *Hardball*, by Christopher Matthews, tells how Lyndon Johnson found a way to use nonstop work to his own advantage. When Johnson was a freshman senator, he wanted to gain access to Russell, a man he deemed, correctly, to be important to his career. Johnson first got himself appointed to the Armed Services Committee, which Russell chaired. Because Russell was a bachelor with no real interests outside the Senate, Johnson reasoned that Sundays would be pretty grim for the Georgia senator. What's to do for a Washington pol on Sunday but watch the talk shows (where *Meet the Press* is known as *Press the Meat*), read *The Washington Post* and *The New York Times,* and wait for Monday? He started inviting Russell over to his home every Sunday, and before long had all but adopted—and, of course, co-opted—Russell, who eventually delivered the support of the southern bloc in the Senate to Johnson when he sought the Democratic nomination in 1960.

Cars or Sundays, whatever it takes. There's a way to crack even the busiest schedule.

LESSON 55

THERE'S BIG BUSINESS IN LITTLE THINGS

John Candy, the eighties reincarnation of Oliver Hardy, got huge laughs in the movie *Trains, Planes and Automobiles* as the quintessential low-rent salesman whose line was shower-curtain rings. The next time you meet a shower-curtain-ring peddler, don't laugh. He's probably making more money than a BMW full of IBM salesmen. It's those tiny, low-tech, invisible niche markets (I call it niche-picking) where the bucks are. Little markets often mean less competition and big, big margins.

Most commodity businesses operate on tiny margins. For a company like ADM, which sells food ingredients like fructose and gluten in enormous volume to manufacturers like General Mills and Ralston Purina, fractional savings of one-quarter cent a pound can mean millions at the bottom line.

Bob Crandall, CEO of American Airlines, is not in a busi-

---

ness that traditionally pays much attention to the cost of peanuts and cocktail napkins. *Business Week* reports that his "Ideas in Action" campaign saved his company $41 million in 1988. Two of the suggestions: Reuse the plastic covers on coffee pitchers (sixty thousand dollars saved) and hold the olives in the dinner salad (forty thousand dollars in the cooler).

Did Bob Crandall dream up these money-savers all by himself?

Well, in the case of the olives, he did. But it was a flight attendant who came forward with the coffee-lid recommendation. Smart companies know how powerful the suggestion box can be in getting the little things done better.

Entire companies can be born out of simple observations based on cost and convenience. There was an article recently in *Forbes* about Sophie Mirman, "the Queen of Pantyhose." Seven years ago, Sophie was managing a group of Tie Rack Ltd., specialty shops in London. She noticed a run in her stockings just before lunchtime and was mightily annoyed. It would take her entire lunch hour to replace them if she had to fight the noon crowds at a department store. Based on this realization, she created her own hosiery convenience store called the Sock Shop. She banked on the fact that other women snagged their hosiery, just as Bob Crandall knew the average passenger wouldn't give a pit about that missing olive.

In a Sock Shop, a tiny store of slightly more than four hundred square feet, a customer can complete a transaction in an average of ninety seconds. Talk about foot traffic! There are now 129 Sock Shops in the U.S, the UK, and France. CEO Mirman is just thirty-four . . . and a multi millionaire.

LESSON 56

●

WHY WASTE WASTE?

When I first started out in the envelope business, I couldn't figure out how to make a profit in it. There was too much competition, the margins were paper-thin (an old and treasured pun), and it seemed as though I was constantly under pressure to go into debt to buy newer, faster equipment. I went to my first trade show, hoping to get a clue, and wound up at the bar of the Fairmont Hotel in San Francisco at two in the morning with a man whose last name is lost forever to me but whose first name I'll never forget. His first name was actually Goldberg, a good old boy from the small town Deep South Somewhere, whose Daddy had given him his "Christian" name in honor of a rabbi he admired.

"How the heck do you make a buck in this business?" I asked him.

"'Pends on how much you all get fo' the scrap," he said.

●

"The what?"

"The scrap! The scrap! The wastage! Your leftover paper. How much a ton you getting up there where you live, boy? You got a good contract, you make out good. Bad contract, you make out good, too, just not quite as good."

I, of course, had been paying some guys to haul it away. Didn't everyone? Apparently not. My competitors were getting $250 a ton from the same guys.

Scrap is now a major profit center at Mackay Envelope.

Which is why I can practically *give* those envelopes away.

For years, the Weyerhaeuser Company, the world's largest forest-products company, didn't know what to do with the tremendous volume of sawdust it generated. It was waste.

The Weyerhaeuser people knew there had to be a better use for it, but they didn't know what it was until finally they developed the technology to compress that waste into solid board. They created a new company, Wood Conversion, now Conwed, and a whole new technology and industry, all based on that determination to be frugal.

There are entire industries—waste, rendering, and recycling—built on what Americans throw away. Hell, there are countries that are built on it. Trying to help Japan recover after World War II, we gave the Japanese technology that we would never have shown our domestic competitors. And now, we're paying dearly for it.

We seem to be learning something, though. What do Americans do best? We sell things to each other. Is there a scrap of unused space that isn't used for advertising?

●

IT'S NOT YOUR IMAGINATION. THE LINES *ARE* GETTING LONGER

When the 1973 oil embargo finally sent Americans crashing down from our post—World War II high as rulers of the world and we saw how vulnerable and dependent we were, one of the first casualties was service.

We learned to pump our own gas. Jobs like usher, elevator operator, hat-check girl, shoeshine boy, and redcap began disappearing in wave after wave of cost-cutting and social upheaval. Family life changed. Working wives became the American family's primary weapon in the war against galloping inflation. Women stopped staying home all day to cook and clean for the male breadwinner. The trend accelerated toward eating chow-line-quality-bus-your-own-dishes fast-food meals.

The paper boy is no longer a boy; he or she is forty years

●

old, drives a beat-up station wagon, and takes care of four times as many customers as I did when I was a paper boy.

Some of these pre-embargo low-paying jobs will always exist, but the ranks have thinned to the point where they are shadow armies. Discount stores charge discount prices because they have so few clerks to pay. Bank lines are going to keep growing until you and I finally learn how to use the automatic teller.

The irony is, the worse the service gets, the more shrill the advertising for it is by the very outfits that give the least of it.

Shop the Friendly Store (if you don't mind waiting in our unfriendly lines, with our signs that say NO RETURNS, NO PETS, NO CREDIT CARDS, NO SMOKING, and NO CHECKS).

People Are Our Number One Asset (we just don't believe in spending any money to train them).

Our Operators Are All Busy Right Now, But Someone Will Be Able to Help You Momentarily (if you'll just stay on the line for the next forty-five minutes and listen to the soothing sounds of Sid Vicious and the Sex Pistols in concert).

We still expect, or at least hope for, service, and as our expectations are more and more unsatisfied, we get angrier and angrier with the people who let us down.

According to a 1987 survey conducted by *The Washington Post* and ABC News, 25 percent of department-store shoppers thought the service was "poor" or "just fair." Their major complaints were long waits and impolite and incompetent clerks and staff.

Professionals don't fare too well, either. A 1985 Consumers Research Center study showed that consumers felt a "pervasive discontent" with the value they received for services of all sorts, including fees charged by doctors, dentists, and lawyers.

The flip side of this reaction is that we're eager to do

business with those few outfits that really do deliver on their promises.

L. L. Bean, the Yankee outfit in Maine with one store and 2 million mail-order customers, teaches its trainees that they're not allowed to say no unless a supervisor approves. At Nordstrom, the Seattle-based retailer, there's one rule on the sales floor: "The customer has to leave satisfied"; and one rule in the employee's handbook: "Use your good judgment." A Nordie's credit card is considered the primary requirement for life on the West Coast, and the chain is a model of profitability for its shareholders.

Would you believe a supermarket with a chandelier? The Byerly's grocery-store chain is such a local attraction in our area that the tour buses stop there. The lines are short, the clerks and carry-out help are many. Quality is high and the prices aren't low, but the volume is so heavy and the word of mouth so good, Byerly's seldom advertises. That's unusual in a business in which competitors constantly strive to out-shout each other's "Special!"s and "Today Only!"s.

Successful service-oriented companies don't all cater to the carriage trade. Rubbermaid makes flyswatters, garbage pails, and twenty-five hundred other common household products. The company spends a lot of time responding to product complaints. The products, however, usually aren't Rubbermaid's. That doesn't stop Rubbermaid from getting back to the consumer within forty-eight hours and sending along a Rubbermaid replacement for the inferior goods, free of charge.

What do these businesses have going for them that most others don't?

Customer loyalty.

Pricing policy won't do it. A business built on price alone is targeted toward customers who will desert you the moment your prices aren't competitive, putting a constant squeeze on margins.

Quality isn't enough. You'll find more variety and up-scale goods at a Byerly's than at most grocery chains, but a can of Campbell's soup is a can of Campbell's soup. Byerly's may be able to sell it at a higher price than the other chains.

It takes service to build a steady, dependable customer base, and you can't fake it.

What difference does it make?

According to the Technical Assistance Research Programs, a Washington, D.C.–based consumer-research institute, if a consumer has a problem with a company and it's resolved, he'll tell five other people about it. If the customer remains dissatisfied, he'll tell ten other people. When it's a big-ticket item, the stakes get bigger, too. Eight people will hear about the happy ending; sixteen will hear about the outfit that messed up. No business can afford to make ten enemies with a sale, let alone sixteen.

These are our policies on *any* customer complaint.

First, we listen. Without interrupting. After all, if we handle it right, we can turn that dissatisfied customer into a satisfied customer for life.

Next, before we start trying to dig up the file, the person taking the complaint, whether it's the salesperson, the book-keeper, the receptionist, whoever, has standing instructions to tell the customer that a written report of the complaint is going to me and that if the customer is not completely satisfied with how the matter is resolved at this level, I, Mackay, will take personal responsibility for taking care of it.

That heads off a whale of a lot of problems.

It sends out exactly the message we want to send: that we care about our customers. It doesn't say we're right or they're right; that's not the issue at this point. It's getting things back on track before our relationship with the customer gets derailed.

Then, like everyone else, we try to dig up the invoice or whatever it is we're supposed to have on the computer or in the paperwork that relates to the complaint. Since the surest way to ensure that an already angry customer will boil over is to put him on hold for ten minutes while you "look up the file," if it's going to take more than a minute to pull it up on the computer, we give our complainant a very specific choice. Our people are taught to say, "If you'd like, I'll put you on hold, but it's going to take me at least ten minutes, maybe more, to find this or the person responsible for this. I'm giving you an ironclad promise here: I'll call you back within half an hour. I'll call you back whether or not I have what we need to resolve this and give you an update. And I'll keep calling you back regularly until the problem is solved. In case I don't, here's the number of the extension to Mr. Mackay's office. Is it okay if we proceed on that basis?"

If we're wrong, and we're only human, I have often told the customer, "This one's on us," and given away as much as five thousand dollars' worth of envelopes. Why? Because it costs me more than five thousand dollars to put the average customer on the books. It's going to cost me a lot more than five thousand dollars, both from his business and the other accounts he'll poison by word of mouth, if I let him go away mad.

If it's a gray area, nine times out of ten I'll eat that, too, or at least make a substantial adjustment. Same reason.

But if the customer's wrong, that's usually the end of it. Most of our customers are reasonable people. A tiny fraction aren't. Then it's a judgment call. Sometimes I'll eat it. Sometimes I won't. If I know he knows it's his fault, if it's a repeat performance by a difficult case who got away with it once before, then I will stonewall until hell freezes over.

It's all right to be the Good Guy, but it's still a jungle out there. Once you develop a reputation as a patsy, customers, employees, and suppliers are going to cut you up into little pieces.

Of course, in some other countries, it's a lot worse.

Yuri is standing in line in front of a Moscow bakery line for the umpteenth time to get his daily loaf of bread.

"I can't take it anymore," he says to his friend Boris.

"Gorbachev promised to change all this. I'm going over to the Kremlin right now to complain."

An hour later, he's back in line at the bakery.

"So what are you doing back here?" asks Boris.

"The lines are longer at the Kremlin," says Yuri.

LESSON 58

———————————————●———————————————

BUT WILL YOU LOVE ME IN THE MORNING?

Customer loyalty is the most valuable asset a business can have and the hardest to earn. There are some businesses that simply do not and cannot command it.

No one watches a program just because it's on CBS or goes to a movie because it's made by Twentieth Century–Fox. If we want to keep our customers, we have to furnish price, product, and service. Every time. The worst business of all for customer loyalty has to be the saloon business. Jim Beam tastes the same wherever you serve it, and if you're not serving it for even a single day, your customers will not patiently wait for its reappearance; they'll get it someplace else. And they might not bother to come back.

It's unusual for a saloonkeeper to own the building. Buster Paige did. And one day, Buster found that his saloon

———————————————●———————————————

stood in the path of progress. The First National Bank of Minneapolis needed his site for its new, glass-sheeted office building.

Buster refused to sell his place, a little one-story job, until a completely new Buster's, identically seedy, was built across the street. When the new place was finally up, and the bottles were lined up on the back bar, and the towels were in the rest rooms, then and only then, and at 2:00 A.M., an hour after legal bar-closing time, did Buster sign the sales documents and run across the street with his license under his arm and let the bank tear down his old place.

Buster may not have expressed the thought in classic marketing terms, but he knew that continuity for his customers was worth more than a thousand marketing textbooks. He knew his customers would find a new place the day he couldn't service them at the old one.

Will your customers go over the hill the instant you're not there?

Do you care to find out?

A friend of mine worked for an advertising agency in Illinois that had a fire. All its film burned. The film was its work product, the ads themselves rendered on negatives in a form called "camera ready," kept handy on the premises so they could be readily reproduced and shipped to various publications where the ads would appear. All gone. And to make matters worse, in the legal sense, once paid for by the client, the film belonged to the client. And the ad agency had lost it. Fortunately, this was Norman Rockwell–land, no client or competitor pressed his advantage terribly hard, and the agency recovered. But not without a terrible scare. Now, everything it does, it does in duplicate, and a copy is sent into off-premises, fireproof storage. Expensive, yes, but saving the milk is still a lot less expensive than replacing the cow.

Computers are wonderful devices, but they have one disadvantage over typewriters: When you write something on a computer, it's locked into the machine until you print it out. I told my secretary never to leave my system alone until we were sure we had printed out a hard copy of every word I'd written. It mattered only once. We had an unexpected cold spell over a weekend, and when we went back to the computer on Monday morning, it had crashed. Something called a "power surge."

"Why didn't you have a 'surge protector'?" the fellow who had sold me the machine the month before asked me.

"Why didn't you sell me one?" I asked him.

Did he think that after selling me five thousand dollars' worth of gear to write with, I would rebel at the prospect of paying another fifty dollars to protect it? My computer lost its memory and swallowed up the first twenty-six pages of this book. If we hadn't printed out every word I'd written on the previous Friday afternoon, I would have lost my mind. Sure, it wasn't my fault. But even so, would you have felt inclined to buy a book with twenty-six blank pages in it?

Whatever your business, you'd better have a backup system in place, because if you're down for any reason—equipment failure, strike, fire, or supplier problems—you may not have a business at all once you start up again.

Customer loyalty is fragile. You owe it to yourself and your customers not to discover how fragile it is by exposing it to unnecessary risks. At some point or other in your business, everything bad that can happen will happen. Your best form of damage control is to anticipate the worst before it happens. Or, as I've said so often, dig your well before you're thirsty.

YOU CAN'T GET DEALT A STRAIGHT FLUSH UNLESS YOU'RE IN THE GAME

One of the authentic characters in our town was Bill Cooley, who went from bricklayer to dogcatcher to political fund-raiser to suburban mayor to big-time real estate developer.

Cooley scored the biggest coup of his career when the site of the old Metropolitan Stadium was sold in a sealed-bid auction. He had heard about it on TV the day before the bids closed, and somehow managed to get his papers in on time. His bid won. It appeared he had snatched the property from under the noses of some of the biggest hitters in the national real-estate development game. For one brief moment, Cooley was the linchpin of the biggest real-estate deal in town. Though Cooley had made the first deadline, he kept missing the ones that followed. He never got the financing he needed to actually develop the property.

But that didn't stop him from playing a very strong game with very weak cards.

His strategy was simple. A lot of money would change hands with any change in the ownership of the property. By positioning himself between the seller and the real buyer, Cooley knew they would have to find a way to provide a few choice crumbs for him before they could deal with each other.

With the help of one of the smartest real-estate lawyers in town, he was able to use his tenuous hold on the property as the onetime successful bidder to force the seller and the ultimate developers to buy him out at a price that left him well compensated for having drawn cards in a wide-open game.

The lesson here is a negative one: Heavy hitters don't want penny-ante players drawing cards against them and getting lucky. When the stakes are big, the ante usually is, too. Cooley was able to find that rare situation in which he could play with only a nominal entry fee, though a substantial portion of the chips he cashed went to pay his lawyer's bills.

Years ago, small businesspeople made nice livings in publishing, restaurants, retail groceries, and other non-capital-intensive businesses. By raising the ante, chain and mass-market merchandisers drove out the little guys. They couldn't compete with the massive advertising, superior facilities, and aggressive pricing policies of their better-financed competitors.

Big guys eat up little guys, both at the poker table and in business. It takes a tremendous amount of talent and guts for a little guy to stay in the game against one of these giants.

Standing pat can destroy big guys, too. It nearly destroyed Timex. Built on decades of promotion as a durable watch with a low price tag, the company stayed with its plain-vanilla strategy while fashion and lifestyle choices drove the watch market. Timex stayed behind the curve until, as one of its designers admitted to *Forbes,* "People apologized for wearing one of our watches. They'd say their real watch was in the shop."

Timex finally found out what time it was. It shifted its advertising from general-circulation to yuppie-oriented magazines like *Sail* and *Runner's World,* developed new designs like the Ironman, for health nuts, and dealt itself into the new game. What do the numbers on the dial say now? Timex has cleaned everyone else's clock with a 33-percent share of the United States wristwatch market.

United Airlines was going to create a whole new approach to serving the American traveler. It built a conglomerate around its airline business that included hotels, a car-rental firm (Hertz), and an airline-reservation system. Consumers didn't buy the package and neither did the financial community. It wasn't long before United went back to being essentially an airline company, another player who learned not to play the other fellow's game, but once again doing beautifully by playing the game it mastered long ago.

A few years ago, CBS had a strong hand and, like United, decided to draw new cards. The managers wanted to convert the company into a diversified conglomerate and bought retail and leisure businesses. But they took their eye off their broadcast properties. The game went so badly for them that they ended up having to sell off one of their crown jewels, the record division, to Sony, in order to protect themselves from being raider-bait.

Traumatized by that experience, and with only one real prime-time TV hit, Angela Lansbury's *Murder, She Wrote,* they started to play their cards too close to the vest. CBS, once the leader, the nabob of networks, developed a skinflint reputation and was reluctant to pay for Lansbury's designer gowns when she hosted the Tony Awards. It has since recovered, and even managed, at great expense, to lure Lansbury back for another season, but not before nearly throwing away its best hand.

The lesson here is not to not diversify; it's to analyze what you're doing right, what's unique about how you do business, and be sure you keep doing it, whether in the new business or the old one. Just because you take a big hit doesn't mean you should change the way you treat your core business or the employees in it. If you still hold a few winning cards, don't freeze and refuse to back them.

Particularly if you're in a creative business. You can't treat creative people like expense items. They're more like exotic tropical birds. With the slightest change in temperature, they tend to fly off to another nesting place.

Recognize also that noncreative-type employees can have creative-type temperaments. You're guaranteed major trouble if you don't treat them the right way. Everybody knows that Lee Iacocca is CEO of Chrysler. But who presided over Chrysler between 1961 and 1975, when the company experienced strong declines in both quality and balance-sheet strength? Lynn Townsend, a bean-counter by training. David Halberstam, in his book about the auto industry, *The Reckoning*, wrote that Townsend ". . . brooked no interference from anyone, whether product man or board member. Those who questioned his authority, no matter how gently, quickly regretted it, for he would lash out at them, demolishing their ideas and humiliating them in front of their peers. . . . Even on his good days he was capable of behavior that fell just short of corporate cruelty. Stories circulated of Townsend grilling high Chrysler executives for hours about real or imagined flaws. . . . Chrysler, for all its shakiness, had not been in debt when Townsend had taken over in 1961. By 1970, however, its debt had reached $791 million, even more than GM's, and was growing all the time."

Dayton Hudson (as described earlier, in Lesson 28),

which had developed a constituency among its own employees and in the entire community, was able to rally itself and defend its independence. In contrast, Chrysler sank in a downward spiral—a demoralized organization in a demoralized headquarters community, greater Detroit. Ultimately, it took a federal bailout and the management efforts of Lee Iacocca to engineer Chrysler's rescue.

Then there are always those who have to ask, "What did you say was the name of this game?"

Dick McDonald is a marketing expert and tells this story: A hospital opened a walk-in clinic in a shopping mall. Being superintelligent, no-nonsense men of science, the doctors called their clinic what it was, the Ambulatory Care Center. The docs knew that "ambulatory" meant "walk-in." Unfortunately, the patients didn't. The center was in the bedpan until a marketing survey showed that 58 percent of its potential customers thought ambulatory meant you came by ambulance. You can bet from then on the new door sign was in plain English.

LESSON 60

IF YOU CAN'T SAY YES, IT'S NO

Some things come more easily than others.

Red Smith, the Pulitzer Prize–winning sports columnist, once said, "Writing is easy. All you do is sit down at the typewriter and open a vein."

I don't tend to agonize when I write, but I do have trouble making decisions about taking on major new projects. I fret. I sweat. I get advice. Then I get more advice. I toss and turn. Eventually, I decide, or rather, my gut decides for me.

After I've spent a couple of months letting my fingers do the walking, I let my stomach do the talking. Somewhere inside, there's a computer processing all that stuff and churning out a conclusion.

Every major decision, from marriages to mergers, no matter how much it's buffered with advice, statistics, reports, and studies, requires a leap of faith. In the final analysis, what your inner voice tells you is the best advice you can get.

Lou Holtz spent one season in the pros. He took the job as New York Jets head coach and left after one dismal season.

"It was the single biggest mistake of my life," Holtz said. "They threw so much money at me. I let the money do the talking. I never really made the commitment."

Holtz said yes when he knew better. Larry Miller, one of the co-owners of the Utah Jazz of the NBA, didn't.

In early 1986, Miller and his partner, Sam Battisone, decided to sell the franchise. They made a deal for $26 million with a Minneapolis group who wanted to move the franchise to the Twin Cities. But when the time came to close, Miller just couldn't bring himself to hit the switch. There were a million public reasons: He recognized the team was starting to jell; he didn't want Utah to lose its only claim to major-league status; he was too much of a fan; maybe it was worth more money.

But the real reason was, there wasn't any reason to sell to begin with. He simply didn't want to sell. He wanted to be the owner of the Utah Jazz.

So Miller bought out his partner, kept the team, and the Minneapolis group went on to pay $32.5 million for an *expansion* franchise just a little over a year later. Since Miller turned down the sale, while the value of all NBA franchises has been heading up, the value of the Jazz has soared. All-Star MVP forward Karl Malone and point-guard John Stockton made them a title contender.

When Miller couldn't find a good reason to say yes, the right answer turned out to be no.

Tapping into your own state of mind is not as weird as it sounds.

Successful traders and successful investors both will tell you that their single most important asset is self-knowledge, not stock knowledge. They know themselves well enough to understand the level of risk they can live with.

Traders let the market tell them whether they're right or wrong. They have the self-discipline to turn on a dime when the market goes against them.

Investors have a different test of character: to stay with a commitment regardless of what the market does on a short-term basis. They have the self-discipline *not* to turn on a dime when the market surprises them.

The surest way to lose money is not to know which breed you belong to: holding on to a loser when you're really a short-term trader looking for a quick turn or selling too soon, whether it's up or down, when temperamentally you're really a long-term investor. Before you make any major commitment, of time, of money, of yourself, you have to be honest enough with yourself to understand how you will react if things happen that you don't expect. If you know you can't handle the bad stuff, if you're not ready to make a total commitment, then you're not ready to say yes, whatever it is.

LESSON 61

———————————●———————————

DON'T TRY ON THE PANTS UNLESS YOU'RE READY TO BUY THE SUIT

Every suit salesman knows he can't sell you a suit unless you're willing to try it on. I ought to know—I worked all through high school and college selling 'em at good old Cook's Men's Store, Robert Street at Sixth in St. Paul. So if you've tried on a few coats and shown the least glimmer of interest in one, the salesman is always going to suggest that you try on the pants "for size." The idea is that once you've left your grungy old threads in the dressing room, then fantasies of power lunches with Donald Trump kick in, and you've sold yourself.

Life is full of these free offers, most of them just as transparent. The free trial subscription, the free sample, the free weekend test drive are no less effective for being ancient come-ons. We accept them as a harmless form of deception. What's a box of Crackerjacks without the prize?

———————————●———————————

257

The problem is when we don't see these curveballs coming. There are certain "free" offers it's dangerous to accept. Don't expect to save any money having the other guy's lawyer draw up the terms of the deal. You can be sure it has as many bugs in it as the American embassy in Moscow.

A friend of mine serves on a church board. That's normally light duty; you wouldn't expect it to bring out the sharks. He was telling me that for fifteen years the church has staged an annual "Soul Liberation Festival." On ten consecutive summer evenings, the church blacktop is filled with the sounds of gospel music and preaching, all conducted in the best tradition of the southern revival meeting.

Only it isn't the South. It's in Minneapolis, where some of the neighbors in this lower-income urban area aren't tuned in to the camp-meeting style and don't see why the church can't stage it somewhere else.

The opposition is small, but it's vocal. The sound has reached the ear of the city council member who represents the area. She must decide whether to sign the permits for the sound equipment and streets that have to be blocked off so Soul Lib can shake that blacktop for ten nights.

She's no fool. Like all politicians, she knows that taking sides, any side, is a losing proposition in the long run. Eventually, even if you always take the popular side, all those dibs and dabs of people you've offended over the years add up to a majority of the voters, and you're gone.

So she has created a Neighborhood Improvement Committee. The committee, which she appoints, makes recommendations to her on tough issues. Stop signs. Garbage collection. Taxes. Soul Liberation Festivals. Local politicians live and die on these neighborhood issues. Editorial writers may want us to worry about aid to the *contras,* but this is the stuff local political careers are built on.

About nine months before Soul Lib was scheduled, the church received a letter inviting it to send four represen-

tatives to a meeting of the committee, to which four representatives of the Soul Lib opposition were also invited.

Sounds fair enough.

Four from one side; four from another. Equality. Reasonable people sitting down and being reasonable together.
America. Democracy.

The church refused.

Here's what the Soul Lib director said, in effect, in his
letter to the councilperson:

Last year, we conducted a neighborhood survey of Soul Lib
and obtained signatures approving your signing of our permits. The people who signed on our behalf represented 90
percent of the people within a four-block area. Though no
one seriously disputes our figures, we're perfectly willing to
take another survey if you so require.

But we aren't willing to submit our case to the committee.

We think the idea of both pro— and anti—Soul Lib appear-
ing before the Committee on an equal footing is going to
lead to exactly the kind of decision that will eventually kill
Soul Lib.

The internal logic of that kind of staged confrontation is
for the committee to formulate a compromise.

Let's see, now. Four of you are for Soul Lib. Four against.
Four want to keep it for the full ten days. Four want to do
away with it entirely. Let's compromise. Let's cut Soul Lib in
half. We should have a five-day and not a ten-day festival.

We're a New Testament church. But we haven't forgotten
the Old Testament. When Solomon was called on to cut a
baby in half, he refused. So do we.

We don't think the solution lies with the committee or
with a compromise. Our ten-day program is designed to give
people a full range of musical and preaching styles, and most
important, enough time to think about what we feel is the
most important commitment of their lives. We do not believe
in denying them the time they need to reach that decision.
We have scheduled Soul Lib for ten days. We will not stage a
two-day festival or a five-day festival or a nine-day festival. It

is you who must decide whether to grant us the permits to stage a festival at all.

As we have every year for the past fifteen years, we are again applying to your office directly for the necessary permits for the Soul Liberation Festival.

And they got them.

Don't get drawn into a proposition in which the process is designed to decide the outcome. Don't try on the pants unless you're ready to buy the suit.

If you are going to control the result, you have to control the process as well.

Whoever sets the table slices the pie.

Whoever states the proposition determines its outcome.

LESSON 62

THEY HAVE TO BE DOING *SOMETHING* RIGHT OR THEY WOULDN'T BE IN BUSINESS

Jack Shewmaker, the former president of Wal-Mart, tells of going with Sam Walton, the founder of the company and one of the richest men in America, into a competitor's store. The place was a total disaster, but instead of sneering and gloating his way through the aisles before stalking out, Walton noticed the one thing in the midst of all the chaos that was working for his rival and said, "Jack, how come we're not doing that?"

You can walk through any plant anywhere, anytime, and even if that company is on the verge of bankruptcy, you can learn something. That's why I have moved mountains to tour over fifty envelope plants.

261

CHAPTER 11

---○---

THEY STILL KEEP SCORE IN DOLLARS

LESSON 63

•
───────────────────────────────

THE FIRST HIRE AFTER YOU HIRE YOURSELF

. . . is your bean-counter. Entrepreneurs are always going broke because their dreams run ahead of their numbers. You have undoubtedly hired wonderful, honest people, and the proof of that is that you randomly audit expense accounts, vouchers, invoices, payables, inventories, and any and all other areas where there may be leakage.

The restaurant business is notorious for losing profits out the back door when the employees go home from work, but it can happen in any business where the owner isn't constantly on top of the books. In the 1950's, two brothers opened a fruit stand in suburban Minneapolis. I don't know what their total internal accounting system consisted of, but I do know that for years they had one of the more novel and effective variations on the theme: They installed their eighty-year-old mother on a stool next to the cash register,

───────────────────────────────
•

and there she sat, day in and day out, saying nothing, doing nothing, sitting there. I'm not even sure she spoke English. But I do know that their business grew to become one of the largest produce and gardening centers in the metropolitan area.

LESSON 64

BASIC BIRD-WATCHING . . . OR HOW TO HIRE AN ACCOUNTANT

Day in and day out, your tax accountant can make or lose you more money than any single person in your life, with the possible exception of your kids.

There are five subspecies of this bird:

The Chicken. Some people fear an audit more than a run-in with the Hell's Angels. An accountant who will take no risks and decides all potential issues in favor of the IRS might as well be working for them instead of you.

The Vulture. He'll try to take a deduction for the high cost of living. By pressing the code too hard, he invites the IRS to challenge everything. Instead of saving you money, he can cost you a bundle in professional fees, assessments, penalties, and interest.

The Bird of Prey. Up to your tail feathers in tax dodges and accelerated-depreciation schedules? Somehow all those terrific deductions don't seem to equal all those not-so-terrific losses your accountant's deals have generated. But then, maybe you'll recoup it all in his next venture: the syndication of his new book, *How to Appeal Your Conviction for Tax Fraud.* The tax-code revisions of 1986 have killed most of these deals, but there are still a few around. Don't be a pigeon, particularly if your accountant or tax adviser tries to put you into a deal in which he profits in any way on the sale—a built-in conflict of interest.

The Dodo. This tiny fellow knows the tax code backward and forward, but acts as though he was born yesterday when it comes to basic economics. "You've got until next April to make your IRA/pension/profit-sharing deduction, so why do it early?" You do it early because the sooner you get the money working for you, the less time it spends working for the government. The IRS doesn't give you fifteen and a half months to make those deductions out of the generosity of its heart. It does it because it understands the time value of money, obviously better than this bird does. The flip side is that you don't pay the IRS until you have to, such as keeping wages in a closely held corporation. The longer you can hang on to the money in the company and have it drawing interest, the longer it's working for you and not the IRS. Withdraw it, and the revenue guys are immediately entitled to the withholding and FICA, and there's usually a state income tax due, too. This stuff isn't in the tax code, it's the basics of money management, and accountants who don't keep you advised of how it can affect your bottom line are short of the professional skills you need.

The Eagle. Here's the one for you. Aggressive, money-smart, up-to-the-minute on the code, willing to take reasonable risks by resolving questions in your favor when the odds warrant it, not attempting to double-dip you by offering you his own deals. How do you find an Eagle? By looking for other Eagles. Ask the nonaccountant you know who most closely resembles the Eagle in attitudes and achievement. That person most likely has an Eagle for an accountant.

THE BEST WAY TO BUY IT IS TO SELL IT

After a couple of years in business for myself, I finally reached the expand-or-die stage without sufficient capital to take the next step: a new plant. Sure, I could have leased, merged, sold equity. If I'd listened to my bean-counter, I would have tried to renovate someone else's old factory. Why not? Envelopes are not an image business. Your customers never stop by to check out your spiffy offices. But settling for a used model was not in my program. For three years, I hadn't dared put my own name on the company for fear I'd go broke. Now that I knew I was going to make it, I wanted something that would be totally mine, from the ground up to the new Mackay Envelope sign on the roof. Besides, a new single-level plant would be more efficient.

You pay for your thrills. Unfortunately, my bankroll did not match my dreams of empire.

I wanted a $250,000 building, big money in those days. I had sufficient cash flow and credit to support a $175,000 building. The difference was what I calculated as the builder's profit.

There was only one solution: persuade the builder to put up the building for me at cost.

"I promise you that if you put up this building for me for $175,000, I will become the best salesman you ever had. I'll get you at least five more buildings of comparable value in the next five years, people I know whom you don't, people you won't otherwise have a crack at. These guys are on the verge of expanding, too. I'm going to be the first one out of the chute. They think they're going to let me make all their mistakes for them. They'll listen to me if I tell them what a hell of a job you did for me. Just keep one thing in mind: Five profits are a lot better than one."

He agreed. But not exactly on my terms. In the first place, like most businesspeople, he had a constitutional aversion to doing anything at cost, so I had to come up with another twenty-five thousand dollars. In the second place, I had to "pre-sell" two of my buddies before he'd fully commit.

But there it was, the forerunner of the Tupperware party. In exchange for playing host, introducing my friends, and letting the salesman use me to peddle his goods, I got a free toaster, or in this case, a true factory discount.

Just for the record, I delivered on my promise. . . . No, I take that back. As the subtitle of the book says, I delivered *more* than I promised: seven buildings, not five.

And I used exactly the same device to get my house built in 1973 when I couldn't afford what I wanted.

The concept is easy. The one thing that everyone in business needs is sales. If you can deliver them, convert yourself from a customer into a salesperson, and whatever it is you want, you can own it for a lot less.

LESSON 66

──────────────●──────────────

BORROWING TROUBLE

The Eskimos have thirty-six different names for snow. Like snow, all money is not alike. Debt and equity are different animals. The explosion in debt rather than equity financing by corporations is the direct result of the tax code. When corporations pay interest, as they do when they issue bonds, they can deduct that interest from their income and reduce their tax liability. Dividends, paid on stock, are not deductible from corporate income and are paid in after-tax profits.

This dandy distinction is what's behind the floor of corporate buyouts, largely financed through the issuance of enormous quantities of bonds.

But there's a risk attached to that benefit, and it's a risk that seems to have been largely ignored in the rush to market these securities. Corporations that are borrowing to establish equity positions in other corporations are buying

──────────────●──────────────

more than assets and tax deductibility. They're having trouble, and they're passing it on to the public.

There's a reason they call these things "junk bonds." Standard & Poor's is one of the two recognized independent investment-rating services of corporate bonds. Here's how it describes a less than investment-grade bond: "[These securities] are regarded, on balance, as predominantly speculative with respect to the issuer's capacity to pay interest and repay principal in accordance with the terms of the obligation. While such debt will likely have some quality and protective characteristics, these are outweighed by large uncertainties or major risk exposures to adverse conditions."

"Adverse conditions"?

Since when were recessions repealed?

Do you want an investment that could tank when "adverse conditions" pop up?

Financing operations with borrowed money depends on your ability to control your cash flow. Interest coverage on junk bonds is often too uncertain and too thin to withstand a recession. Junk-bond issuers pile up so much debt orchestrating these buyouts that, when an economic downturn hits, the underlying equity they've bought won't generate enough cash flow to cover it. Unlike dividends, which can be cut when profits are down or the company simply wants to hang on to the money, debt is a legal obligation the corporation must pay, or it faces the prospect of being driven into bankruptcy court by the bondholders.

A Harvard study reported in *The Wall Street Journal* found that "investors who bought and held a portfolio of all junk bonds issued in 1977 and 1978 would, by November 1, 1988, experience a default rate of more than 34%."

Stay away from this stuff. The 5 or 6 percent extra interest you can squeeze out of these high-yielding securities isn't worth the huge chunks of principal and interest that will be lost when these lenders default.

All bonds are not alike. Playing with bonds as if all you have to do is find the highest yield is no smarter than taking any deal on the basis of price alone.

It's like the story of the guy with the elephant. He runs into his friend on the street and says to him, "I've got an elephant for sale. It's a thousand dollars. You wanna buy it?"

"Are you crazy?" says the friend. "What am I going to do with such a thing? I'm a tailor. I live in an apartment. Seventh floor. Three rooms. I've got a wife and a kid. I can barely make ends meet. Besides, a thousand dollars is too much. I'll give you five hundred."

Even the pros, just trying to make an honest zillion or two, and investing in the highest investment-grade U.S. government bonds, can be pulverized.

Don't assume that just because an investment is a bond it is automatically safer than a stock, or any other investment. Even if it is of unimpeachable quality, don't underestimate the power of a bond to cause you a world of pain, particularly if you've borrowed money to pay for it.

All investments are unforgiving of human error. There are no exceptions.

WHY YOUR ADS DON'T WORK

For the first seventy-five years Hershey was in business, it didn't advertise. You should be so lucky.

Finally persuaded that a multibillion-dollar consumer food business couldn't compete using a marketing strategy whose key element was cajoling restaurants into displaying its candy bars near the cash register (although it had worked for years), even Hershey felt compelled to begin an advertising program.

For every hundred ads that run, only ten are effective. About eighty-five sink beneath the waves unnoticed; five are noticed and give off such negative sparks they work against the advertiser.

What's the difference between good advertising and bad advertising?

More often than not, it's good clients and bad clients.

Unfortunately, advertising is one of those soft sciences in which everyone regards himself as an expert. The results often are ads that are designed for a target audience of one, the guy who pays the bills. Agencies will offer opinions, but there aren't many that are going to refuse a client who insists on having his own way just because the ads are weenies.

How do you tell?

Here's Harvey's Short Course on that Mad, Mad, Mad, Mad World of Advertising.

Rule 1: Stay Out of the Picture. For every Lee Iacocca, there are 1,001 jerks who insist on having their own faces leering out from amid assembled multitudes of refrigerators or used cars because "the public knows me" or, fantasy of fantasies, "the agency wants me to." Sure, and the agency wants to sell you an ad, too. Save that gorgeous smile for the Hollywood career that's just a phone call away. Personalissimo sells creative products like movies or books, but unless you led the league in homers last year or cracked the Nielsens, don't try to do your own testimonials. For most bread-and-butter goods and services, the value is in the product itself, not in the people who make it or sell it. Stay out of your own ads. People looking for a new fridge don't care to see your mug popping out of the freezer compartment.

There's another disadvantage to starring in your own advertising: *Your* image comes to overshadow the company's product. I saw that graphically illustrated recently when I escorted Victor Kiam, the "I bought the company" Remington shaver mogul, to the airport. At least a half-dozen people sidetracked him to request his autograph. They know the *product,* but when he challenged each of them to name his company, all he drew were blanks!

Unless you're immortal, like Colonel Sanders or Mickey Mouse, the new owners are going to have to invest in a whole new image for the company when you're no longer around. That makes the company worth less to a potential buyer. Just another hidden cost of ego-tripping.

Rule 2: Don't Be Your Own Copywriter. This is the common failing of intelligent people, particularly lawyers and CEOs (the kind who write lots of memos), and all the glib types who make their livings selling words to other people. The only problem is, they make their livings selling the wrong kind of words as far as advertising copy is concerned. They sell big words—and lots of them. Advertising people sell tiny words, and as few of them as possible. They know effective advertising isn't about products. It's all about the benefits people get *from* the product. People don't want a bar of soap. They want clean hands.

Naturally, intelligent people like this dismiss the efforts of professional copywriters as too flashy and commercial. They want to "educate" the public. Mostly they want to say what they want to say the way they want to say it. So they insist on leaden, copy-heavy monsters, which lie on the page unread. Surprise. The public doesn't want to be educated. If you went back and looked at ads from thirty years ago, most of them would be copy-driven, with scant visual impact. Television has changed all that. Advertising is a visual, not a verbal, medium, whether in print or on the tube. Graphics tell the story. Headlines deliver the graphics. If the body copy gets read, it's a miracle.

Rule 3: Disband the Advertising Committee. Hire an advertising manager. This is a tough one because so many corporate cultures are so committee-driven. The problem here is the too-many-cooks syndrome, the ad that's passed through lots of hands, all of which are waving wildly in the air trying to make a point. There's no safety in numbers.

This ad is characterized by visual and verbal clutter. It tries to tell you everything you didn't want to know about a hundred different features: price, quality, specs, uses, availability, appearance, with a little corporate image, sex appeal, and a free offer thrown in just to keep the pot boiling. The mind boggles. The page turns. With a thousand or so ads fighting for our attention every day, no one is going to stop to figure one out. It has to be simple and understandable. It hits you immediately, or it doesn't register. One ad = one image = one idea. Or forget it.

There's one exception, those ads with the head shots of one hundred or so salespeople who have been named members of the "President's Round Table," or "the Million-Dollar Club," or whatever. They're directed not at the people who read the publication but at the people in the ad itself. They're a form of recognition, not advertising. If one purpose of advertising is to bolster corporate pride by showing your own people that you care about them, this is the ultimate expression of that sentiment.

Rule 4: Don't Play It Safe. The most common mistake of all is the "safe" ad. It doesn't make any obvious mistakes. It isn't narcissism. It isn't garish. It isn't a visual mess.

But it's in the 85 percent category. It just isn't interesting enough to be noticed amid the 999 other ads clamoring for attention. It's a gray-flannel suit in a sea of gray-flannel suits.

For some advertisers, that doesn't matter. Procter & Gamble has earned a very nice reputation for marketing and an even nicer living with Mr. Whipple—quality advertising. It seemed almost afraid of being too clever for fear of offending Middle America. So it drove home its messages with repetition. Mr. Whipple got more airtime than the Ayatollah ever did. If you spend a couple hundred million or so on advertising every year, maybe you don't have to take any chances. You can buy market share. But in the last year, even P&G has recognized the need not just to drive its message home but to entertain its audience. Mr. Whipple and Mrs. Olson are being replaced by ads that get noticed and aren't as "safe."

For the rest of us, it has to be good enough to be noticed or it won't work.

Rule 5: Hire an Agency the Same Way You Buy a Suit. First, Consider Quality. You can define quality as demonstrated success in working with companies similar to your own, with budgets similar to your own, and winning awards for those campaigns.

I don't expect ads to sell products. Only salespeople can do that. But I do expect ads to be noticed. I like hard data from readership surveys. I like high response levels to the bingo cards they put in the back of magazines. I like—hell, I insist on—campaigns that stay within budgets.

How good is the agency's stuff? Well, the industry gives awards in the ad game for everything but punctuality, and some awards are more significant than others. Awards from the Art Directors Club of New York (Addys), the One Show (Effies), Communications Arts, the Clio Awards, or the Cannes Festival (Lions) are in the top tier. But I think any award is important. They're an indication of quality, concern, and pride by an agency in its work product. Creative egos are fragile. They crave recognition even more than the rest of us. Agencies that cater to those egos by nurturing creative talents and entering shows tend to produce the best advertising.

I would tend not to hire an agency that believes "awards aren't important. They don't sell product. They're just to impress clients." Well, I like to be impressed. When your agency wins awards, part of that pride rubs off on you and your employees. Their winners will help you build your winners.

Rule 6: Next, Consider an Agency's Style. There are two types of bad agencies: account-driven and creative-driven.

If the account people dominate, you're going to get terrific service. But what about the ads themselves? If the creative types dominate, you'll get great ads all right, but they might be wildly expensive and wide of your target, too. Substituting Itzhak Perlman and the New York Philharmonic for Mr. Whipple might turn some heads on the awards panel, but it probably wouldn't sell toilet paper.

You need an agency that has strong account services plus creativity.

There are all kinds of clues. How long does the agency hang on to its accounts? Short life spans sometimes are the result of weak account services, like blown budgets and missed deadlines, not weak creative. Ask for references— current accounts and former accounts. What kind of teams is the agency willing to commit to your account? Are the creative people who produced the award-winning ads they're showing you to win your account going to be the same ones who are assigned to your account once they get it? If not, let's see some stuff from the people who are going to be assigned to your work. Who's your account exec going to be? Someone with a year or two of experience or a real pro? Keep asking questions like these, and you'll have a pretty good idea of the agency's strengths and weaknesses and how much the agency will value your business.

Rule 7: Then Make Sure You Have a Fit. You want an agency that isn't so big you'll be lost in the shuffle and not so small it doesn't have the wide range of talents or media-buying capabilities you need.

You want to be sure, too, that the personalities mesh. If your advertising manager is a three-piece-suit kind of guy making x dollars a year, you don't want to pair him off against the agency's Mr. Funky, who's making x plus y a year. The chemistry would be wrong.

Make sure there are no conflicts of interest. The Bible says, "No man can serve two masters." Some folks in the agency game haven't read that chapter. The last thing you need is an agency that's trying to juggle your account along with someone you're competing with. That's like discovering your lawyer also represents the other side in your lawsuit.

Rule 8: Now, Set the Price by Contract. Agencies can, and do, make a profit on you in three different ways. First, the "traditional" 15 percent on the ads themselves. That's the agency commission. The media usually bills the agency directly for the space or time, less 15 percent of the gross.

Then there's the markup on any production costs, outside materials, or services they've purchased on your behalf, like typesetting or photography. The markup here runs 15 to 20 percent. You mean you didn't know about that? Well, that's another one of those advertising "traditions."

Finally, on some services, like PR or media buying, there may be an hourly charge, which is usually itemized in the billing.

The good news is, it's all negotiable.

If you're a big enough media buyer, you may not have to pay the 15 percent agency commission. In fact, you can often negotiate the right to place your own advertising, which, if you're running the stuff in the same publications issue after issue, can save you a bundle. Usually, the publication claims it will give the discount only to "accredited agencies," but all that means, if it gets sticky, is that you establish a house agency with its own name.

Most commonly, for small accounts the agency retains the agency commission, but you can get it to shave the markup on production costs considerably and even dispense with the hourly rates. In the end, you should get what you pay for. The good agencies will be open with you and discuss their fees. Many will negotiate.

Rule 9: Reread Rule 1. You have to stay out of the picture figuratively as well as literally. Unfortunately, this rule is the hardest one of all to follow, because advertising is one of those businesses, like managing a baseball team, in which everyone thinks he's an expert.

Think of it as hiring an employee who's in charge of installing and maintaining the most complicated piece of machinery in your shop. Tell him where the switch box is and if the machine is doing what it's supposed to, but don't tell him how to do his job.

LESSON 68

•

BUY IT BEFORE IT'S FOR SALE

Maybe not today, but someday. And the best things that are for sale don't have For Sale signs on them. Nobody hung a sign around Kraft or RCA.

When you see something that interests you, make your interest known. I've even knocked on doors, of businesses and homes, handed over my card, and seen those pleasantly startled expressions when I said, "If it's ever for sale, please let me know." The door may slam in your face if you're offering vacuum cleaners, but not when you might be offering currency. And when you let it be known that you could be in the market, word gets around very quickly, even to those places you haven't contacted.

It doesn't mean you have to buy. It does mean you stand a good chance of getting the first look. While the truth is, most sellers have an inflated sense of the value of their property, occasionally one will come along who doesn't. Or who simply wants to dispose of it with the minimum amount of hassle.

I must have tried it twenty times. It worked just once. I bought a company from a manufacturer who had diversified in hopes of keeping his son interested in the family business. Neither the son nor the new line had worked out, he was embarrassed, and he wanted to unload quickly and quietly.

Just once. But in this case, once was enough.

LESSON 69

●

ECONOMICS IMITATES ART

Building a new plant or office? Before you succumb to the lure of the suburbs, take one last look downtown.

Is there an old building you can renovate? Not tear down but renovate, recycle, preserve?

Our national motto used to be: "This is America. Throw it away." It's been that way with our cars, our clothes, our spouses. Should our buildings have been any different? Without considering the real value, we've torn down thousands and thousands of old buildings because we've been programmed to like what is new.

Then came the oil embargo and a 21 percent prime rate, and we decided that some of the same buildings we'd dismissed as useless piles had hidden qualities that made them worth saving. I'm talking about tax breaks that are available for the costs of historic preservation and for locating in "enterprise zones."

●

Another hidden quality is the long-term benefit you bring to the community by preserving a piece of its history. You become a civic hero, scoring a public-relations coup that's visible every day of the year.

And finally, you're going to reach a pool of potential workers, many of whom may be underemployed now and whom you won't be able to reach in the suburbs. That's another long-term social benefit that combines both PR potential and good economic sense. You may have to drive a few minutes more to get to work, but the core of your work force can come right from the neighborhood. You won't even have to buy as much space for parking.

Before you throw up another cinder-block-sheet-metal monster, take a pass through the city with the industrial-development people. Then talk to a good preservationist, an architect who's done this kind of job before, and see if he or she can make one of these buildings work for you. Most important, walk the streets in the neighborhood. There's an almost dead-sure way you can tell if one of these areas is coming back: Look for the artists.

Check out the restaurants. The galleries. The bookstores. Find the lofts.

A couple of beards, funky outfits, or Get Out of Central America posters are worth more than all the site evaluations you'll ever pay for through the nose. They're the single greatest indicator of undiscovered real estate value there is, like finding gold by finding copper.

The pattern in urban revival is *always* the same:

First come the artists. Free-lance writers, painters, art directors, photographers. They're looking for cheap space, for each other, and for that certain cachet that their eyes can detect before ours can. Then come the galleries and the restaurants that service them.

Then come the boutique advertising agencies and small architects who want to give off an aura of artsiness.

Then come the yuppies.

Then come the tourists.

And with every new wave, property values go up.

Until eventually the artists who started it all get priced out of the market and have to go somewhere else.

A couple of years ago, a large advertising agency had the chance to buy an old warehouse but instead took a more traditional path and stayed within the boundaries of the established business district.

It took a fresh eye, in this case an investor from West Germany, to see the beauty and value the local agency had passed on. He bought the building for $325,000, did some relatively minor renovation, and within five years the city had assigned it a market value of $1.5 million.

So, hey, we're not talking financial sacrifice here.

Here's a way you can do well by doing good.

LESSON 70

●

PUT ME DOWN FOR THE MINIMUM

I may talk tough, but I'm not immune to the siren song of the stockbroker. Occasionally, very, very occasionally, I'll bite. When I do, I'll limit my investment to 10 percent of what I'd normally invest if I were serious about it.

If it goes up, at least I've made a small profit, and if I do decide to take the plunge and buy the remaining 90 percent, my initial average cost is going to be below the current market, thanks to that small original investment.

If it goes down, well, I haven't lost too much.

And up or down, I've got a rooting interest in the stock and a reason to track it, something I would never do if I had ignored the advice and put nothing into it.

It's worked for me quite a few times, both on the upside and on the downside.

The beauty of it is that when it works on the upside, it works exactly ten times better.

HARVEY MACKAY'S
SHORT COURSE ON PEOPLE

CHAPTER 12

---○---

BEWARE THE NAKED MAN WHO OFFERS YOU HIS SHIRT

FOUR OF A KIND

There are honest mistakes, and then there are not-so-honest ones. It still pays to count your change, even when it's the small change from the Coke machine. There will always be people who make a living from the naïveté that often sprouts the strongest branches when it's fertilized by greed.

Let me tell you about four remarkable dream merchants, all experts at selling the shirts off their naked backs to furnish the emperor with his new clothes.

If you looked at a photo of Edith Reich in *Fortune,* you'd see a sixtyish, silver-haired grandmother with the kind of look that goes with winning the apple pie bake-off at the state fair. Between 1979 and 1981, Reich bilked Dayco, the big Ohio manufacturer of rubber and plastic products, out of $13 million in advance commissions. She conned Richard Jacob, the chairman of Dayco, named one of America's ten toughest bosses by *Fortune* magazine, into believing that $120 million of faked orders from the Soviet Union were real. Reich ended up in a non-state-fair state program where apple pie doesn't get blue ribbons; they eat it off metal trays.

Then there's John Ackah Blay-Miezah, who once served time in prisons in Pennsylvania and Ghana and who now spends time in tonier digs in London's West End. Blay-Miezah contends, according to *Forbes*, that Kwame Nkrumah, Ghana's first prime minister, stashed away a fortune alleged to be worth $20 billion in European banks and made Blay-Miezah sole beneficiary and trustee. The money was supposed to be used to develop Ghana. Blay-Miezah was happy to oblige American and European "investors," including professional people and company presidents who wanted a share of the Ghana mother lode, by relieving them of some $100 million in exchange for handsomely engraved notes from the Oman Ghana Trust Fund that promised returns of 1,000 percent and more.

Adela Holzer parlayed the contacts and publicity from a small investment in the hit musical *Hair* into a fantasy world as the pretend wife of David Rockefeller and a big-time Broadway producer. She offered investors 40- to 60-percent returns on deals involving murky contracts to transport boatloads of commodities to exotic places, according to *New York* magazine. There was the "maxi-deal," which returned a profit in three to four months (investors had one week to wire her the money); the "mini-deal," which returned a profit in three to four weeks (the money had to be there in two days); and then there was the "micro-deal," which became profitable in ten days (Holzer had to receive an investor's money that very day). According to the New York district attorney, all the deals were the same: variations on the Ponzi scheme. There were no shipments. Money from new investors was used to pay off old ones. From April 1988 to February 1989, many supposedly sophisticated New

Yorkers fell for this one to the tune of $7 to $8 million, despite Holzer's already having served two years in state prison in the 1970's for running the same kind of game. Holzer was just days away from opening another major Broadway play, financed by wealthy investors, when she was indicted and arrested.

The nine hundred or so people who gave Ken Oxborrow $58 million, it is contended, thought they would be earning 2.5 percent on their money, weekly. Part of the investment was to be placed in commodities futures. The Oxborrow incident was written up in the book *Investor Alert!* by Wilbur Cross and in *Barron's. Barron's* describes Oxborrow as "an ex-unsuccessful spud farmer with no investment experience in commodities futures, and no license to sell unregistered securities." For his efforts, Oxborrow became a guest of the state of Washington.

It isn't superior selling skills that make these con artists so successful. Oxborrow, undeniably an expert on the subject, told *Barron's,* "When people want a good return, they don't look at the risk. When people want it, no matter what is in print, they're not going to look at it. They're going to start rationalizing." Actors call it "willing suspension of disbelief," allowing yourself to believe something you know deep down can't be true but that can't be fully experienced and enjoyed unless you suppress that doubt.

You can defend yourself only by getting in touch with your true feelings and recognizing that you're driven not by belief but by greed so strong that it makes you want to believe what you know in your heart isn't, can't be, true.

All of us have our greed streak. What allows these deals to happen is the weakness in us, the self-delusion, more than the manipulation by others. An anonymous investor, quoted in *Forbes,* says, "I've seen [Blay-Miezah] in a room with a group of Germans. I swear he didn't say 20 words, just smoked a cigar. Everybody left the room believing a story he never told."

When the naked man sells you his shirt, remember, it was your own blindness, the dazzling vision that danced before your eyes, not his skill, that closed the deal.

LESSON 72

•

DEALER'S CHOICE

It's a good thing you won't be around to watch this scam unfold, because it would break your heart to see it, and it's all your fault.

This takes place shortly after your untimely, deeply mourned demise.

The scene is a stamp dealer's store. Or coin dealer's. Or baseball-card dealer's. Or an antique-gun collector's. Or your own living room. (Pardon me, former living room.)

There are two people present: your surviving spouse and a stamp/coin/gun/whatever dealer.

Your widow/widower speaks:

"George/Georgette collected for years and years, but never told me what these things are worth. What would you be willing to offer me for the collection?"

•

The dealer is only human. Rarities collecting is the only business in the world in which the dealers and their customers compete for the merchandise on equal terms. Most material, particularly good material, is bought and sold at auctions, where it doesn't matter to the seller if you're a collector or a dealer, as long as you're the high bidder. However, usually only dealers have access to "private treaty" estate purchases. Where else would a naïve non-collector go?

So the dealer in our living-room scene swims into the shark/shark-bait waters. Not wishing to appear too interested, he takes only a few moments to examine a collection that has been assembled over a lifetime by loving hands.

"Gee, I'm afraid we really don't have too much call for this kind of merchandise anymore. G/G was about the only one really interested in this stuff. If you want me to, I can take it down to the shop and give it a full appraisal. If I had to make you an offer on the spot, I could give you a few thousand, maybe even four thousand dollars."

Your survivor, deeply disappointed that your collection seems to have so little value, seizes on the dealer's remark, hoping to take advantage of what appears to be a casual slip of the tongue—the dealer's willingness to pay as much as four thousand dollars, not just two or three, for the collection.

Perhaps he or she asks for six thousand dollars, and the dealer lets himself be talked into paying five thousand. Perhaps the dealer is permitted to examine the collection in the shop, but probably not, for fear he may damage something. Whatever the outcome, the spouse is helpless and totally unprepared for the encounter.

Why?

Because you didn't want to tell your spouse how much you had spent over the years on your little hobby. But don't think of it as a total loss. At least you will have provided another high point of the next dealers' convention. At the nightly bull sessions at the bar, where the boys gather to try and outbrag each other, you can be sure one of these vultures will be able to describe every item in your collection to a knowledgeable audience. He'll also be able to recount exactly what he sold that thousand-dollar collection for. Ten thousand dollars. Fifteen thousand dollars. Twenty-five thousand dollars. None of these amounts is unusual—*for a single collectible item.*

Sure, you might not want your spouse to know how much it cost. Sure, you want to avoid any estate taxes if you can. Okay, so don't tell your spouse.

But for God's sake, tell somebody. Right now, put down this book and begin to make an inventory of every item. How much it cost. How much it is currently worth. Then mail it to your estate lawyer (and if you don't have a will, you'd better get one).

Another copy should go to the trust officer at the bank, assuming it's a bank that will be handling your assets after the estate is settled. Give both of them specific instructions to tell your spouse, after your death, that the collection is potentially valuable, should not be sold until a court-supervised appraisal is made and a court-supervised plan of dispersal is drafted and carried out. Since you are the expert on the value of the collection, you might even suggest *several*—not just one—experts who can be consulted and would be willing to make that appraisal under sworn oath.

As for your concern about estate-tax consequences, they generally don't kick in unless your estate is valued at over $600,000 and even then they're a lot less than taking a 90 to 95 percent beating from an unscrupulous dealer who knows that your survivor is selling to him directly in part to avoid estate taxes and lowballs his bid accordingly.

The American Philatelist comments on the tale in this lesson: ". . . may this brief true story remind ALL accumulators NOT to leave the hoards that have given them so much pleasure to be plundered by strangers, who may deceive and rob their widows and orphans."

LESSON 73

AND A NEW WAY OF SKIMMING THE POT

While I can get indignant about the classic scams I've mentioned, this one kind of tickles. I suppose I'd feel differently if I ran an airline. Around Easter and Christmas, when planes are loaded to the gills, airlines always overbook.

College kids will take advantage of this by buying a seat on the busiest flights on the schedule, showing up at the airport at the appointed time, and volunteering to be bumped—in exchange for a free round-trip ticket—when the airlines announce an overbooking. Then it's on to the next flight, and the next, parlaying a single ticket into a fistful of free ones.

Now, that's not a scam. It's the American free-enterprise system at work. Or is it?

LESSON 74

———————————•———————————

WHAT DID YOU SAY YOUR TITLE WAS?

Big corporations discovered long ago that a way to keep a number-two or number-three person happily on board was to give him or her a title that sounded as if, well, maybe, that person was number one. Thus, we have the president, the chief executive officer, the chief operating officer (or COO, I love the sound of that one), plus the chairman, plus the chairman of the executive committee.

Who's in charge here?

The ultimate expression of title-itis was the Nixon presidential campaign of 1968. It was Alice in Wonderland time ("Everyone shall run the race, and everyone shall have a prize"). Let's say you were a podiatrist and wanted to help the campaign. If you walked into a Nixon headquarters in Peoria and volunteered, instead of sending you over to a dingy corner to lick envelopes, the Nixon people would say,

———————————•———————————

"Congratulations, you're chairman of Peoria Podiatrists for Nixon. Now, go out and raise some money from all the other foot doctors in town, and run a big ad in the paper that says 'Podiatrists for Nixon,' and everybody gets to see their name in the paper signed at the bottom of the ad."

And they did.

One group, "Mayors for Nixon," had more steering committees and policy committees and issues committees than Congress. Since Republicans don't control many big-city city halls, it was made up mostly of the kind of mayors who are employed elsewhere by day and are mayors of suburbs, pop. 5,000, "the friendliest city in the state," by night. They raised and spent some forty thousand dollars of their own money, money that never would have found its way into the campaign if the Nixon people hadn't thought of a way to give their supporters some recognition in exchange for their cash.

From the standpoint of someone outside the institutional culture, this practice is usually harmless.

Where it really gets aggravating is when you cut a deal with someone and then find out that person doesn't have the authority to close—after you've put your best deal on the table. It's a trick as old as the "I'll have to clear it with my sales manager" number. Always, always, before you start any negotiation, look beyond the title and make sure that the person you're dealing with is in a position of authority to sign off on the agreement.

If not, don't deal until you can sit down with someone who is.

LESSON 75

———————————————•———————————————

THE DEADBEAT

Once you've done the deal, you still have to face the challenge of getting paid.

There's no way I know of to cure the slow-pay artist, but I do have a remedy that will ease the pain. You build an aggravation factor into every bill. That way they're paying interest on their balances, whether it's charged directly or indirectly. One of the most common slow-pay devices is the check written on the out-of-town bank. Why would anyone in New York City keep his account in Billings, Montana, for any reason other than to squeeze an extra day or two float out of his funds? If the amounts involved are substantial, and there's a steady flow, or if you're concerned about the possibility of insufficient funds when your check is presented for payment, then the solution is to open your own account at exactly the same bank in the same remote corner of the

———————————————•———————————————

world. When you get the other guy's check from Billings, you send it by overnight mail to your own account in Billings, and it's collected the next day.

But although slow pay is bad enough, *no* pay can be death.

When I was starting in business, at age twenty-six, I got my first really big order from an outfit in Chicago I'd never heard of before. I should have been suspicious, because freight is such a high part of the cost and at that time, the envelope business was largely local. But I was too naïve and too hungry for the big three-thousand-dollar score to sense something was wrong.

After we made the shipment and waited the customary thirty days, I began to get antsy and started calling my customer with those polite little "How're you today, and by the way . . ." messages. Terrific news, he was just fine, and by the way, we could expect payment any day now.

Another thirty days of getting the runaround finally woke me up to grim reality. My valued customer intended to stiff me. Totally. If I wanted to recover a nickel, I would have to sue.

I drove down to Chicago wearing old beat-up clothes. It was nine in the evening by the time I got there, and because I was still counting every penny, I literally slept in my car, waiting for the place to open up. Finally, the next morning, after an army of workers had climbed over my body hunched in the doorway, my customer showed up.

While I'm tugging on his sleeve, he's heading for the sanctuary of his office. The door slams. He's made it into the inner sanctum, one of the rows of executive offices that line the walls of the building. I'm left to wander around the bullpen, the windowless interior where the peons work and the sun never shines. There's no chair for me. So I sit down on the floor next to the iron gates outside his office.

And I begin to cry.

Softly at first.

Then more and more loudly.

"If he doesn't pay, it's bankruptcy."

More sobs.

"Why won't he even talk to me?"

All work has stopped. All eyes in the bullpen are focused on me.

Some are curious; some seem sympathetic; and surprisingly, none appears hostile.

It's obvious he's stiffed others before me. And probably a few of them are in this very room. Anyone who stiffs his suppliers is not above stiffing his employees.

Now, there is some activity inside the office. Scurrying in and out.

Muffled curses. Finally, his secretary emerges—with a check for twenty-five-hundred dollars. A jerk to the end, he has to beat me out of at least five hundred dollars.

I told this story to a friend of mine, and he told me his version. He'd been sold a defective roof. After the first winter, the shingles started to curl, and getting no satisfaction either over the phone or with letters, he showed up at the offices, too, but with his wife and two daughters, ages four and seven, in tow.

"You're lucky you didn't get arrested," my friend said to me. "That's why I brought the whole motley crew. I told the girls I had to see my Uncle Willie, and that he was awfully shy, but a real nice guy, so they didn't have to worry about not touching things or not running around, like when I took them down to my office. They were playing tag in the aisles when Uncle Willie decided to see me. I got my new roof the next week. For years, the kids asked me when they could go down and play in that office again and meet the mysterious Uncle Willie. They had a wonderful time."

You don't have to sue to catch up with a deadbeat. Be creative. The sixties may be over, but some of the protest techniques that were used then are just as potent today if you know how to use them. Pay him a visit. Bring some friends, and maybe a banner or two. A TV reporter wouldn't hurt, either. Smoke him out. He'll be glad to see you. Glad to see you leave. Glad enough to pay you for it.

LESSON 76

•

WHO ASKED YOUR OPINION?

It is not the critic who counts; not the man who points out how the strong man stumbles, or where the doer of deeds could have done them better. The credit belongs to the man who is actually in the arena, whose face is marred by dust and sweat and blood; who strives valiantly; who errs, and comes short again and again, because there is no effort without error and shortcoming . . . ; who knows the great enthusiasms, the great devotions; who spends himself in a worthy cause; who at the best knows in the end the triumph of high achievement, and who at the worst, if he fails, at least fails while daring greatly, so that his place shall never be with those cold and timid souls who know neither victory nor defeat.

This excerpt is from a speech frequently called "The Man in the Arena," given by President Theodore Roosevelt in Paris in 1910, a year after he left office. It had a brief

•

rerun during the Nixon administration's darkest hours. Nixon no doubt thought he had found a presidential soul-mate.

The critic stands high on the list of life's more unwelcome visitors.

Max Reger, an early-twentieth-century German classical composer, is better known today for his response to a critic than for his music.

"Dear Sir: I am sitting in the smallest room of my house. Your review is before me. Shortly it shall be behind me."

How you handle giving and getting bad marks says a lot about you.

John Wooden, the most successful basketball coach in history, won ten NCAA championships, including seven in a row, while compiling a 620–147 win/loss record. Wooden, now seventy-nine, was asked by *Investor's Daily* how he dealt with mistakes. "If you correct the situation as it happens, you don't have to harp on it. But I never embarrassed a player who was out of line in front of others."

That isn't the way they do it in some places. Anyone who's ever been to boot camp knows that the drill instructor's M.O. is to work over his recruits with such thoroughness that he destroys their sense of self-worth and individuality so they can be remolded into a unit that will operate on automatic pilot, obedient and unquestioning. It may be the only way to get an eighteen-year-old kid mentally prepared to lay his life on the line, but it's not the way to build self-confidence or morale in a corporation. Act like a D.I. at the office, and you'll get the same kind of response that Frank Lorenzo did at Eastern Airlines.

Do I always bite my tongue and smile when I'm on the receiving end?

Hell, no. My mind seethes with dreams of revenge, unfulfilled thankfully, or I'd probably be writing this in pencil on a Big Boy tablet and trying to get it smuggled out on visitors' day.

Alas, what hurts most is that there usually is a nugget of truth in even the most mean-spirited criticism.

The mind trick that works best for me is to try to extract something I can use out of it.

I know of one salesperson, Don Michaels, who picks one enemy and puts his or her name at the bottom of every weekly schedule he fills out. "Sometimes it's a guy who beat me out of an order by bad-mouthing me. So I dedicate my week to closing every account we're both competing for," says Michaels.

"Sometimes, when I can't think of anyone else, it's Miss Fogelman, who ridiculed one of my reports in front of the whole sixth-grade English class, and very nearly turned me to a life of crime and bad grammar. When I put her on the list, I call on all my good-old-boy accounts and use 'ain't' every chance I get."

Michaels has managed to find a constructive use for the anger we all sometimes feel toward our critics.

A friend of mine got married late in life to a much younger woman. It didn't work out, and their split was not an amicable one. The settlement seemed, on its face, to be generous to her. She got the house and he got the payments, including the utility bills, but she still wasn't happy. Throughout the winter, she kept the windows and doors of the place open and the furnace running full blast to run up as big a heating bill as possible. Sometimes getting even carries a pretty high price tag for both parties.

I think Machiavelli may have had the best answer of all. When he was on his deathbed, the priest attending him asked if he had renounced the Devil. "This is no time," he said, "to be making new enemies."

CHAPTER 13

POLITICIANS AND LAWYERS

A NONPOLITICIAN'S GUIDE TO POLITICS

Of all the American subcultures, politics has always seemed to me to be the most useful as a commentary on human behavior. Watching pols is a kind of out-of-body experience in which you can stand apart and imagine yourself doing the ridiculous things they do, but not quite. It's like learning what drives your own behavior by studying someone else's language or history.

This ability to learn by observation is especially useful for businesspeople.

What makes politics so fascinating is that while the activities that politicians and businesspeople engage in, like chairing meetings and giving speeches, are the same, politicians tend to take an entirely different view of these events and how they should be played to squeeze out their maximum benefits.

Why? Watergate may have put a few superficial restraints

on the way pols are supposed to conduct themselves, but it's still the only game where the rules of competition are quite so openly cutthroat. Macy's may not tell Gimbel's, but at least Macy's did not publicly accuse Gimbel's of engaging in alcohol abuse, womanizing (manizing?), and the like.

Also, politicians have only one product to sell, themselves. They see gain in situations where the rest of us see pain and vice versa. Do you want to avoid the big crowds at the game by ducking out early? They want to stay, to pump a few hands. Do you avoid funerals? Pols go to lots of them. They want to be seen. Take a drink at a party? Pols will seldom be seen with a drink in their hands at a local get-together. Drinking in public is for out-of-town gatherings.

And they will never let themselves be photographed holding anything that could be misconstrued as being alcohol. As the photographer drifts into view, the experienced pol will perform a maneuver known as the "Washington Embrace," reaching an arm behind the back of the person beside him in a gesture of friendship that conceals the drink in his hand from the photographer's lens.

Lyndon Johnson had his own refinement on the liquor situation. He was a scotch drinker, but when he became president, he refused to admit it. Knowing that scotch is often considered a rich man's drink, and an imported one to boot, Johnson always claimed that his glass held bourbon, the more proletarian product of his native South. White House bartenders were given stern instructions to support the fiction in case the press tried to pursue the issue.

So you see, it's a whole different world out there when seen through politicians' eyes. Let's look at a few common situations and see where some of their techniques could apply to the rest of us.

THE POLITICIAN'S GUIDE TO RUNNING A MEETING

A friend of mine who works as a speechwriter and political consultant told me this story.

He was attending a meeting chaired by a campaign manager and attended by eight or ten staffers, all volunteers, to
discuss the kickoff of a statewide campaign of a senatorial
candidate who had made his pile in business and decided he
wanted to cap his career by running the world for a while.
Like a lot of these patrician types, the candidate didn't want
to *be* a senator, he wanted to *have been* a senator, so that
after he'd served a term or two and retired, his country-club
friends would have to spend the rest of their lives saying
things like, "I think your ball is away, Senator."

After the meeting had been under way for an hour or so,
the candidate himself slipped into a chair beside my friend,
took in about five minutes of the meeting, then motioned
him out of the room, and they left to work on some speech
revisions.

My friend sighed. "I knew then he wasn't going anywhere. This guy is not ready for prime time. That isn't the
way a pro does it. You have to understand why people volunteer to work on a political campaign. It's exciting, it's history, it's usually a one-time-only experience, and it's an ego
trip; your rewards are strictly personal. These people will
lay down their lives for you if you ask them to, and their
enthusiasm is infectious. Jack Kennedy knew how important
they were. He had a saying, 'One Paul Revere is worth ten
Hessians.' Most people don't realize this, but the biggest job
a candidate has isn't flinging zingers at the other guy, it's
keeping his own volunteers going. They tend to be extremely sensitive. A skilled politician doesn't want to give
anyone the impression he's playing favorites. If he wanted to
see me alone, he'd never get me out of that meeting himself.
He'd send someone to fetch me.

"And if a pol does go into a meeting, any kind of meeting
or gathering, he has to acknowledge the presence, the great
contribution, that everyone there is making. The whole purpose of the thing is to get him elected. They're all sitting
around talking about him. He has to show he's aware of that.

He thanks everyone for being there, he goes around the table, name by name, thanking, squeezing shoulders, thanking some more.

"This guy's head was still at his last business meeting. He's still acting like he's running his company. He didn't realize that for politics you have to reinvent yourself as the world's number-one cheerleader. People don't break their backs for you just because they like your stand on farm subsidies. They do it because they like you and they think some of that power you're going to get is going to rub off on them. They want to think that when you get elected, they can walk into your office, put their feet up on your desk, tell you what countries not to lend money to, or whatever, and you'll listen like they just passed on the biggest slice of political wisdom since Jefferson wrote the Declaration of Independence.

"You want to get elected? Here's what a pro does. Every time he goes into a room, he makes this his objective: He wants to make everyone in that room know that he's been there and feel better that he was there. Every time. Every room.

"Politics is the ultimate retail business. Votes are gathered one at a time. Every person a pol meets over the age of eighteen is either going to be for 'em or agin' 'em. Even when you're running for president and need upwards of thirty million votes to win, these personal contacts are the key to victory. George Bush spent the better part of a lifetime laboriously writing personal notes to everyone he came in contact with and a few million he didn't, in hopes they'd be convertible into votes someday. Seems like they were. So every day, every meeting, every person can be the margin between winning and losing. The politician's career depends on doing it right."

Is it just pols who can benefit by learning to take people's feelings seriously? 3M thinks it's so important the company makes it a matter of company policy. According to *Business Week,* "Division managers must know each staffer's first name. When a division gets too big, perhaps reaching $250 to $300 million in sales, it is split up."

Of course, politicians do take the idea a bit further.

They used to say that when Hubert Humphrey went into a public rest room, he would never pick the fixture on the end, always the one in the middle. In case two other guys came in, he could shake hands with one and talk with the other while he was taking care of business.

And Kennedy's grandfather, "Honey Fitz" Fitzgerald, a former mayor of Boston, was said to be able to do Humphrey one better. He was the only man in the world who, at a political gathering, could talk to one guy, shake hands with another, and be winking and nodding at a third, all at once.

But then, he had an advantage. Unlike Humphrey, he was facing his audience at the time.

THE NONPOLITICIAN'S GUIDE TO RUNNING A MEETING

Time for another meeting?

When John Kennedy launched his New Frontier administration, the Peace Corps soon became the symbol of the youthful vigor and idealism he wanted to project.

Since nothing like it had been tried before, there weren't any "This is the way we've always done it around here" bureaucrats to deal with, but there were plenty of untested, off-the-wall ideas.

To get up and running, the new agency needed everything. Congressional approvals, structure, training, budget, rules, plans. All were decided on during endless rounds of *ad hoc* committee meetings. There was an air of purpose and excitement about the place, and no time to nurse sensitive egos. The meetings had to be run quickly and efficiently if any semblance of order was going to be established. Kennedy's brother-in-law, R. Sargent Shriver, the first Peace Corps director, had an effective means of cutting off office gadflies in midflight. He would bring along a yellow pad and a pencil to every meeting. When someone spoke, if the speaker was making sense, Shriver would take copious notes. If he wasn't making sense, he would begin twiddling his pencil up and down; the more ridiculous the comments, the faster the pencil twiddled.

If the speaker still didn't get the message, Shriver would snap the pencil in half.

One guy was so caught up in his own oratory that Shriver had to go through two pencils before he caught on. That was the speaker's last Peace Corps meeting. He had flunked the Peace Corps edition of the *Gong Show.*

Gadflies have their uses, but sometimes you have to get out the gadfly-swatter. The pencil trick is a good way to do it.

What's the difference between Hubert Humphrey in Part I and Sargent Shriver in Part II?

Hubert Humphrey was a wonderful politician, but no one ever said administration was his strong suit.

Sargent Shriver was a hell of a good administrator, but he never got elected so much as dogcatcher.

If you can combine the strengths of each, you'll do just fine.

THE POLITICIAN'S GUIDE TO SPEECH-MAKING

Politicians and preachers speak for a living; they have to be good at it. The good ones realize that we absorb the spoken word differently than we do the written one. When you're reading, you can always reread what you don't understand. But if you're hearing a live speech, you can't very well raise your hand and ask the speaker to repeat something if it flies by too fast. The standard outline of a political speech is:

Tell 'em what you're going to tell 'em.

Tell 'em.

Tell 'em what you told 'em.

It's not a bad outline for any speaker.

THE POLITICIAN'S GUIDE TO TURNING A WEAKNESS INTO AN ADVANTAGE

Hubert Humphrey, one of the better stump speakers, frequently opened his speeches by telling the story of how, on one occasion, his wife, Muriel, who was sitting on the speaker's platform, passed him a note on a napkin just as he rose to speak. Written in lipstick was the word: "K.I.S.S.*" Humphrey, deeply moved, shared her warm message with the audience. Just as he was about to stuff the napkin back in his pocket, he noticed that underneath the word she had written: "*Keep It Simple, Stupid."

Sometimes, Muriel would change the message on the napkin to read: "Hubert, remember, you don't have to be eternal to be immortal," which always got a good laugh.

Having ribbed himself for his well-known long-windedness, Humphrey would go on and deliver one of his stemwinders, knowing you can't knock a guy who's already knocked himself and that he had the audience on his side for admitting his own weakness.

Jack Kennedy was a master of that device, too. In 1960, after winning the West Virginia primary against Humphrey in an election widely believed to have been bought by the Kennedy millions, he quipped that his father had chided him, saying he was perfectly willing to buy enough votes to ensure a victory, but Jack had no right to ask him to pay for a landslide.

Don't be surprised if you find John Tower working the same vein on the speaker's circuit, using his reputation as a one-man Shriners' convention to poke fun at himself. You won't have to shed any tears for Tower. With the notoriety surrounding the rejection of his nomination for secretary of defense, his speaking fee has jumped to fifteen thousand dollars a pop.

THE POLITICIAN'S GUIDE TO TAKING ADVICE

An officeholder in one of the western states was being considered as a potential candidate to run for his party's endorsement for governor against the incumbent, a member of his own party who had come to be widely regarded as an ineffectual hack. He wrestled with the decision. Should he stick with his safe job and wait until something opened up, or should he pry his way open by helping to dump the tired old governor?

He asked one of his colleagues for his advice, and made him feel how grateful he was to have received his wisdom.

Of course, 8,000 other people gave him the same advice, and 8,001 people gave him the opposite advice. But it is the peculiar genius of the gifted politician to make each person feel his opinion is appreciated.

What would he say to those who had given him advice opposed to what he had followed? Why, of course he would say, "Gee, I wish I'd taken your advice. I'd be governor now!"

Smart pols give credit to people who give them advice they follow. Even smarter ones know how to give credit to people whose advice they don't follow.

Smart pols remember; smart people remember, too.

THE NONPOLITICIAN'S GUIDE TO MAKING A DONATION

The following advice may seem a bit calculating, but it is, nevertheless, another illustration of the way things work in the real world. Most people do not contribute to political campaigns strictly out of a sense of civic virtue. They do it to advance their own interests. There's nothing wrong with that. It's textbook democracy. The collective total of everyone acting to serve his or her own interest is the public interest. If you ever decide to donate money to a politician, or to anyone else, never send it in one of those envelopes they provide for the purpose. If you're smart, you won't mail it at all.

Big money is always solicited personally. Put your check in an envelope (you know who makes the best ones by now) and *hand-deliver* it to the person who solicited you.

If you do contribute by mail, then toss the envelope they've sent you and mail in your check to a *specific* person, ideally the candidate, or the head of the organization, the campaign manager, the campaign secretary, a staffer, a relative, preferably someone you know.

Why?

Two reasons:

First, it will never hurt you if the check goes to the *wrong* person, that is, someone supposedly not in the loop to handle contributions. That's because you want that check to pass through as many hands as possible before it gets deposited. You want lots of people to see it, to be aware of it.

Second, you want to be sure that at least one of those people is someone with a name and a face; someone who will get credit within the organization for having received your bounty; someone who will remember you; someone who, if the candidate wins, you can reasonably expect to

have access to. If the time comes when you need the support of the candidate or head honcho, just as he once
needed yours, you want to maximize your chances of getting it. One other rule of political giving is that early money
is worth a lot more than money that comes on board when
the election is already in the bag. It's like any other investment: The returns are the greatest when you can pick a winner long before the crowd does.

I learned that one the hard way. Some years ago, I got a
call from a friend, a local political consultant named Mike
Berman, who was trying to drum up a few bodies to attend
a fund-raiser for an obscure ex-governor from the South
who had the notion he could get elected president. By the
time he got to me, and I was far down the list, he was having trouble finding eight people to pay one hundred dollars
apiece to attend a Minneapolis reception for a politician
named Jimmy Carter. Even though I turned out to be the
eighth, I didn't pony up any additional funds, but the fellow who did probably wound up with a new first name:
"Ambassador."

LESSON 78

•

HOW TO HIRE A LAWYER, PART I

You are involved in a breach of contract or an accident in which you sustain personal injuries. It was the other guy's fault, or at least you think it was. You want to sue to recover damages, but first you have to hire a lawyer.

Here are some things you should know:

Lawyers sometimes handle claims for damages on a "contingent fee" basis. Under this arrangement, the attorneys' fees are based on a percentage of the amount that is recovered for you or if the lawyer recovers nothing on your claim, there are no attorneys' fees.

Lawyers not only handle personal-injury cases on a contingent fee, but sometimes will handle other claims for damages on the same basis, such as a breach-of-contract suit for damages, a condemnation proceeding where a person's real estate is taken by governmental authorities, and other matters.

•

The big advantage is that the lawyer is highly motivated to work for a successful result, and if for some reason he is not successful, you don't have to pay any fees. Thus, there is no risk.

As you probably know, nine out of ten lawsuits are settled out of court. But what you may not know is that the high settlement ratio is not attributed to American jurisprudence. It is partly because plaintiffs' lawyers on contingent fees make more money settling cases than trying them, and defendants eliminate substantial costs and risk settling a case rather than going to trial.

Notice I said "plaintiffs' lawyers" and "defendants" do better. I did not say "plaintiffs" do better. Plaintiff, that's you.

A lawyer can settle twenty cases in the time it takes to try one.

Trying a lawsuit takes a lot of time. There is preparation of witnesses, legal research, the trial itself, and possible appeals. It can take years and years before the lawyer on a contingent fee sees a dime of the defendant's money (and that is *if* the plaintiff's lawyer wins the case).

So, though a plaintiff may wind up with less than he would have if the case were tried, plaintiffs' lawyers have a very strong personal incentive to encourage their clients to settle. By settling as many cases as possible, lawyers more than make up in volume what they lose by not getting the big score in any individual case.

Remember, you, as a client, are the "individual case," and he or she, as the lawyer, is trying to grind out settlement after settlement as the most cost-effective way of running his or her law practice. Bear that in mind the next time you hire a lawyer on a contingent-fee basis, when he urges you to settle the suit, pointing out there is "no risk" of what a settlement will be and "saving you from the ordeal of a trial," and "you'll get your money a lot sooner this way."

No doubt about it, a trial is an ordeal. But taking too little money for a claim would seem like more of an ordeal to me.

Don't forget, when you hire a lawyer on a contingent-fee basis, though it may appear on the surface that the lawyer's interests and your interests are the same, they aren't.

You and the lawyer have a built-in conflict of interest, because it is more to the lawyer's benefit to settle than it may be to yours.

How do you protect yourself? By hiring a competent, reputable lawyer who specializes in this area of law and negotiating the contingent fee whenever possible. Since most attorneys would charge a similar percentage contingent fee, try to select the most successful and skilled lawyer in the field. Check with two or three lawyers in whom you have confidence who do *not* handle cases of this type. Ask each for two or three names of the top attorneys in the field. Interview three of the top lawyers on the list, but be sure that no referral fee is being paid to the lawyer you initially consulted. If a referral fee is paid, the lawyer who handles your case will have less incentive. His fee will be significantly smaller because of the referral fee, and he will be even more motivated to settle the claim.

Before you sign a retainer agreement with an attorney, ask a few questions:

"What is your experience in trying cases similar to mine?"

"When was the most recent case you tried?"

"What was the result?"

"What was your biggest verdict?"

"When?"

"Will you give me the names of some former clients who would tell me about you?"

"If I find after talking with them that I don't care to have you represent me, may I void this agreement?"

"If I hire you, do I get you or do I get some associate to try the case?"

Take notes on the answers.

Most people also don't realize that even after you have signed a retainer agreement with an attorney on a contingent-fee basis, if you're not satisfied, you can at any time fire the lawyer, with or without cause, and you would owe only the value of the services already provided on a time basis. The lawyer would then be obligated to turn the files over to another attorney even if you didn't pay the fees at that time.

A lawsuit is not a pretty thing. It is based on the principle of the crucible. Put two different elements in a bowl, mash them together, and the mixture produces something that's beneficial. Take the two competing sides in a lawsuit, let them have at each other in fairly unrestrained fashion, and you come up with the truth. It takes a pretty tough frame of mind to go through the whole program knowing the other side is going to try to crush you and destroy your credibility. But that's how the system works.

Before you walk into the lawyer's office, if you want the maximum recovery you're entitled to, get yourself in the frame of mind to accept that kind of experience.

You're supposed to tell your lawyer everything? There are a couple of things you better not tell your lawyer.

At some point, he or she will "reassure" you that the case will probably never go to trial. You'll be spared the terrible ordeal.

That's when you state that you *want* to go to trial, unless you get a good settlement.

- *Never indicate to your lawyer in any way that you would prefer to settle the suit.*

- *Never give your lawyer the right to settle the suit on your behalf.*

- *Never indicate how eager you are to "get it all over with."*

If you do, then the lawyer *knows* he will never have to try the suit.

Ask the lawyer when he will evaluate your claim and try to obtain his opinion regarding what a reasonable settlement would be *before* settlement negotiations begin. That way, it will be difficult for the lawyer to later recommend that you accept less than the amount you were told earlier the case was worth.

Make your lawyers do the work. That's what you're paying them for. There'll be plenty of time to settle before the case actually goes to trial. And the closer you get to trial, the more the settlement offer is likely to be. Defendants have costs and risks, too. They want to avoid them just as much as you do. The more you make them think they will incur them, the more money you are likely to recover.

HOW TO HIRE A LAWYER, PART II

Now about that contingent fee—in personal-injury cases.

Lawyers will try to tell you that 33⅓ percent is the standard fee, as if it were chiseled in granite somewhere. *It isn't.* It's negotiable. Sometimes, if the case is clear-cut or the damages very substantial, you can negotiate a contingent fee of less than one third or a percentage over a certain amount.

You should always attempt to negotiate a deal that provides for a lesser percentage fee if the case is settled before trial.

If it settles, the lawyer gets less. It's less work and less risk.

If the case is actually tried, that is, *tried to a verdict,* then you can sit still for a higher recovery by the lawyers, say, one third of the total amount. Also, don't agree to a contract that leaves room for the lawyer to receive any percentage higher than one third, even if the case goes up on appeal. In other words, if the wording reads, "We agree to represent you through the *trial phase* of this lawsuit for one third," change it to read "entire lawsuit."

They'll yell; they'll scream; they'll be indignant that you should question their fees, their qualifications, their very integrity—after all, you sought them out. And even if they don't, lawyers are *always* encouraging trade; you have no reason to apologize for cutting the best deal you can for yourself.

It's your money and your life we're talking about.

LESSON 80

•

HOW TO HIRE A LAWYER, PART III

Let's change the scenario. Now you're the defendant, or we're talking about a commercial transaction, like drafting a complicated lease or contract.

No contingent fee here. The lawyers are paid by the hour.

Here's some advice that's saved me a lot of money.

First, you want weekly time charges and weekly bills.

Not monthly.

Not "when the job is over."

Weekly.

Therefore, you won't have any surprises, and if you think you're being overcharged, now is the time to change lawyers.

Again, they'll yell; they'll scream; they'll be indignant that you should question their fees, their qualifications, their

---
•
---

very integrity—they'll say their "computers aren't equipped to handle your request."

Oh, yes, they are.

There isn't one lawyer in a hundred who can tell you what his computers can and cannot do. Instead, the lawyers are telling you what they want and don't want to do.

Second, try to obtain from the lawyer in advance his best estimate of the time and charges that will be involved in doing the work. If you're told this is difficult or impossible, persist. Ask for a "ball-park" figure. You will then have some idea about the total costs, and the lawyer may ultimately be reluctant to charge you much more than the initial estimate.

If he doesn't agree with these reasonable requests, fine. Go to someone who will agree.

LESSON 81

HOW TO HIRE A LAWYER, PART IV

Very, very carefully. See parts I, II, and III.

CHAPTER 14

MISSING PERSONS

TWO OF MY FAVORITE ROLE MODELS

Let's start by disposing of three common myths.

MYTH: THINGS ARE GETTING BETTER FOR WOMEN IN BUSINESS IN AMERICA.

Fact: In some ways, they're getting worse.

Item: Eaton Swain, an outplacement firm specializing in finding jobs for executives, reports that 25 percent of the outplaced (that is, laid off or fired) executives it now counsels are women, although women make up less than 5 percent of the managerial and executive work force. "In other words," says Jane Evans, who has spent her career as a fashion-industry executive, "women are tumbling *off* the corporate ladder in proportionately far greater numbers than men."

Item: Although approximately 50 million women in this country are in the work force, only three New York Stock Exchange—listed companies are headed by women, a grand total of only fifteen publicly held companies are run by women, and of these, only five have revenues of over $50 million.

MYTH: YOU CAN TRUST THE BEST AND THE BRIGHTEST.

Wrong again. Affluent, well-educated males are often less accepting of women in leadership positions than are blue-collar males.

Start by examining election returns. When the voice of *all* the people is heard, not just the voice of the board of directors, the result is a representation of women in high public office that exceeds that of women in the head office. That's true worldwide: Norway, Iceland, Great Britain, Israel, and even traditionally male-dominated societies like India, Pakistan, the Philippines, and Grenada have elected women heads of state.

Election returns show that lower-income workers, male and female, support women at the polls in much higher percentages than do upper-bracket types. During the early years of the civil-rights movement, says Michael Novak in his book *The Rise of the Unmeltable Ethnic,* when election results were analyzed, the much-maligned blue-collar voter, rather than being a wellspring of bigotry, supported pro-civil-rights candidates in much higher percentages than did upper-income-bracket voters. Given the wide publicity about the attitudes of the limousine liberals, it's easy to forget that the greater percentage of liberals in this society is at the bottom of the heap, not up where the decisions are made.

Bias against women may be expressed more delicately by a Harvard Business School man, but it is the blue-collar male who has shown a greater willingness to overcome it.

In 1965, the *Harvard Business Review* did a survey in which only 9 percent of the men questioned said they held "strongly favorable" views toward women executives. In 1985, the figure had grown to 33 percent. But what about the other 67 percent? A 33-percent approval rating doesn't win too many elections, or top jobs.

While there is a growing acceptance of women in middle-management positions and while new areas like public relations have opened up as kind of velvet ghettos, it's still lonely—and male—at the top.

Women who do make it, like Christie Hefner, president of the NYSE-listed Playboy Enterprises, and Katharine Graham, who heads *The Washington Post* and *Newsweek,* might never have had the opportunity to demonstrate their undeniable talents were it not for family. For others, the route up the corporate ladder is all but closed. Those who find success often do so based on pure entrepreneurial grit. In fact, women are increasingly recognizing that the entrepreneurial route is the *only* route. A 1989 Small Business Administration study of sole proprietorships registered in 1986 shows that women are starting businesses at a rate twice that of men.

One such self-starter is Lillian Katz, who founded Lillian Vernon, a mail-order house, at her kitchen table in 1951 with a borrowed two thousand dollars. She built it into an operation that earned $8.1 million in 1989 on revenues of $140 million.

When she agreed to meet me at a restaurant, it didn't take me long to demonstrate the limitations of my sensitivity training.

"How will I recognize you?" I asked, realizing this was something I might not have asked a man.

"I'm six-nine, young, and beautiful," she replied.

Pointed humor can work as well as irritation . . . without leaving those "she's-too-abrasive" scars on the fragile male ego.

Katz gets as well as she gives. "Make me laugh, and Lillian doesn't hear problems" is one of her catchphrases.

Katz's story is vintage "Only in America" stuff based on determination, timing, and talent. The added wrinkle is that, for a woman, determination, timing, and talent weren't enough. She had to have a sixth sense, what her associates call "awareness"—and what I call a sense of humor—that enabled her first to cope and then to motivate others to help her build her company.

"One of the major problems I had in building this business," she said, "was that a good man is hard to find. Most men just don't take women seriously as business associates, particularly as bosses. I am serious, and I mean to be taken seriously; but part of the trick to managing men is to walk that thin line between making it clear who's in charge while not treading too heavily in the process. A sense of humor helps.

"In a way, though, it's fortunate that it takes an exceptional man to hitch his wagon to a woman, because that's what every business needs. Exceptional men. And exceptional women. And that's what we've got."

When I asked her how she was going to spend the remainder of the day following our meeting—it was a Sunday brunch—I got the classic Type A entrepreneur's response: "I'm going back to the factory. I've got some things to do." For the Lillian Katzes of the world, male or female, there will always be a few things to do.

Jane Evans, whom I quoted earlier in this chapter, may have chosen an even harder path than Lillian Katz. She took the corporate route. She was a retailing superstar who skyrocketed from assistant buyer to merchandise manager in less than a year. When Maxey Jarman, chairman of the board of her employer, Genesco, heard about her, she was all of twenty-five. By the time she'd had five years' experience in the business, Jarman, who had gone through eleven presidents in fourteen years at Genesco's I. Miller subsidiary, was willing to take a chance. Even on a woman.

At the time, I. Miller Shoes, like most of its customers, was old and tired. Evans turned the company's image around with stunts like hiring the cast of the Broadway musical *No, No, Nanette* to tap-dance its way into I. Miller on Fifty-fourth Street for the store's grand opening. It drew national media attention, showcasing both the store and Evans's talent. From I. Miller, she went on to a number of executive jobs with the likes of Charles Jourdan, Izod, Ship 'n Shore, Lark (luggage), and Monet Jewelers. Today she is president and CEO of Hawaii Retail Group, a division of Interpacific.

Evans, like Katz, has had her share of problems with the male ego. She said, "I ran into this problem when I became president of Butterick and Vogue. I inherited an all-male team of vice presidents who made it known throughout the company that they weren't especially pleased that a woman—a thirty-year-old woman—was now their boss.

"In fact, the vice presidents went so far as to hold a strategy meeting on what to do about this miserable turn of events. The setting was perfect—the men-only bar at the New York Athletic Club. Encouraged by this chummy atmosphere, and by a few rounds of drinks, they all voted to resign. Except for one, a family man with four children to support, who turned the argument around. Said he, 'We'll give her three months, and if she doesn't shape up, then we'll resign.'

"Playing under protest, I suppose. Well, you can imagine my reaction when I heard about the 'Treaty on Fifty-ninth Street.' I called in the troops and explained the situation as I saw it. That they had more to prove to me, as the senior executive, than I had to prove to them! That came as a bit of a shock to them, for up to that point they had looked at me as a woman—not as their *boss.* Things went fine after that. But the point here is that there is still a degree of hostility and suspicion toward women in the male-oriented corporate world. And as far as women are concerned, if we're going to be accepted as equals, we must be intellectually and emotionally prepared to accept the fact that most men are accustomed to meeting women on a limited set of terms. There are still so few of us in the top-management ranks that the majority of men have never had the opportunity to work with, much less *for,* one of us divine creatures. At times I feel a bit like Mae West—so many men, so little time.

"It is incumbent on *women*—by demonstrating their abilities, competencies, intellect, and sense of humor—to encourage and persuade our male cohorts to allow and help us advance in the business world, in order to provide a larger pool of leadership talent in the future for the betterment of our corporations."

MYTH: YOU CAN TEACH PEOPLE TO HAVE A SENSE OF HUMOR.

You can teach anyone damn near anything, except to have a sense of humor, because everyone already thinks he has one.

Katz and Evans really do. While they may credit their success to the usual entrepreneurial and managerial abilities, a large part of it is because their humor is so natural, so close to the surface, and so totally on target that they don't need to strike poses or threaten others to make their points. It's a gift that more male bosses could use, and one that currently is almost indispensable to women.

LESSON 83

MS. BUTTERFLY

One of the popular myths Westerners entertain about Asians, particularly the Japanese, is that despite the powerful economic models they've constructed, their social norms are semifeudal. There's some truth to it. Japanese society is very structured, its xenophobia is world class, and women are all but invisible to the average foreigner except in the most subservient roles. However, there's a lot more going on than what's visible to you and me.

We assume Asian women are submissive homebodies, walking six steps behind their mates in public and sipping green tea while hubby stops off at the geisha parlor for some relaxation after work.

Ah, so? Not so.

Japan's massive life-insurance company, Nippon Life, has sixty-nine thousand salespeople. Fully 90 percent are women.

Merle Higa, forty-eight, is president of Japan's largest frozen-pizza firm. Before you dismiss her as a small cheese, you should know that her two factories spin out 5 million pizzas a month.

Even in arch-conservative Korea, women manage the assets of wealthy families more often than not, and Korean *bok buin* ("speculator wives") have become a potent new force in Korean and even U.S. real estate deals. Then there are the American women of Asian descent making it big in the States, like CBS anchor/correspondent Connie Chung and General Motors vice president Shirley Young.

Talent is talent, Asian or Caucasian or any other color of the rainbow, male or female. Maybe that's another lesson we have to learn from our toughest competitors. We probably should have learned it from the Bible. After all, the first successful salesperson was not a man. It was Eve.

CAPITALISM IS EFFICIENT. PREJUDICE IS NOT

John H. Johnson is head of Johnson Publishing, whose best-known magazine is *Ebony.* His early experiences are described in his book *Getting It Together,* which also tells the stories of a number of other successful black business-people.

In 1942, Johnson was working for Supreme Liberty Life Insurance, probably the largest black business outside the South. Johnson realized that if there was a market for life insurance specifically targeted to blacks, there was a market for a magazine, too, and he conceived *Negro Digest,* which he started with five hundred dollars borrowed from a small loan company on the security of his mother's furniture. With that money, he launched a direct-mail campaign, using Supreme Liberty Life's mailing list to offer policyholders a charter subscription for two dollars. Most direct-mail solicitors count themselves geniuses if they can get a 2 percent response. Johnson got 15 percent.

Having found a market that white publishers didn't realize existed, Johnson set out to convince the white advertising industry of the advantages of targeting black consumers. He wrote letters to the presidents of dozens of major companies simply asking for an appointment. He used the novel argument that if the chief of state of even the smallest foreign country came to the United States, he'd get an audience with the president of the country. Therefore, Johnson, as head of a company serving a market that then represented 10 percent of the population, should be entitled to a hearing from a company president.

It drew blanks.

Until Johnson wrote to the president of Zenith, which became his first major national advertising account. Johnson so impressed Zenith that he later served on its board of directors from 1974 to 1988.

Johnson became a millionaire many times over. He overcame every obstacle you could throw in the path of a businessperson to become successful, and one obstacle, prejudice, that is more corrosive, more lethal, than most white businesspeople ever think about. He is a role model for anyone, black or white, who ever nurtured a dream.

Here's your early warning system for the next seismic shift in the business cycle. It will not win the Nobel Prize for economics, but it sure worked for one guy.

Otis Sims ran a trucking operation in Houston. In 1981, his business started to slow down for no perceptible economic reason. He sold it at a decent price while it was still solvent and moved back to Minneapolis. His timing couldn't have been better; he bailed out just before the collapse of both oil prices and the Houston economy.

"For the first time in my life, I was glad I was born

black," he said. Invariably, black businesses are the first to feel the downdraft. They're like the canary in the mine shaft. When they stop singing, it's time to get the hell out of the mine shaft.

In a series of decisions, the U.S. Supreme Court recently severely limited the requirements for affirmative-action programs. This was a major legal setback for minority rights in business, and more important, a clear signal that the judicial branch, like the administrative and legal branches, is closing the door to further legal protection for minorities and leaving affirmative action up to the private sector.

If you think that takes care of that issue for another hundred years, you're going to be very surprised as the rate of minority economic strength continues to accelerate, not slow.

Capitalism is efficient. Prejudice is not. Modern capitalist states do not function efficiently when a substantial segment of the population is economically disenfranchised. Blacks are not getting their share. They represent 12.2 percent of the population; they own only one tenth that amount of our total business assets. For every black earning thirty-six thousand dollars, there are twelve blacks living below the poverty line. Not surprisingly, these figures represent the situation of many other minority groups as well.

That will change, because eventually everything in this country, including public morality, is rooted in economic fact. Prejudice is a lousy business practice. It's a terrible drag on the economy, because everyone below the poverty line has to be carried on the back of someone above it.

Minorities have long since passed the point where they will tolerate being shut out of the benefits of our economic system. With my generation in charge, they have been. When the younger generation is in charge, I don't think they will be. We were brought up on stereotypes. Younger people have been taught to be more sensitive to minority concerns. As the forum for civil rights shifts from the courtroom to the boardroom, smart businesspeople will gain by recognizing the great untapped national human and economic resource that minority groups represent.

Of course, you don't have to get ahead of the curve. You're not legally required to change your marketing plans, or your product mix, either. But you do it when you think you have anticipated a trend. Well, here's a trend that's more certain than any: Minority representation will continue to grow at every social, political, and economic level in this country. What have you done to prepare yourself for it? You can benefit from it as a businessperson—and incidentally, as a person person.

Ulric Haynes, Jr., a black businessman who, as ambassador to Algeria, was instrumental in the release of the American hostages from Iran in 1981, had several white mentors: J. Irwin Miller of Cummins Engine, W. Averell Harriman, a former governor of New York, and former president Jimmy Carter. In an article in *The New York Times,* Haynes credits them all for taking an interest in his career and for acting as role models. "I remember my first days representing Cummins in Iran, when I was told that if I wanted to get our engines through customs in a timely fashion, I would have to pay off the customs officials. That was against company policy—and later, United States law—but many American businessmen felt they had to play the game. I refused, and gradually the Iranians accepted that decision. Without ever asking, I was confident that Irwin Miller would back me to the hilt."

Of course, Haynes himself is a role model.

It's incumbent upon *all* responsible businesspeople to do more to seek out and serve as mentors for other John H. Johnsons and Ulric Haynes, Jrs. Otherwise, where will future generations of minority children find their role models? Somewhere in your company there is, or should be, a black, Hispanic, or another minority person, within a lap or two of you on the corporate running track. By the simple act of taking the trouble to give opportunity to a minority person, you will touch the lives of others far into the future.

THERE ARE NO SEVENTY-YEAR-OLD BURNOUTS

Arthur Miller, one of America's great playwrights, is noted for his outrage against the relentless grinding away of the individual by the industrial machine. He probably would be even more outraged to be characterized as a prime author of one of this age's most pervasive forms of discrimination: ageism.

But it's true.

Miller's Willie Loman, the protagonist of *Death of a Salesman*, is the quintessential image of the pathetic aging worker in the American mainstream.

The reality is something quite different.

In my experience, the older worker, particularly the *really* older worker, tends to be the best on the floor.

Why?

Most people who work beyond retirement age are

always motivated, because so many of them are working when they don't have to. And when you do something you don't have to, it means you want to, and when you want to, it means that you're good at it.

It's crazy that we don't do a better job of harnessing the energy and abilities of older workers.

You know all the standard examples of people who seemed to accelerate rather than slow down with age: Albert Schweitzer, Grandma Moses, George Bernard Shaw, Golda Meir, Armand Hammer, Bob Hope, George Burns.

Here's one of my personal favorites.

Seventy-one-year-old Jeno Paulucci has passed the two ultimate tests of the entrepreneur: He did it twice, and he kept it both times. You'll find him in the *Forbes* 400. Paulucci started out in Duluth, not exactly the mother church of the entrepreneurial faith, and found a way to make a fortune using the lowly and abundant bean sprout as the base of a new food concept: packaged and frozen chow mein. That was Chun King, which he sold to R. J. Reynolds for $63 million. Then he started Jeno's, another food concept: pizza rolls. He did a little better this time. Pillsbury bought it from him for $150 million.

Admittedly, Paulucci has slowed down a bit. He now gets up at five in the morning instead of four. Among his considerable holdings are three thousand acres of prime land now turned into a city where you can live-work-play and shop. It's near Orlando and called Heathrow.

He told me recently what happened when he tried to pitch the American Automobile Association on moving its international headquarters to Heathrow's International Business Center. AAA had narrowed the list down from eighty-two to eighteen possible sites. Heathrow had made the cut, and Paulucci called Jack Stephenson, who was in charge of the relocation for AAA. Stephenson told him that the project had been assigned to a study firm and that it "will get back to you in six months."

That afternoon Paulucci called him back.

"Your six months are up!" Paulucci said and after a long conversation finally persuaded an extremely reluctant Stephenson to see him.

Knowing how loath Stephenson had been to give him an audience, Paulucci was taking no chances on any foul-ups. He even made sure that his regular limo driver, Julius, had made a dry run to AAA headquarters in Falls Church, Virginia, so he knew exactly how to get there without getting lost and making Paulucci late for the meeting.

When Paulucci flew in to Dulles on his private plane, Julius performed flawlessly, and Paulucci was able to persuade Stephenson to hold a second meeting, a week later, this time with Jim Creal, the president of AAA.

Stephenson told Paulucci quite forcefully that this meeting would begin promptly at 9:00 A.M., and would last for exactly fifteen minutes, no longer.

Again, Paulucci made his meticulous arrangements, but when he arrived at Dulles, he was shocked to see no Julius. The limo company had sent a different driver.

"Do you know where Falls Church is?" Paulucci asked him.

"Of course," said the driver.

But after they had gone past it twice, missing the correct cloverleaf both times, time had just about run out. With only minutes to go before he was due at the meeting, and the building in plain view as they were about to pass it by again on the opposite side of two expressways, Paulucci told the driver to stop the car.

"The limo stopped at the entrance to a cloverleaf and I started climbing up this forty-five-degree hill, carrying a clipboard, a legal pad, and wearing the newest and most beautiful suit I'd ever owned.

"I got across the first two lanes of traffic, and then the median, and then another two lanes, but then comes a twelve-foot barbed-wire fence." Paulucci is about 5'5" tall.

"The building is just over that fence. I ran along the fence, but I couldn't get around it. So I ran along it the other way, and there's still no end to it. All the time, the clock is ticking and there's the building. I don't want to ruin the beautiful suit. But there's no other way. I say to myself, 'Jeno, fetch!' like I'm a golden retriever, and I toss the clipboard over the fence, hang on to the family jewels, and go over the top."

With thirty seconds to go, he's in the office of the president, where of course, he steers the AAA man over to the window.

"See that four-lane highway? I crossed it on foot to get here. See that median? See that six-lane highway? I crossed them, too. See that hill? See that fence? I climbed them both. Now do you think I would have done that if I didn't believe that Heathrow had exactly what you need for your new headquarters?"

And do you have any doubt about where AAA decided to locate its new international headquarters?

Strange, the unusual places the message seems to be getting through: The Peace Corps, which has the image of a place for young idealists to spend a few years after college before settling on a career, does some of its most vigorous and successful recruiting among retired workers. Unlike younger people, they don't bail out from homesickness when the going gets tough.

What about you? Want to prove that just because there's snow on the roof, it doesn't mean the furnace is out? Here are some tips, laid out the paint-by-the-numbers way:

Step 1: Use what you've got. Your Rolodex can be worth more to you than your company retirement plan. Someone sixty-five years old knows more people than someone twenty-five or thirty: people you've done favors for, people who know your capabilities. Before you leave your present position, make sure those IOUs are not only current but built up as much as possible. Be the one to introduce your suppliers and customers to your successor, so he or she can hang on to your account. In the next breath, make sure that those suppliers and customers are aware of your next move, so they can be in position to give you some business in return.

Step 2: Surprise! You need a plan! This time, it should be built around your natural advantages: your contacts, your experience, the capital you've built up. If you examine these three assets, chances are you have them in much greater abundance than most people younger than you. They are worth their weight in gold; don't throw them away in an attempt to do or be something if your age is a liability. The bad news: You won't make it as a tango instructor on a cruise ship. The good news: That doesn't mean you can't make it as the bridge instructor.

Step 3: Don't try to do it on the cheap. This is a business, not a hobby, even if the business you've chosen is to make a lifelong hobby pay. If you're going out on your own, give yourself a payroll to meet, even if you're the only one on it. Never work out of your home if you can help it. Even though it saves you a few bucks, get out of that house and go to an office. Your spouse married you for better or for worse, not for lunch. What you're really doing if you're staying home isn't saving money; it's making it easier on yourself to fail. Staying home will undermine you psychologically. Home isn't where you work; it's where you live. Act as though you mean it to yourself, or you'll never be able to convince anyone else.

Step 4: Spend at least *10 percent of your budget on the best professional advice available before you spend a nickel on anything else.* Don't buy that franchise. Don't make a down payment on that business. Don't enter into a contract for that land. Don't lease that office. Not until your head is swimming from more advice than you ever thought you'd need.

Whatever it is you're planning on doing, *this time* you have infinitely more riding on it than you did when you were young and broke and could afford to make every kind of mistake known to man.

The money you spend up front investigating the prospects for the business and for screening out the scams is a cheap price to pay for insurance against disaster.

Step 5: Build an escape hatch. It's not your failures you've got to worry about; it's the other guy's.

Even after you've made up your mind, if you're investing in a business, make sure the sales contract sets forth the seller's representations and can be revoked if any of them are false. Also, you want built-in performance clauses that must be met before the full purchase price is paid.

Step 6: Hire a shill. Even though you can *do* the work better than someone half your age, you'll find that the hard part is getting it.

The most common late-career moves involve converting a hobby into a business or becoming a consultant to your old clientele. After a while, you'll usually reach the point where you've exhausted your previous lifetime supply of prospects among your old friends, and you realize you're going to have to figure out where you're going to get some new ones. It's not the end of the world. Every business always needs new customers. The additional challenge you have to overcome is age discrimination.

Here's how one fellow designed a way to get around it. He used a little camouflage.

This gentleman was a former preacher who graduated to a career in consulting on church fund-raising. After a few years, most of the people who knew him had retired or died, so he decided he'd better get a new act. He is no longer the president of his company. His son is. The son, MBA and all, is much more successful than dad at scheduling appearances before hard-eyed church boards looking for the latest in "modern" fund-raising techniques. Sonny closes, Dad disposes.

Step 7: Step up your networking. Keep up whatever clubs or professional associations you belonged to before and join some new ones. Be more, not less, active in them. If you'll be speaking or presenting, advises communications consultant Lynne Lancaster, get some coaching. A videotape won't lie the way your spouse or best friend might. Be visible socially. Dress better than you did in your old job; not more youthfully—don't change your style—just better.

Step Eight: Take some college-level courses. Didn't you always say you were going to go back to school when you had a chance? Well, now's the chance.

Be sure that the class is not a straight lecture, but small enough so you can discuss the course material during class sessions.

My advice is to try the liberal-arts courses, like literature. Here's your best single opportunity not only to stretch yourself, but to get in touch with the people one-third your age under circumstances in which they'll really let you know what they're thinking. And unlike any attempts to interact socially with them, where they'll only think you're ridiculous, the classroom is a setting where they'll show some respect for your opinions. (Alas, part of the reason is that you will actually have read the assignments, while they were making an on-site inspection of the cute item in the next row.)

Step 9: Get in an exercise program. One of the new business forms that came into its own in the shake-'em-up period of the eighties was the outplacement outfit, the specialists in helping people who got sacked to get it together again. If they have one ironclad rule, it's to get their clientele on some kind of an exercise schedule. Naturally enough, you feel better about yourself when you feel better physically, and that, of course, is what exercise does. The same idea applies here.

Step 10: Have some fun at it. Your first career was for the money, the prestige, the security, whatever. Well, you've proved to yourself and the world you can do all that, so what else is there to prove? Now you're doing it because you feel more alive and useful at it than anything else you could be doing. For the first time in your life, you're naming the game; you're calling the shots. That means if school's out every Wednesday afternoon so you can play golf, well, then, that's the way it's going to be. This time, this time for sure, *you,* your needs and concerns and wishes and quirks, are running the business. The business isn't running you. If you can't do it that way or find anyone who'll let you do it that way, then any progress you make on steps 1 through 9 simply isn't worth it. If it ain't fun anymore, head back down the staircase.

But if you do stick around for the second act, there's one last thing I want to share with you: Now it's your turn to be a mentor for someone else. You've accumulated a lifetime of business experience and insights. Don't waste it. Take someone who's starting out and give him or her the benefit of your hard-won knowledge. There isn't a better legacy you can leave than making it a little easier for the next guy.

This time, don't take my advice. Give them yours. Pass it on.

And that's the thought I intended to leave you with, but I have more to say . . .

CHAPTER 15

QUICKIES

QUICKIE 1

———————————•———————————

EVERYONE WANTS TO WIN ON SATURDAY
AFTERNOON . . .

. . . but the guys who do are the ones who practice the other six days of the week, says my favorite football coach.

If you're going to give a speech, even if it's ghost-written, take the trouble to be your own advance man. Some years ago, I was a commencement speaker at Iowa Wesleyan. Three weeks before I was scheduled to give the speech, I went down to the campus in Mount Pleasant, unannounced, and spent the day going to classes, meeting students and faculty, dribbling beer on myself at the local hangout, and generally acting like the world's oldest freshman. It helped me personalize my material by giving me an insight into the school that I was able to use to make it a better speech. It proved to my audience that I did write it myself. It showed them I cared enough about them to try to get to know them

———————————•———————————

better, not just stop by to pick up an honorary degree. That experience worked out so well, I've done the same thing when I've gone on radio or television.

Those of you who read *Swim with the Sharks Without Being Eaten Alive* know I never made a cold-call sale. I never make a cold-call appearance, either. You'll always do a better selling job when you've done your homework.

QUICKIE 2

NOTHING WORKS ALL THE TIME

I once described how you can convert almost any public restaurant into your own private club. Ron Fellows, who organizes and arranges international seminars, took my advice—always a leap of faith. Here's what happened:

"My guest was Dr. Yoshiro NakaMats from Tokyo. Dr. NakaMats is one of the wealthiest men in Japan. He invented the floppy disk and holds 2,630 patents, making him the world's most prolific inventor. He is nearly as revered as an emperor.

"I had arranged dinner for twenty at one of our finest restaurants. As you outlined, no menu was to be presented, no mention of cost, no bill was to be brought to the table. All was prearranged. Everything went perfectly—until the waitress dumped his salad all over him.

"As you know, it is nearly impossible to read the Japanese face to determine a reaction to such a misfortune. Though the dinner proceeded without further incident, I was still concerned about what had happened. After the dinner concluded and I said good night to my other guests, I found Dr. NakaMats outside the restaurant, standing alone and facing out toward the nearly empty parking lot.

"I asked him what he was doing.

"'Drying my pants,' he said."

QUICKIE 3

DON'T TAKE A BACKSEAT TO ANYONE

Do you, like me, automatically gravitate to one of the backseats during any kind of lecture or religious service? It must be a carryover from my school days. You've heard me brag about everything else, but not my grades.

Notice how the better students seem to sit up front? Is it their thirst for knowledge, their determination not to miss a single word that drops from the professorial lips?

I asked a friend of my son's where he sat.

"I sit up front, because that's where the smart kids sit," he said. "You can read the small print under the small print, and you don't have to turn up your hearing aid. Besides, if you're close enough to see the teachers really well, then they're close enough to see you. You're not just a name in a gradebook; you actually become human. It's like they tell you to try and make friends with your kidnappers. It makes it harder for them to harm you."

Take the front row at the next meeting and try to look interested. You're a tiny bit less likely to be left twisting in the wind later on.

QUICKIE 4

THE COOKIE FACTOR

I've been addicted to overnight-delivery services ever since Federal Express came on the scene about ten years ago. Like Post-it notes and VCRs, Fed Ex invented both a product and a market for the product, and then made them seem indispensable to human existence. Though overnight delivery services are now somewhat threatened by FAX machines, there's going to be room for both.

Will there be room for delivery companies that don't compete on the basis of either speed, like FAX, or price, like the United States mail? UPS has had to find a different route. It handles size. It handles local deliveries. But when it competes with the rapid-delivery guys, it has to give a little something extra.

A friend of mine was waiting for an overnight delivery. A couple of hours after it was given to UPS, Mr. Big discovered it had been sent to his home address rather than his office. It was of such cosmic importance that he stayed home that morning to wait for the delivery.

As the day wore on, Mr. Big's already short fuse crept ever closer to the flash point.

"Why don't you take Grover for a walk, dear?" said his wife, sensing an explosion in the making.

To her astonishment, Mr. Big stopped his pacing, roused an even more astonished dog from a comfortable nap, and headed outside. They had taken only a few steps when the UPS truck pulled up. Mr. Big was all set to unload on the to-his-mind tardy driver in his famously obscene and unbridled fashion, when the driver reached into his pocket, pulled out a dog cookie, and stuffed it into Grover's drooling mouth.

"Good-looking pup, aren't you?" he said. "What's his name, sir?"

"Er, it's Grover," grumbled Mr. Big.

"Boy, he's lucky to have a master like you, even as busy as you are, who takes the time to show him some attention. I just don't do enough with my little guy."

"Well, it's not as if . . ."

"I believe this is for you, sir. Could you sign here for me, please?"

End of problem.

UPS prides itself on being owned by its management, and "management" doesn't mean a few folks in an executive suite. There are sixteen thousand active managers in this privately held company, and no one person owns more than 2 percent of the stock. Turnover is low, and the drivers are treated like the professionals they are.

Another thing about the company: The trucks are washed every day. In January, when cars change color, UPS trucks do not. They're always squeaky clean.

UPS will find a way to keep on trucking, regardless of how fast or how cheap the other delivery services become.

QUICKIE 5

SPENDING WATER LIKE MONEY

The greenhouse effect, the gradual warming of the Earth's atmosphere, is having a powerful effect on our economic future. It's causing fresh water to evaporate, and that puts a real premium on water supplies. *Business Week* reports that in Colorado, ninety farmers will give up much of their present farming business having sold their water rights to Public Service of Colorado for a cool and refreshing $25 million.

ADM, the giant food-ingredient processor, paid $36 million for a 15 percent stake in Illinois Central Railroad. Why? In 1988 the level of the Mississippi River was down twenty feet and in the future may not be able to float grain barges. In years to come, ADM may need to train the grain.

If you're a "trend" buyer of stocks, you might start to look in the direction of companies like Lindsay Manufacturing, which makes the continuously moving electrically powered giant sprinkling systems for irrigating farmlands.

Or you might ride the wave by considering the consumer end of the business.

Health-conscious consumers are drinking less booze and coffee and more bottled water. The Coors brewery company is watering down its beverage line and forging another Silver Bullet as it takes aim at Perrier to become the number-one water bottler in the U.S. Bottled water, says *The Wall Street Journal*, is the fastest-growing beverage in the United States, averaging 10 percent growth a year and already totaling $2 billion annually.

In 1988, on Beverly Hills's fashionable Rodeo Drive, a bar opened up that sells—you guessed it—nothing but water: 120 different kinds of it. It gives a whole new meaning to the term "watering hole."

It's a good thing W. C. Fields isn't around to see it happen.

QUICKIE 6

"IT'S A GREAT COUNTRY, BUT YOU CAN'T LIVE IN IT FOR NOTHING."—WILL ROGERS

A study by the International Monetary Fund reveals that in 1986 the United States government subsidy to the dairy industry was the equivalent of $1,139 for every cow in the country, a figure that is greater than the average annual income of half the world's population.

In 1986, the National Park Service purchased a small parcel of land next to Fort McNair in Washington, D.C. In December of last year, it learned that the parcel was already owned by the federal government and had been since 1914.

Last year the IRS lost its right to appeal a case, which the federal appeals court said it would have won, because it missed a filing deadline. The amount of the tax deficiency in question was $102 million.

The IRS's own internal studies reveal that the agency loses 2 million tax returns and related documents annually.

QUICKIE 7

YOU PAYS YOUR MONEY, YOU TAKES YOUR CHOICE

A printer friend of mine has a sign up where his customers can read it:

PRICE.
QUALITY.
SERVICE.
PICK ANY TWO OUT OF THREE.

QUICKIE 8

TIP ON TIPPING

When you go to a resort for a week or two or take a cruise, you're expected to tip a fairly standard fixed percentage of your total bill on the last day of your stay.

The best way I've found to ensure the kind of service I want is to tip on the first day of my stay, not the last.

Why fly in the face of custom?

For two reasons: I'm a good tipper, and I'm a demanding guest.

364

I've found I've had much better results with the tennis pro and the golf starter if they know that I'm a live one and not a stiff before we get under way than if they have to wait until the end of the tour to find out.

QUICKIE 9

ANYONE CAN WIN—ONCE

In the past ten years, ten different teams have won the World Series. There have been no back-to-back repeaters in professional football over that same period, either.

The conventional wisdom is that talent is a) getting spread thinner or b) getting spread more evenly.

I don't buy it. Professional skills don't change that much in a single season. But professional heads do. That's why I think there's another, much more significant reason.

Success breeds the seeds of its own destruction. Winning is often accompanied by a tendency to forget the sacrifices and the team spirit that got you there. The mindset is: "Okay, I proved I can do it. Now that that's over with, it's my turn." When that happens, it is all over with. The "me-ness" that had always been lurking beneath the surface, surfaces, and the "us-ness" vanishes. The skills may still be in the game, but the head isn't. Guys who might otherwise be making $4.55 an hour pumping gas become truly insulted when they're offered only $7.9 million in response to their demand for $8.1 million. Internal conflicts overshadow the conflicts with the guys in the other uniforms. Player X is offended because Player Y is getting more money. Player Y is offended because Player X is getting more deodorant and underwear commercials.

And on it goes. You can't keep the kind of corrosive attitudes those responses generate off the playing field.

Anybody can win once. Jack Fleck did. One U.S. Open. And then he never won another major tournament in his life.

The St. Louis Browns did. One pennant in 1944. And not another one, before or since.

They were winners, all right. The record books may not show it, but in our heads, we put an asterisk next to those names every time we see them. We remember those kinds of wins as flukes.

Flukes or champions? The difference is how you handle success.

With champions, success lies in the journey, not the destination.

With champions, success is never unexpected; it's a natural result that comes from continuous, unselfish, unrelenting determination to win, never letting down, never letting outside influences into the game.

Champions know it's not having the talent to win that makes a champion; it's having too much pride to lose. Season after season. Year after year. Championship after championship.

Lombardi's teams never lost. Occasionally, they just ran out of time.

QUICKIE 10

PURE DOGGEDNESS

The dominant sports media personality in our market is not a handsome young newscaster with fifteen thousand dollars' worth of capped teeth, a dazzling prose stylist, or a Geraldo clone. He's a deeply middle-aged sports columnist who never played any of the games he writes about and never made it to college, much less journalism school.

Sid Hartman's columns don't really have beginnings, middles, and ends. They simply trail off, stream-of-consciousness style, in a series of unconnected snippets he calls "jottings." He's also become the most popular radio personality in town, with a broadcast style that's no more polished than his writing style.

Hartman has blown away half a dozen competitors, all of whom he would be the first to admit are superior writing and broadcast talents. Those who have had Something Important to Say About the Games We Play are no longer saying it on our sports pages, while Sid, who has yet to offer his first insights into the social significance and inner meaning of sport, marches on.

The Hartman mystique is that there is no Hartman Mystique. He doesn't use his considerable public platform to sensationalize or harangue or take cheap shots. Hartman is as bland as Minnesota cottage cheese. His success is rooted in pure doggedness. If you live in Minnesota and are of the athletic persuasion and any good at just about anything,

Hartman knows who you are by the time you're in high school. He calls. You become column fodder. Your name pops up in one of his loosely jointed sentences or he interviews you on one of his innumerable sports shows. He keeps calling. He follows you through high school. He knows your background, your record, your coach. He tracks you through college. He tracks you through the pros. He tracks you when your athletic career is over and you're getting on with the rest of the story. Once you're on Sid's Rolodex team, you don't ever get cut. You're on it for life. He knows more about athletes, coaches, and owners than any other sportswriter anywhere. And when some of these become really big pro stars, coaches, and executives, he has greater access to them (and often through them to other stars) than anyone else—because he dug his well before he was thirsty.

And he also owns the U.S. Mint of sports reporting: the biggest, most reliable network of sports sources of any journalist in the country. One of the times he used it was when Woody Hayes, the Ohio State coach and perpetual loose cannon, had made national headlines on the behavioral-science front and then rendered himself as elusive as a Shiite in Tel Aviv. Hartman was on the case and called a number in California a source had given him.

It was 5:30 A.M. Sunday morning on the Coast as the phone rang. "Hello, Sid," said a sleepy Hayes, as he picked up the phone. "How did you know it was me?" asked Hartman. "Who else could it be?" said Hayes.

When Roger Maris was in the midst of his assault on Babe Ruth's single-year home-run record in 1961, he was under such enormous pressure from the press and the public that his hair was falling out by the fistful. Maris, who had grown up in Minnesota and North Dakota, regarded Hartman as his only real friend in the press corps. Hartman had access to Maris like no one else in the national press corps got. They remained friends until Maris's death.

One of Sid's great strengths is that he's never adopted the reporter's traditional cynicism about the people he covers. He's as much a fan as any fan. His sources are his friends.

Even George Steinbrenner, who does not count many sportswriters among his friends—and vice versa—counts Hartman as one.

Sid may never make it to the Baseball or Football Hall of Fame, but if they ever get around to building a Rolodex Hall of Fame, he'll be the first one they call. Talent is a gift, but like many gifts, we often take it for granted. If Sid Hartman had applied equal energy, dedication, and perseverance to another career—such as sales, for example—I'm positive he would have achieved the same great success he attained as a sportswriter.

Give me the guy who uses 110 percent of what he's got. He'll find a way to get the job done when no one else can.

QUICKIE 11

ONE MORE REASON THEY CALL IT "THE ONE THAT GETS USED"

A major telephone company executive told me this story:

A young hustler, just out of college, borrowed some money from his dad to go into business. What business? I don't know yet, Dad, I'll have to look in the Yellow Pages.

That he does, going down to the phone company offices and cajoling Yellow Pages for twenty different cities.

First, he looks under "shoes." Too many shoe stores. He

tries "hardware." Too many hardware stores. And so on. He finally tries "building maintenance." Most cities had fifty to seventy-five different firms in the business, but he found one city that had only seven. There he went, and there he made his mark with a successful janitorial service.

With so many different types of marketing surveys being peddled, this strikes me as one of the more imaginative.

It also meets GM chairman Roger Smith's criterion as a fifty-cent solution to a million-dollar problem. Another executive, probably anticipating a big study and even bigger capital investment in a new heating and ventilating system, once asked Smith what could be done about the poorly heated executive offices at GM.

"Do what I do," said Smith, unbuttoning his jacket. "Wear a sweater."

QUICKIE 12

WHY YOU CAN RUN A TWENTY-SIX-MILE MARATHON EVEN IF YOU'VE NEVER RUN HALF THAT FAR BEFORE IN YOUR LIFE

Because the crowds carry you.

At least that was my experience when I ran the New York Marathon in 1987.

Recognition is the best means of motivating us to achieve more than we ever thought possible.

When we lose key employees at Mackay Envelope, chances are it's not the salary or the perks, it's that someone at another firm is romancing them, making them feel wanted, and they like it. Same reason people change spouses. They like the attention the new partner gives them—for a while.

I have yet to receive my first note from someone telling me I'm giving him or her too much recognition.

QUICKIE 13

THE MEXICAN RUG DANCE CAN BE A LOT MORE EXPENSIVE THAN THE MEXICAN HAT DANCE

On a trip to Mexico, I wanted to know the seller's true selling price on a Mexican rug.

Reconnaissance by a Mackay suicide squad (everybody works in this family, even the kids) had established that the seller's asking price was three hundred dollars.

I divided $210 among four different pockets. I started negotiating, pocket by pocket.

He shook his head back and forth each time. Three no's.

I emptied the fourth and final pocket. As I stood there, all four pockets inside out flapping in the breeze, waving fistfuls of dollars and pesos, I told the seller that it was all I had left. If I didn't catch my cab, waiting over there (much vigorous pointing in the direction of the cab stand) and get back to the pier, my ship would sail without me.

"We're just here for two hours. Just long enough to do a little shopping and get back to the boat. You'll never see me again. I'll get in the cab and be gone. And you won't have the sale. There may not be another buyer for ages."

A fourth shake of the head. "No."

I started walking toward the cab.

Here's the payoff.

If he lets me get into the cab, then I know absolutely for sure he will *not* change his price to $210, but with each step toward the cab I have a chance that he will holler and say "Mister, I will give it to you for two-ten."

I got to the cab.

I opened the door.

I shut the door.

He never called me back.

I had the cab drive around the block and then walked back to his stand and said, "Okay, you win. I want the rug; here's the three hundred dollars."

He nodded solemnly, took the money, counted it very slowly, and handed me the rug.

"Maybe you want me to deliver it to your hotel?" he said.

"Hotel? But, I'm on the—"

He held up his hand to stop me and shook his head no for the last time. "I waited on the table next to you at the hotel last night. My brother, Manuel, has been your waiter all week. He says you take real good care of him, mister. We check out all the tourists. That's our business, you know. Thank you. I'm sure you'll enjoy the rug."

Moral: It's one thing to be a moderately successful amateur bargain hunter, but when your livelihood depends on knowing more than the other guy, then you don't play amateur games. You make it your business to know.

QUICKIE 14

ONE LINE THEY'VE NEVER HEARD BEFORE

Occasionally, I'll start a negotiation by saying, "I don't want to overpay . . ." That remark is invariably greeted by the usual grim gray faces across the table. Then I continue ". . . but I don't want to underpay, either." Now, there are tiny puzzled smiles on the other side. I'm not sure what impact it has on the final outcome, but it sure as hell stops conversation for a while, and gives me a chance to see if they "read" at all when they hear something unexpected.

Do they think I'm nuts? No, I hope to get a few points for a sort of peasant cunning.

Every time I've ever used the line, it invariably gets thrown back in my face later, even months later.

At which time I always say, "Gee, I'm glad you remembered my saying that two months ago. Just proves nothing gets by you, so you must also have heard me say, 'I don't want to overpay, either.'"

QUICKIE 15

WHEN YOU SHOULD OVERPAY

On the first totally rotten hand you hold in a poker game with strangers, to establish your absolute stupidity in hopes of luring in a few callers when you are dealt cards.

And when you're buying a piece of real estate that no one can put a value on but you. In a sealed-bid auction, I paid twice the next highest bid for our Minneapolis plant site. The other bidders, who had consulted highly regarded site specialists, thought I was nuts, and after I saw what they were willing to pay for it, I thought they were right. I'd be able to sleep through a nuclear alert, but for two weeks after the big sale, I was literally a zombie.

Today, the land is worth ten times what I paid for it.

But it wouldn't matter to me if it were worth one tenth what I paid for it.

What matters with anything you intend to use is what you can do with it, not what you can get it for. If I had played it smart, I'd never have owned the property, or Mackay Envelope, for that matter.

A dream is always a bargain, no matter what you pay for it.

QUICKIE 16

NOTES ON NOTES

You may never look at them again—and then again, you may. Top negotiators, top athletes, and top poker players debrief themselves after every major session. They always keep "a book," not only on themselves, but on their opponents. You never know when that information may be solid gold.

Your notes have all kinds of weird and wonderful uses.

I travel a lot, more since I hit the author circuit, and I've kept notes on every out-of-town trip for as long as I can remember. Not the usual stuff about what hotel to stay at in each city, but much more detailed than that. What floor to stay on and even what room to ask for. Will it be ocean view or mountain view? Every hotel has its rooms overlooking a mine shaft or next to the dumbwaiter or that were skipped over in the last renovation. Some desk clerks can be encouraged to make a good assignment, some can't, but they all know which rooms are which. And more often than not, so do I. It can make the difference between a pleasant and an unpleasant experience for me, but I would never be able to do anything about it if I hadn't made it a lifetime habit to keep notes.

In his book *Intellectuals*, Paul Johnson reports that Bertrand Russell, the English philosopher and peace activist, kept a lifetime record of every dollar he'd ever been paid for his writings. Since he wrote more than sixty books, and only he knew how many potboiler articles, it was a considerable list. Russell kept his records in a little notebook he always carried with him. In rare moments of despondency, he would take out the notebook and go over it fondly, slowly turning the pages and examining the numerous entries and the tidy sums of money after each. His spirits restored, he would put the notebook back in his pocket, and get on with his life.

I doubt if many books would be written, even fiction, if authors didn't constantly make notes and keep journals of material that they can mine when they need it.

QUICKIE 17

BLAME SOMEONE ELSE FOR THE GOOD NEWS

Killing the messenger was the ancient practice for the bearer of bad tidings.

Let someone else carry the good news, too.

When they relate to business, good tidings about you are best passed on by someone else. Also, make sure they're described as the result of the good work done by a third party on your behalf. Don't overestimate how eager other people are, even your friends, to hear from you of your good fortune and mighty accomplishments.

Often, friendship can stand bad news a lot better than it can stand good news.

QUICKIE 18

ONLY ELVIS DOESN'T READ WHAT THEY SAY ABOUT HIM IN THE PAPERS, AND THAT'S BECAUSE HE'S ON THE ROAD

I know several celebrities. They all tell me they never read what is written about them. Well, maybe the president of the United States doesn't read what's written about him, not all of it anyway, but that's because he can't read Swahili. Everyone else reads every word.

No one makes you become a celebrity. You choose the celebrity profession, in part because you like the attention, including the press. It comes with the territory. It *is* the territory. So you read about yourself. They all do.

I think what the alleged nonreaders must mean is that they don't remember the good stuff they read, only the bad.

QUICKIE 19

WHY PR PEOPLE COULD USE SOME PR

I get a ton of annual reports in the mail. These documents are referred to in the communications business as "collateral," not advertising, so they are generally prepared by the "public-relations professionals" and "corporate-communications specialists," not by the agency that handles the advertising.

Annual reports are the mother lode of bar charts, all of them marching upward to the heavens, left to right, across the page. I'll give a free box of envelopes to anyone who can show me a bar chart in an annual report where the little bars are heading down, unless it's something good, like expenses.

I received an annual report for Texas Utilities, a public utility whose earnings were down for 1988, and were even lower than they had been in 1984.

Was there a bar chart showing the earnings decline? Nooo. That kind of news was buried in the back of the book under "Financial Statistics."

But there was a bar chart right on the front cover. *Something* was heading up, up, up each year. It was the number of customers served and the company's estimates, glowing of course, of rapid increases in this vital area in 1993 and 1998.

Growth, you gotta have it, even if it means finding it in places where only a PR person would have thought to look.

QUICKIE 20

YOU ARE WHAT YOU AREN'T

PR people are expert at papering over weaknesses and making them appear to be strengths.

There's a bank down in Texas that was among the first to computerize its operations, and in the process developed a reputation for being aloof, remote, and cold-blooded.

PR to the rescue. Among the new image-building devices was an "identity change" for the company. The old logo was abandoned, and in its place was a black-and-white line drawing. The style was old-fashioned, very detailed. Drawn from behind, it showed a somewhat scruffy-looking, hardworking old cowboy leading a little-boy cowboy by the hand. The little boy was gazing up at his mentor, eyes filled with hero worship as they walked off along the dusty trail, into the sunset. Beneath the new corporate symbol was the legend HELPING TEXAS GROW.

Same PR company. Another bank. This time the outfit was a quill-pen operation with an image of not-with-it-ness. The new image consisted of a stylized logo set in computer type, like a dot-matrix printout. The old corporate name was changed. It wasn't a bank name anymore, it was a bunch of initials. The new slogan: BANKING ON THE FUTURE. Both campaigns worked. Subsequent market surveys showed that the negative perceptions of each had largely been overcome.

That's why we have PR. It's a lot cheaper to change the image than it is to change reality.

QUICKIE 21

WE'RE NUMBER THREE . . . WE TRY EVEN HARDER

In *Swim with the Sharks,* I said that the ideal position for any company or salesperson to be in was number two. If you position yourself as second in enough situations, sooner or later some number ones are going to mess up or drop out, and you'll find yourself moving up.

Well, wonderful things can happen even if you're number three. An example is Progresso Soups, as it was written up in *Fortune* in May of 1988. In 1986, the dominant canned soup was Campbell's, as it has been ever since Campbell invented the alphabet and put it into cans. The formidable marketing people at Heinz had tried for years to develop a position against Campbell, but they finally decided to turn in their ladles and withdraw from the consumer market. Some very shrewd people at IC Industries, now Whitman Corporation, scouted around and found that next in line after Heinz was Progresso. They bought the company from Ogden Corporation and integrated it with their other food subsidiaries, Old El Paso and Pet. Progresso then mounted a revitalized campaign, introducing more serving sizes, six new recipes, and a much more vigorous marketing program. Sales gains have been running about 25 to 30 percent annually.

As Chris Evert said about losing her top tennis ranking, "Would the number-three brain surgeon in the world retire?"

QUICKIE 22

WHY IS IT THAT YOU CAN NEVER BRING AN EXPERT TO NEW YORK?

Because that's where they all come from. And as everyone knows, no one in New York ever believes anyone outside New York knows more than he does about anything.

Even though all New York's experts are originally from Peoria, too.

Currently, the rights to broadcast the New York Yankee baseball games in the local market cost about $50 million a year. A business analyst of sports franchises puts the value of the team itself at about $150 million.

Who owns the New York Yankees? The principal owner is a fellow from Cleveland named George Steinbrenner.

Who'd he buy it from? Those prototype New Yorkers, the corporate moguls of CBS, who sold it to Steinbrenner's group for $10 million.

The next time you hire an expert, don't rely on a New York address or any other fancy credentials as being a guarantee of wisdom. The definition of an expert is still anyone more than fifty miles away. Do your shopping at home first. You're a lot less likely to be disappointed.

QUICKIE 23

TELL ME A SECRET

My father, Jack Mackay, who was an Associated Press correspondent in Minnesota for three decades, always warned me against telling anyone how I voted, because "Once they find out what you are, Harvey, they'll know what I am, and I like it the way it is. The Democrats think I'm a Republican, and the Republicans know I'm a Democrat."

Ask me today and I'll still tell you, "That's why they have a secret ballot."

The late David Niven used to describe how, on Academy Award night, before the awards were announced, he gave the same assurance to each competing nominee. "I voted for you," he'd say, beaming and winking, as he glided by the nervous candidates.

Back here, where they don't give Oscars but still hold elections, one of the local city-hall lobbyists used to spend election night waiting for the returns to come in and then make the rounds of the postelection victory parties. "We won! We won!" he'd tell the winners, automatically including himself in the ranks of the victors. Maybe *he* should have won an Oscar!

Nothing's tougher than getting an accurate head count before a secret ballot is taken. Or separating the real supporters from the bandwagon jumpers-on after the fact.

And the more politically savvy the electorate, the tougher it gets. Once every few years, the Senate and the House have a turnover in one of the leadership positions, and a couple of members compete with each other for their colleagues' votes for an open slot. Invariably, the loser will say something like, "If everyone had voted for me who said they were going to vote for me, I'd have won this thing by a landslide."

Alas, the secret ballot, like other secrets of the heart, is seldom revealed.

Don't count on any promise that isn't made in public or isn't in writing. And then don't count on those too much without a good lawyer in your corner.

QUICKIE 24

WHY SOME PEOPLE NEVER FAIL

After Edison's seven-hundredth unsuccessful attempt to invent the electric light, he was asked by a *New York Times* reporter, "How does it feel to have failed seven hundred times?" The great inventor responded, "I have not failed seven hundred times. I have not failed once. I have succeeded in proving that those seven hundred ways will not work. When I have eliminated the ways that will not work, I will find the way that will work."

Several thousand more of these successes followed, but Edison finally found the one that would work and invented the electric light.

Failure is an attitude, not an outcome.

QUICKIE 25

SPEND SOME TIME IN THE TRENCHES

There is no dirty work in your business. One way to prove how important every job is and everyone is, is to take on the job yourself.

If you believe there is no such thing as a good job with a shovel, then so does the guy who has the job. You can't expect his attitude to be any better than yours.

At least once a year, I'll spend a day at one of the jobs at my company generally regarded as menial. It's not a stunt; I don't announce it in advance or announce it afterward, either. I don't hire a photographer to record it; the house organ does not carry a story about it. I just do it. Believe me, that's enough. Word gets around.

And more than once a year, I will go out with a salesperson on his or her calls. That works, too.

QUICKIE 26

FIND ONE GOOD IDEA, AND YOU CAN USE IT FOREVER

Ronald Reagan had two: lower taxes and rebuild our military strength.

Charlie Hires had only one: If you're selling a new kind of carbonated sugar water to hardscrabble Pennsylvania coal miners, better call your product "root beer" instead of "root soda pop."

One may be all you'll ever need.

QUICKIE 27

IT'S A TRADITION

Until recently, newspapers were printed on machines well lubricated with heavy grease. Pressmen, to avoid having the stuff drip onto their heads, would make a paper hat each day from a newspaper, folded in a special way, to wear during their shifts.

The old-time presses have been replaced by electronic ones, which require no grease, but the hats remain, a symbol of the pressman's trade.

Cadillacs were the status symbol of the 1950's hotshot salesman and were used as a comic metaphor in the movie *Tin Men*, a spoof of the roofing and siding game. Every business and trade has its special traditions and rituals.

Some are good. Some are not so good. The tradition of the hard-drinking, heavy-spending salesman is gradually giving way to a more professional image. Sexism and racism are more deeply ingrained but gradually giving way to more open-minded attitudes.

But no matter how good or bad, you can't tangle with these traditions lightly, particularly if you're the new kid on the block.

Don't expect them to change by waving your magic wand. You have to provide reasons, motivation, both positive and negative, and leadership by example if you expect the change to take root.

And if they're simply expressions of status, style, or

pride, like the paper hats or the Cadillacs, let them be—or even encourage them.

They give people identity.

If you've gone to a pressman's funeral and seen him buried with his paper hat on, you'll realize just how important they are.

QUICKIE 28

IT AIN'T A CLASSLESS SOCIETY

And apart from using "ain't," the quickest way for others to get a fix on your background comes when you sit down at a table to eat. Rudimentary etiquette, particularly table manners, probably ranks number one as the most totally abandoned tradition in American life, but it can matter hugely to your career.

We may have learned good table manners from our parents, but we seldom pass them on to our kids. The change in life-styles is the culprit. Since today's families dine together much less often than in previous generations, the day-in, day-out practice of enforcing some discipline at the family table has been lost.

It's not uncommon to see a newly arrived executive, turned out to perfection in a fifteen-hundred-dollar suit, doing a pretty good Three Stooges imitation at the dinner table.

They don't teach etiquette much anymore, but if you ever have to choose between Incredibly Advanced Accounting for Overachievers and Remedial Knife and Fork, head for the silverware.

Somewhere along the line, someone who can do you a lot of good is going to invite you to join him at the table instead of the office. He or she may have already seen how you handle your pocket calculator. Now, the person wants to see how you handle yourself. Don't expect to fake it. If you haven't had much practice, it's going to show. Sissy manners stuff? Don't kid yourself.

It's the seemingly unimportant stuff like this that separates the people at the peak from those in the pack.

QUICKIE 29

TABLE STAKES

My town, Minneapolis, is one of the world's milling capitals, home to General Mills, Pillsbury, and International Multifoods.

I was having lunch with an executive from one of the big milling companies. His ancestors had been among the founders of the city's milling business, and he was very proud of their long historic ties to the industry and their deep roots in the community.

There was a third person at the table, a top salesperson with a packaging company who was also something of a health nut.

It was not really a business lunch. We were trying to organize a charitable event, but we both called on the same executive as suppliers when we were performing our business roles.

The salesperson, who for years had seemed to subsist on

grass and twigs, surprised me by taking a roll, which he buttered lavishly and ate with great relish.

"That's kind of unusual for you, isn't it, Eddie?" I asked, after we had a moment to ourselves. "I mean, haven't I heard you say that sugar-fortified bakery rolls and congealed animal fat are hostile to the human body?"

"Harvey, my man," he said, "when you dine with a miller, you break a roll."

If you want to keep your bread buttered, be sure you've done your homework. There aren't any lunch breaks for salespeople who want to stay on top.

QUICKIE 30

THERE'S NO MARKET FOR BAD NEWS

In a lifetime of reading projections of sales, rentals, profits, population trends, consumption, market share, and sundry other forecasts, I have yet to see one where the little blue line didn't go from the bottom left-hand corner to the upper right-hand corner. They can all be summarized in three words: up, Up, UP.

Why are they always, always, far too optimistic?

Because there is no market for bad news.

Planners and gurus have no one to sell it to, because no one wants to hear it.

Would you have bought a book titled *If You Swim with the Sharks, You're Damn Well Going to Be Eaten Alive*? There are always a few nay-sayers around, but for the same reason people like to read horror stories and go to scary movies: It's fun to be scared when you know as soon as you've finished the book or the lights go back on, it's all over. No one reads or sees them to believe them or act on them.

Optimism is encoded in our genes. Without it, we wouldn't breed the children who are essential to our survival as a species. But don't let genetics stop you from viewing any projection designed to separate you from your net worth with a healthy degree of skepticism. If somebody tells you he's going to give you an absurdly high percent of return on your investment, it's probably too good to be true.

Here's Mackay's Rule for Projecting a Return on Your Investment:

If you are quoted a return on your investment that is more than 20 percent, figure that is what you are going to lose—not gain—every year.

Thus, if your return is projected at 50 percent annually, you can expect to *lose* 50 percent of your money the first year and 50 percent of what's left every year after. Thirty percent? You're lucky. You should lose *only* 30 percent the first year. Works every time for me. And I've got a wall papered with stock certificates to prove it.

QUICKIE 31

HOW TO KEEP YOUR TRAIN OF THOUGHT

There are two ingredients to make this work.

You have a short-term assignment that requires intense concentration.

There's a passenger train you can take.

I'm not going to try to sell you on the joys of train travel as an everyday kind of thing. But I can tell you that when you're working on a project that requires a short burst of total, uninterrupted concentration, nothing beats it. They're comfortable; they're easy to move around in; you can arrange to have some privacy; there's something to look out the window at when you need a break; and they're sufficiently novel to most of us that there's a fun element that planes don't have. I know one fellow who had to edit a three-hundred-page report who boarded the Twin Cities–Chicago train in the morning, did his edit, then turned around and flew back home that afternoon.

Beats telling the office you have a cold so you can stay home all day and get some work done.

Choo-choo-choo.

QUICKIE 32

HOW TO GET A BANKER TO SMILE AND SAY YES—OR MAYBE NOT SMILE AND SAY YES

I received a letter from Arnold Grundvig of Salt Lake City, who just finished getting his MBA because he figured that it would help him discover what the great secret was to running a business. He discovered it. "Believe in yourself and work as hard as necessary to succeed."

He also has a pretty good feel for how you borrow money.

Your first move is to make your banking connection before you need the money.

A good way to start is to pry your banker away from his desk for lunch. Describe your business, tell him you don't need to borrow now, but there will be a time when you will.

Make it clear that you can structure your cash flow to cover expenses and debt service because you're such a tiger about planning things in advance.

Plop your financials in his lap, and then go away for about three months.

When you do need the money, you've laid some solid groundwork.

Move two: You now need the money.

Be specific: x dollars for x days. Don't wait for an answer. Start haggling about interest rates.

He will respond by ignoring your assumption that the time to talk about interest rates is prior to the time the loan is approved and introduce the concept of "committee approval." Register mild disappointment. After all, you told him you were going to need the money, didn't you?

"This scenario does two things for your banker," says Grundvig. "First, it puts him at ease that you know what you're doing. Nothing turns off a banker faster than a borrower who 'will lose everything' if he doesn't get this loan. Such poor planning betrays your business incompetence and eliminates his confidence in you. Second, the banker will trust your plan for repayment. After all, you did accurately forecast this need several weeks, even months in advance."

And, of course, your loan will require "committee approval" and be at whatever interest rate the bank decides to set.

Grundvig also discusses the practice of making a similar arrangement at a second bank to pay off the first, but I wouldn't recommend that. It's a red flag that you're in trouble and undermines the relationship with the first banker.

Dance with the guy who brought you, Arnold.

QUICKIE 33

MEMORIES ARE MADE OF THIS

One of the persistent contradictions of the deeply rooted prejudice against older people is that we accuse them both of forgetfulness and of over-remembering the events of the past. Sometimes they remember all too well.

A year ago, I had a late-night dinner in Chicago with Dr. Norman Vincent Peale and his wife, Ruth. He was ninety. She was eighty-three.

They had just returned from Japan and were, as usual, vibrant, energetic, and keen in their observations. During the course of this three-hour dinner, Norman illustrated his points with amusing anecdotes, and after one particularly appropriate story, Ruth couldn't resist exclaiming, "Why, Norman, how perfect! You haven't told that story in forty-five years!"

"Ah, but I repeat myself," said Norman, not missing a beat.

QUICKIE 34

WHY COMMUNISM IS IN TURMOIL

For all of our mortal terror about the Communists taking over the world, they have their work cut out for them at home. We've all heard about the long lines for scarce food items in the Soviet Union. According to Sovietologist Marshall Goldman, Kremlin officials are straightening the problem out in typical Communist fashion. They have subsidized the price of bread to keep the consumer happy and subsidized the cost of grain to keep the peasants happy. As a result, bread is cheaper than raw grain. The Soviet peasants who grow the grain sell it to the government, then turn around and buy the bread and feed it to their cattle, which adds to the demand for bread, which increases the need for grain, which creates even longer lines around the bakeries.

Business Week reports that one of the tallest skyscrapers in Warsaw was planned twenty-four years ago and rises thirty-two stories on Marszalkowska Boulevard. It's the home of Poland's Foreign Trade Office. Its purpose: to symbolize Poland's emergence as a new force in East-West trade. Only one problem with the symbolism: They haven't finished the building yet.

In East Germany, the showcase of the Communist system, the most common domestic auto on the autobahn is the domestically produced Trabant. The Trabant is a two-cylinder eggbeater that would make your kid's Big Wheel look like a Ferrari. There's a joke going around East Germany: "Can a Trabant take a curve at a hundred kilometers [sixty miles] an hour?" The answer: "Yes. Once."

QUICKIE 35

WHY OUR SYSTEM WORKS BETTER

"This is America. You can do anything here."
—TED TURNER

"That's why I love it."
—HARVEY MACKAY

I've been delighted to hear from many of the people who have read and enjoyed *Swim with the Sharks,* and I'd be pleased to hear from you regarding *Beware the Naked Man.* You may write to me at:

Mackay Envelope Corporation
2100 Elm Street, S.E.
Minneapolis, Minnesota 55414

Thank you.

INDEX

Adams, Cedric, 160
Adams, Steve, 160
Adizes, Ichak, 130

B., Raymond, 197–199
Babson, Roger, 38
Bailey, Martin, 208–209
Battisone, Sam, 255
Bechtel, Stephen D., 161
Beethoven, Ludwig van, 70
Berman, Mike, 320
Berry, Ray, 228–229
Blay-Miezah, John Ackah,
    292–294
Bosold, Don, 186–187
Bradley, Bill, 228
Brower, Charles Hendrickson,
    113
Brown, John Y., 111–113
Bryant, Bear, 53
Buffett, Warren, 71

Burns, George, 348
Burr, Don, 87
Bush, George, 131, 314

Caine, Michael, 68
Candy, John, 236
Carlson, Arleen, 89
Carlson, Curt, 73, 89, 187, 234
Carnegie, Andrew, 84, 213
Carnes, Julian, 68
Carson, Johnny, 84
Carter, Jimmy, 131, 320, 345
Cazel, Lyle, 193, 196
Chung, Connie, 341
Cioran, E. M., 229
Clausewitz, Karl von, 71
Cooley, Bill, 249–250
Crandall, Bob, 236–237
Creal, Jim, 349
Cross, Wilbur, 293
Curley, James Michael, 88

Da Vinci, Leonardo, 70
Durocher, Leo, 208
Dyer, Wayne, 83–84

Edison, Thomas A., 383
Eisenhower, Dwight, 211, 213
Evans, Jane, 333, 336–338
Evert, Chris, 380

Fellows, Ron, 358
Fitzgerald, "Honey Fitz," 315
Fleck, Jack, 366

Gehrig, Lou, 3
George, Phyllis, 113
Gibran, Kahlil, 137–138
Goldman, Marshall, 393
Goldwater, Barry, 129
Gorbachev, Mikhail, 245
Gottlieb, Linda, 86
Grager, Robert A., 205
Graham, Billy, 208–210
Graham, Katharine, 335
Grundvig, Arnold, 390–391

Hahl, Bob, 67
Halberstam, David, 252
Hammer, Armand, 348
Harriman, W. Averell, 345
Hartman, Sid, 367–369
Hayes, Woody, 53, 368
Haynes, Ulric, Jr., 345
Hefner, Christie, 335
Higa, Merle, 341
Hires, Charles, 384
Holtz, Lou, 4–7, 10, 36, 73, 91
    131–132, 151, 228–229,
    255
Holzer, Adela, 292–293
Hope, Bob, 348

Hopkins, Anthony, 233–234
Hubbard, Elbert, 163
Humphrey, Hubert H., 129,
    315–317
Humphrey, Muriel, 317
Hunt, Lamar, 13–14
Huston, John, 68

Iacocca, Lee, 252–253, 275

Jacob, Richard, 291–292
Jarman, Maxey, 337
Johnson, Brett, 87
Johnson, Jimmy, 5
Johnson, John H., 342–343,
    345
Johnson, Lyndon, 13, 235,
    312
Johnson, Paul, 375
Johnson, S. C., 122

Katz, Lillian, 335–338
Kennedy, John, 313, 315–317
Kiam, Victor, 39, 275
Kotler, Philip, 231
Kroc, Ray, 24

Lancaster, Lynne, 353
Lansbury, Angela, 251–252
Leahy, Frank, 5, 10, 132
Lombardi, Vince, 53, 366
Lorenzo, Frank, 50, 307
Lynn, Mike, 14–15

McDonald, Dick, 253
Machiavelli, Niccolò, 308
Mackay, Jack, 381
McKnight, William, 85
Malone, Karl, 255
Maris, Roger, 368

Marriott, J. Willard, 82
Matthews, Christopher, 13, 235
Mayer, Louis B., 95
Meir, Golda, 348
Metz, Robert, 230
Michaels, Don, 308
Miller, Arthur, 347
Miller, J. Irwin, 345
Miller, Larry, 255
Miller, Rudolph W., 82
Mirman, Sophie, 237
Moses, Grandma, 348

NakaMats, Yoshiro, 358–359
Napoleon, 183
Nelson, Marilyn Carlson, 12
Newhouse, S. I., 160
Nietzsche, Friedrich, 86
Niven, David, 381–382
Nixon, Richard, 54, 300–301, 307
Nkrumah, Kwame, 292
Novak, Michael, 334

Olivier, Laurence, 233–234
Oreffice, Paul, 38, 70
Ottomanelli, Nick, 230
Oxborrow, Ken, 293

Paige, Buster, 246–247
Paulucci, Jeno, 348–350
Peale, Norman Vincent, 113, 392
Peale, Ruth, 392
Picasso, Pablo, 70
Pillsbury, Phillip, 158–159

Ratner, Harvey, 231
Reagan, Ronald, 55, 57, 131, 384

Reger, Max, 307
Reich, Edith, 291–292
Rein, Irving, 231
Reynolds, Burt, 123
Riggs, Bobby, 39
Rockefeller, David, 292
Rockne, Knute, 5, 132
Rogers, Will, 363
Roosevelt, Franklin Delano, 95
Roosevelt, Theodore, 306
Rozelle, Pete, 13
Russell, Bertrand, 375–376
Russell, Richard, 235
Ruth, Babe, 70, 368

Satterlee, Nita, 222
Savage, Marilyn, 35–36
Schenk, Nicolas B., 95
Schrage, Michael, 233
Schweitzer, Albert, 348
Self, Dr. Thomas, 151
Shaw, George Bernard, 124, 348
Shewmaker, Jack, 149, 168, 261
Shriver, R. Sargent, 316
Sills, Beverly, 36–37
Sims, Otis, 343–344
Smith, Red, 254
Smith, Roger, 370
Stanky, Eddie, 208
Stein, Bob, 108–110
Steinbrenner, George, 369, 381
Stephenson, Jack, 348–349
Stockton, John, 255
Stoller, Martin, 231

Tinker, Grant, 210
Tower, John, 318
Townsend, Lynn, 252
Truman, Harry, 211, 213
Turner, Ted, 394

Walton, Sam, 261
Watson, Thomas, 94
Weinberg, Irwin, 161
Winchell, Walter, 54
Winfrey, Oprah, 48

Winter, Max, 14–15
Wolfenson, Marv, 231
Wooden, John, 307

Young, Shirley, 341

ABOUT THE AUTHOR

HARVEY MACKAY is chairman and chief executive officer of Mackay Envelope corporation, a business he founded in Minneapolis in 1959 and built into a 60 million dollar company today. He lives in Excelsior, Minnesota, with his wife, Carol Ann. The Mackays have three children and two grandchildren. *Swim with the Sharks Without Being Eaten Alive* is Harvey's first book. It was on the *New York Times* bestseller list for 54 weeks and rated the Number 1 business book in the United States for 1988. *Sharks* has been translated into 35 languages and distributed in 80 countries around the world.